Developmental Couple Therapy for Complex Trauma

Developmental Couple Therapy for Complex Trauma provides therapists with comprehensive and practical guidance for integrating DCTCT into their work with traumatized couples. The book includes an evidence-based framework which emphasizes the importance of containing conflict and helps clients to build emotional regulation and mentalizing skills. The framework is an invaluable asset to all clinicians working with couples dealing with the ravaging impacts of complex trauma, who may not be able to benefit from traditional forms of couple therapy due to challenges in regulating emotions, mentalizing, and other aspects of the complex trauma response that limit capacity to engage in relationships and couple therapy.

The chapters guide you through the four key stages of DCTCT: Psychoeducation, Building Capacity, Dyadic Processing, and Consolidation. Each stage has accompanying activities and narratives in which to engage traumatized couples and includes a variety of case transcripts to illustrate the approach. Throughout the manual the author provides the reader with:

- insights from real-world scenarios based on her extensive clinical experience;
- worksheets that can be used as part of the therapeutic process;
- systematic analyses of the therapeutic process from the therapist's point of view;
- comprehensive recommendations for further reading so that you can develop your expertise in any area of DCTCT.

Never losing sight of the fact that the therapist plays an essential role as a coach and mentor for those undertaking couple therapy, this manual is a valuable tool for any clinician working to engage traumatized couples and equip them with the skills they need to develop and maintain a strong and vibrant couple relationship.

Heather B. MacIntosh, PhD, is a Clinical Psychologist and Associate Professor in the MScA Couple and Family Therapy in the School of Social Work at McGill University, Montreal, Quebec, Canada, where she is the recipient of the 2017 H. Noel Fieldhouse Award for Distinguished Teaching.

Developmental Couple Therapy for Complex Trauma

A Manual for Therapists

Heather B. MacIntosh

Routledge
Taylor & Francis Group
LONDON AND NEW YORK

First published 2019
by Routledge
2 Park Square, Milton Park, Abingdon, Oxon, OX14 4RN

and by Routledge
52 Vanderbilt Avenue, New York, NY 10017

Routledge is an imprint of the Taylor & Francis Group, an informa business

Library of Congress Cataloging-in-Publication Data
A catalog record for this book has been requested

ISBN: 978-0-415-79361-2 (hbk)
ISBN: 978-0-415-79362-9 (pbk)
ISBN: 978-1-315-21094-0 (ebk)

Typeset in Sabon
by Apex CoVantage, LLC

To Patricia,
My safe haven and secure base, without whom none of this would be possible.

Contents

Acknowledgements

First, I must acknowledge the many couples who have laid themselves bare and worked so hard as they shared their struggles and pain in therapy and showed me what it means to take risks and be vulnerable despite devastating traumas. These couples demonstrate the resiliency and tenacity of the hope of finding a safe haven and secure base in one another. The students of CAFT613 2016/2017 played an invaluable role in the ongoing research on DCTCT including, Danelle Barnard, Sarah Burley, Jessica Fortin, Caroline Hoppenheim, Stephen Legari, Anita Mehta, Elsa Perez, and Carole Sandy. Finally, to P. Rose Primeau for her assistance in the preparation of this manuscript.

Chapter 1

Introduction for therapists

By the time I was 22 years old, I had two young children, my marriage was crumbling beneath me, and feelings, images, sounds, and sensations were intruding on me, night and day, overwhelming me. I was forced to come to grips with the loss of my intended career as a classical singer as the long-term effects of an early traumatic injury began making themselves known in my body and mind. I had no other identity than that of a singer, no family, and no relationships that could help me buffer against the tsunami of converging forces that thrust themselves on me as I navigated motherhood without a model of what a mother should be. I didn't understand what was happening to me. I didn't know how to exist haunted by constant terror, but I was desperate to provide my children with a childhood different from my experience in my adoptive family. In that environment, shame was served up liberally as a side dish with every meal, while sexual boundaries only existed to protect the "real" family. Meanwhile, as the adopted child, I was fair prey for stray desires and wandering bodies. So I got out of bed every morning and put one foot in front of the other, trying to be the mother I had never experienced, myself. I had no way to afford good therapy, but someone suggested I read an article by Bessel van der Kolk, "The Body Keeps the Score" (van der Kolk, 1994). I began to understand what was happening to me, albeit in an entirely intellectual, cognitive way. I began to make sense of my experience: the words on the page contained my experience and gathered me up into meaning. This marked the beginning of a lifelong journey to understand the impacts of trauma and to help survivors fight their way out of the paper bag of their lonely terrors. The more I came to "know" about trauma, the clearer it became to me that the "knowing" wasn't enough. As much as I longed for love and connection, I was still unable to wrest myself free of the avoidance that had caught hold of me in the bid for survival in a family of emotional and sexual intrusions. I began to learn of the powerful disconnection between insight and experiential change; simply understanding something doesn't help you change it when it is driven by forces that exist outside of one's awareness. While I understood the impacts of my own trauma on my capacity to connect with others, I was not able to change the feeling that I needed to pull away as soon as anyone got close to me. Over many years of education, a million hours of therapy, and an extended practice of intellectual containment, I found my way into a relationship with a woman who had a healthy capacity to tolerate my needs to manage our level of closeness, combined with just enough pursuit to be the glue in our relationship. That was over 20 years ago; over those years I have been living the parallel process of learning how to tolerate being close, loving, and being loved, while also working on developing ways to work with survivors who are struggling in their longed-for but distressed relationships. This book reflects that journey, the journey of one survivor struggling to balance her longing for love with her terror of connection and the journey of a clinician researcher working to help couples brave the pain and vulnerability of bridging the gap between their desire and their terror, to build loving relationships of hope and healing. I hope that, in these pages, you may find some answers to your questions about how to work with these challenging couples who want so much to be freed from the pull of the past living in the present, and encouragement for your persistence and commitment to this difficult but vitally important work.

Why is this manual needed?

Childhood trauma can fracture the basic fabric of human relationships. When children are harmed, especially by those in positions of trust, they may later struggle with developing and maintaining strong, stable, and loving relationships in adulthood. For survivors of childhood trauma, the difficulties that arise from their traumatic experiences are not just those related to the after-effects of trauma that might befall an adult who had been traumatized, such as flashbacks, nightmares, and avoidance of reminders of the trauma; they are more complex. These more complex trauma responses are those that interfere with the web of human relatedness, trust, safety, and the skills that help a person develop and maintain a relationship with a primary attachment figure (Herman, 1992). In spite of these challenges, survivors of childhood trauma continue to long for an attachment relationship that is not fraught with fear and pain but rather is loving, gentle, safe, and secure.

What is it that fuels the longing of childhood trauma survivors to find people to love them, and to love in return, in the face of remembered traumas often inflicted by the very people who should have been protecting them? I reflect on this question every time I sit with a couple that seeks intimacy and security yet struggles to navigate the consequences of devastating childhood attachment relationships and violent, destructive traumas. What is it that defies the lesson of history – people are dangerous – and allows them to try, against the odds, to find love? There is no easy answer to this question, but I am awed by the forces that drive attachment as a basic, primal, human need. And so, therapists who sit with these couples need to find ways to help balance the forward momentum of attachment seeking with the backwards-leaning terror and power of destructive models about how to be in relationships.

Traditional models of couple therapy provide practitioners with important skills to intervene with couples, but inherent in these interventions is the baseline assumption that partners in these couples possess the basic skills of interpersonal engagement, the developmental self-capacities, with which to tolerate, engage in, and benefit from the therapy. For many of the couples with whom I work, these basic developmental capacities are simply not present; all efforts to engage in the give and take, the ebb and emotional flow of couple therapy lead to crisis, emotional escalation, and in some cases, interpersonal violence and dramatic relationship ruptures. The goal of Developmental Couple Therapy for Complex Trauma (DCTCT) is to provide competent, effective care to couples poorly equipped to engage in traditional couple therapy. This model takes a developmental, step-by-step approach to building skills in the couple context, focusing on containment and growth while preparing the couple for the later "meat and potatoes" of stages focused on healing and processing trauma.

Why couple therapy?

While we know that couple relationships may moderate the impact of childhood trauma, clinical research over the past 30 years has concentrated on the development and validation of individual models of treatment for childhood trauma survivors. In fact, until very recently, couple therapists would turn away trauma survivor couples under the premise that survivors should engage in individual therapy prior to embarking on couple therapy. It was believed that following extensive individual treatment, trauma survivors could be "healed enough" and ready to shift their focus away from themselves and towards their partner and the couple relationship. It has also been suggested that couple therapy with childhood trauma survivors in active healing would be too tumultuous and chaotic to be safe and productive. What then happens to these couple relationships while waiting, potentially for years, for the survivor to be "healed enough", and how could that determination be made?

Emerging into adult couple relationships, childhood trauma survivors often evidence insecure attachment styles and display fearful avoidant ways of being with their partners, leading to painful struggles with maintaining closeness and potentially intolerable conflict (Alexander, 2009; Cloitre, Stovall-McClough, Zorbas, & Charuvastra, 2008). When survivors do develop and maintain relationships, they are often plagued with distress, interpersonal violence, severe difficulties with communication, and significant struggles in their sexual relationships. The dance of connection is often characterized by competing and fluctuating needs for closeness alternating with avoidance, typical of fearful avoidant attachment styles (DiLillo, 2001; Godbout, Runtz, MacIntosh, & Briere, 2013; Rumstein-McKean & Hunsley, 2001). Survivors' relationships are often full of the pain of longing for connection contaminated with the terror of intimacy and closeness.

For partners, being in a relationship with a childhood trauma survivor can be challenging. Partners report isolation, pain, anger, frustration, challenges with communication and intimacy, sexual difficulties, and general dissatisfaction (Reid, Wampler, & Taylor, 1996). Partners talk about feeling as though they need to shut down emotionally and they tend to make negative assumptions about their survivor partners and their relationships (Millwood, 2011). Partners also report feeling left out of the individual therapy process, and they complain that individual therapists do not help the trauma survivor with important relational issues such as developing intimacy and repairing sexuality. Many partners voice the fear of becoming associated with their partners' perpetrator when they express their sexual needs or more difficult emotions. Partners often end up feeling that they are waiting for their turn – when the individual therapy has come to an end – so that they can resume their relationship (Dimitrova et al., 2010; Runtz & Schallow, 1997; Whiffen, Judd, & Aube, 1999).

When asked, childhood trauma survivors also perceive their partners in a negative light. They see them as less caring or supportive, and more controlling, insecure, dependent, immature, and exploitative, compared to the way partners without a history of childhood trauma describe their significant others (DiLillo, 2001).

What is known about working with childhood trauma couples?

The literature about working with childhood trauma survivors in couple therapy has begun to grow, as more survivors seek support in their relationships and express dissatisfaction with therapists' limited understanding of the role of trauma in relationship distress (Zala, 2012). Up to one third of couples presenting for couple therapy have a history of childhood sexual abuse in one or both partners (Anderson & Miller, 2006). Meanwhile, the process of couple therapy with childhood trauma survivors can be extremely challenging. Adding an attachment figure to the therapy process can accentuate survivors' challenges with attachment insecurity, emotion regulation, and tolerating or even imagining their partner's perspective. In my research, the most challenging moments in couple therapy were those where one partner expressed a need for something from their partner or a hurt that was caused by their partner: traumatized partners had difficulty listening, hearing, and responding to what their partner needed to some extent without becoming defensive or overwhelmed with difficult emotions (MacIntosh, 2013; MacIntosh & Johnson, 2008). Our analyses of the process of couple therapy with childhood trauma survivors have established key developmental self-capacities – attachment security, emotion regulation, and perspective taking or, more broadly, mentalizing capacities – which were severely compromised in childhood trauma survivor partners. The compromise of these capacities appeared to impede to play a vital role in the capacity of the survivor to tolerate and fully engage in the couple therapy process.

Why address developmental issues in childhood trauma couples?

Challenges with emotion regulation and mentalization are thought to underlie many of the difficulties that childhood trauma survivors experience in their couple relationships and in couple therapy. For children to develop the capacity to regulate their emotions, they need to experience the help of an attachment figure when dealing with distressing emotional states in early years. Over time, the help they receive from caregivers within secure attachment bonds becomes internalized as a self-capacity they will retain throughout their lives (Sroufe, 1996). Otherwise, distress becomes intolerable for infants and young children, and they do not develop the capacity to regulate their emotional distress. Lost in the sea of their own distress, without attachment figures to regulate and soothe them, these survivors may eventually turn to self-injury, dissociation, alcohol, sexual compulsivity, eating disorders, and other impulsive or self-destructive behaviours to distract, soothe, and numb themselves from their tumultuous inner worlds (Briere, 2006; Cloitre, Cohen, & Koenen, 2006; Linehan, 1993; van der Kolk, 1996; Zlotnick et al., 2003). Childhood trauma survivors can experience severe challenges with emotion regulation, even more than those who experience trauma in adulthood (Pelcovitz et al., 1997). For survivors, these problems can manifest in the form of emotional distress arising from seemingly small stresses, severe emotional responses, and subsequent difficulty calming down and letting go of upsetting events (Cloitre, 2002; Rorty & Yager, 1996; Zlotnick et al., 1999). Imagine the struggle, then, when survivors face the complex emotional challenges of romantic relationships without access to these vital capacities to regulate their own emotional states. Couples have described their emotional lives together as chaotic, frightening, painful, and exceedingly frustrating, as an experience of never being able to get out of the dark woods, no matter what direction they take.

Mentalizing is an interrelated self-capacity, a form of imaginative mental activity to make sense of others and of ourselves through the understanding of mental states. These capacities allow us to infer meaning to both explicit and implicit mental processes. Mentalizing is connected to emotion regulation; this capacity also develops throughout infancy and early childhood in the context of attachment relationships with those close to us. Caregivers who are responsive and try to understand our needs and distress help us develop the capacity to mentalize. They understand when it is time to help a person to become calm, soothed, and settled and when it is time to play, roughhouse, and laugh. Throughout these experiences, children learn that their feelings and mental states are their own and are acceptable, tolerable, and understandable. In learning how to mentalize well, they begin to think about, reflect on, hold, and explore emotions, thoughts, and mental states. Strong mentalizing capacities are fundamental to a person's ability to navigate the social world.

Survivors of childhood trauma frequently have difficulty in mentalizing well (Fonagy, 2010; Stein & Allen, 2007). Early studies have identified associations between childhood adversity and mentalizing difficulties in adulthood (Fonagy et al., 1996; Stein, Fonagy, Wheat, Kipp, & Gerber, 2004). In addition, mentalizing may play an important role as a mediating factor between childhood trauma and later psychological and relational functioning (MacIntosh, 2013). In general, those who report higher levels of abuse in childhood tend to have lower mentalizing capacities. In addition, those who experienced childhood trauma yet subsequently developed mentalizing capacities appeared to experience lower levels of distress, and difficulties in functioning, in adulthood. For survivors in couple relationships, it seems that mentalizing acts as a buffer against the development of some of the problems that traumatized couples experience in managing conflict and closeness (Fonagy et al., 1996). Thinking about how mentalizing capacities develop, through the consistent and responsive interchange between children and their attachment figures, it makes sense that survivors of childhood trauma often struggle in this area; someone who abuses a child is clearly unable or unwilling to imagine that child's inner experience. What child would feel safe and curious about the inner contents of the mind of someone who would abuse them?

At the same time, mentalizing is a capacity essential for partners to develop and maintain a healthy romantic relationship. Without being able to tolerate and reflect upon one's own thoughts, feelings, and behaviours, and those of one's partner, being in a couple relationship is very difficult indeed. Mentalizing allows us to acknowledge and take responsibility for ourselves in relationships, to have empathy and compassion for one another, to be vulnerable and open, and to have safe and clear boundaries with partners. However, old patterns, including those set by abusers, are likely to arise in intimate relationships that call on our most basic fears, longings, hopes, and needs. These patterns are often outside of our awareness. For childhood trauma survivors, who may previously have missed the opportunity to develop these vital self-capacities, emotion regulation and mentalizing – navigating the emotional complexities of relational life – can be a daunting task. But grounded in a therapeutic attachment that provides a safe base for exploration, a couple dealing with the ravages of scars left by childhood trauma may begin to engage in the emotionally challenging process of repairing and strengthening their couple relationship.

What is Developmental Couple Therapy for Complex Trauma?

Developmental Couple Therapy for Complex Trauma (DCTCT) was developed to provide couples dealing with the impacts of childhood trauma with a form of therapy that integrates a specific focus on the development of attachment security, emotion regulation, and mentalizing skills within the couple therapy context. The educational and skills-based focus early in the process allows couples to be prepared for, to tolerate, and then to fully engage in the deeper work of trauma processing and resolution of couple distress characteristic of later stages. This manual provides you, the therapist, with a basic framework with which to approach this work. Each section provides information for you, for your own knowledge development, along with a general outline of tasks and goals accompanied by segments of clinical sessions to illustrate them.

How the manual is organized

This manual is organized based on a model built to reflect the work I have done with couples in clinical settings. As with all manualized treatments that outline interventions in stages and steps, all couples differ, and each of them will require a unique approach that might involve more or less time at each stage. Many couples will have the capacity to tolerate difficult conversations right from the beginning of the process; meanwhile, others require many months of gentle preparation and relationship building before becoming ready to dive into conversations about traumatic memories, triggers, sex, and the role of past traumas on current relationship distress and conflict. Be mindful not to undermine the remarkable resiliency of survivor couples. Review each section and move at the pace of the couple's capacities.

Moving through the manual, you will find that early chapters, in Stage One, focus on providing the background and resources needed to engage in the psychoeducational modules. These provide a kind of buffet that allows you to adjust your selection of psychoeducation and interventions to the specific needs of each couple. Some couples may need to dive right into sex and sexuality, while other couples may need to focus on the impact of trauma on individuals and couples for many weeks before other topics can be explored. Each module of this section will be accompanied by psychoeducational handouts to help you explore these themes with clients. Moving into later stages of treatment, the manual will provide you with appropriate background, suggesting readings to expand upon particular topics and transcriptions of sessions that demonstrate how to get into the moment-by-moment process with a couple.

As a DCTCT therapist, your work changes during the successive stages of treatment. Beginning as a teacher, model, and mediator, then becoming a containing trauma therapist at certain intermediate stages, practitioners eventually act as a couple therapist, coach, and validator during the later stages. Over the recommended course of treatment, sessions move from weekly to bi-weekly to monthly and then taper off after 6–8 months. It is essential that couples not feel that their success in couple therapy is tied to losing you as their therapist. Go slowly, help them pull out of challenges and double back for more consolidation when they find applying their new skills and abilities to be too difficult, and cheer them on as they move towards autonomy.

Chapter 2

The couples

Throughout this manual, three representative but fictional couples will offer an in-depth look at the stages and steps of the process of DCTCT. Their backgrounds and struggles will be presented here; these couples will return and will contribute, through transcripts and commentary, weaving their way through the themes and processes of treatment. I have chosen to develop fictional cases based on composites of the many couples that have participated in clinical research over the years to protect their identities and confidentiality. Given the extremely painful and vulnerable process of engaging in couple therapy, where so much traumatic history is played out in graphic detail, I felt it necessary to disguise clients as much as possible while staying true to the clinical experience. In these discussions, I frame myself as the therapist and these couples as having completed the DCTCT process.

Amira and Anush

Amira and Anush are a young couple that has been married for 10 years following a long-distance courtship. The couple lives in a modest home, which they own, in a major Canadian city. The couple is devoted to their two young children, and describe their marriage as highly compatible in relation to parenting and managing the household. This couple came from a culture where both sets of parents were in arranged marriages to people chosen and approved of by their own parents; both partners also grew up in intergenerational households. Amira and Anush have both dated outside of the culture; however, they, and their families, were very happy when they decided to marry within the culture. Both Amira and Anush are very close to their families and treat their extended marital family as their own.

Anush was the eldest child, and the only boy, in his nuclear, first generation, Middle Eastern Canadian Muslim family. His parents came to Canada as refugees during a period of military unrest in their country of origin. Anush feels certain that his parents witnessed atrocities and were traumatized by their experiences as refugees. However, he is very aware that most others have never spoken about their experiences. He was raised to have strong identification with the role of eldest male, family protector, and caretaker.

Anush reported in the first session that his uncle, who lived with the family after he was sponsored to immigrate to Canada, sexually abused him from the ages of 10 to 12. Anush did not disclose this abuse to anyone. When it began, Anush was forced to sit with his uncle while he watched pornography and fondled Anush's genitals. The abuse progressed over the course of 2 years and involved forcing him to watch pornography while making Anush "jerk him off". Anush reported a confusing combination of revulsion and arousal that stayed with him from pubescence into adulthood, which severely impacted his comfort with his own developing sexuality. Anush indicated that he could never tell his parents about the abuse because of what he feared the revelation would do to them. Anush believed that his parents had been through enough and that telling them about his abuse would be unbearable. He also acknowledged that his own fear, confusion, and shame about his arousal during the abuse made it very difficult for him to situate the experiences into a perspective from which it was not his fault. He found it difficult to discuss his abuse in early sessions, but he was able to provide an outline and to let me know that he had not disclosed this to anyone, his parents, siblings, friends, or even Amira, until the previous year. The disclosure only came when Amira told him that she was going to leave him if things did not improve.

Amira was the youngest child in a large family of five girls, also a first-generation Middle Eastern Canadian Muslim family. She grew up with an overbearing father who constantly berated her mother and physically abused some of her older siblings with no warning for small transgressions. Amira was never physically assaulted by her father, although she was terrified that it would happen. There was no predicting when, and against whom, her father would strike. He could be gentle and tender with her one moment, and then viciously and brutally attack one of her siblings the next. Amira couldn't make any sense of this and fell into a pattern of hiding from her family, spending most of her time in the community library. Over the course of her childhood, her mother fell into several serious depressions, which resulted in hospitalizations and lengthy recovery periods. Amira did not label her childhood as having been traumatic, although she did acknowledge that it was confusing and stressful.

This case represents a childhood trauma survivor couple where many aspects of development unfolded as they should. However, Anush's experience of sexual abuse, and Amira's experience of witnessing interpersonal violence and the confusion of not being able to predict or understand her father, were excessively stressful and damaging. The abuse and interpersonal stress cast a long and dark shadow over the couple. Anush and Amira both developed the capacities needed to regulate their emotional states, to develop and maintain basic attachments, and to mentalize. These essential developmental capacities help this couple navigate the painful impact of the partners' prior experiences on their relationship. Both partners agreed that their marriage works in most ways: they are compatible, enjoy one another's company, complement each other as parents, and are devoted to their families. The couple also share core values about family and finances, are well-educated and engaged in their careers, and have little conflict about how they spend time or money. However, the couple struggles sexually: Anush cannot find his way to initiate and engage in sexual intimacy with Amira, but he has an addiction to internet pornography that takes him into deeper and darker places, separating the couple more and more over time.

Gary and Geoffrey

Gary and Geoffrey have been together for 12 years, but their relationship has been rocky from the start. The couple reported that over the course of their relationship they have broken up many times followed by increasingly tentative reconciliations. The couple would agree that each of these relationship ruptures wore down their trust and closeness a little more. To add to their stressors, the couple struggles financially and lives in a small subsidized apartment that feels a little claustrophobic to both partners.

Gary works part-time as a telemarketer and Geoffrey is struggling to make it through a university programme he has worked on for 7 years. Both partners report histories of significant trauma but neither has had access to trauma-informed mental health care due to limited finances.

Gary grew up with a father who was kind and loving at times, but who would fly into sudden, violent rages, hitting and kicking Gary until he was bloody and cowering in a corner. His mother left the family when Gary was 4 to live with a man in another city. Before she left, Gary's mother would go into Gary's bedroom at night in her nightgown, crawl into his bed, and rub her body up against him. Gary did not understand what she was doing and only knew that he felt "yucky" and uncomfortable. When Gary entered adulthood and learned about sex and sexuality, Gary realized, in horror, that his mother had been masturbating in the bed, cuddled up close to him, while he tried to pretend to sleep. Over the course of his childhood, Gary saw very little of his mother, who went through a string of boyfriends in many different cities.

Gary's father remarried when Gary was 5 years old and the couple had three daughters. Gary's father travelled for work, so Gary was left with his stepmother, who treated him like an uninvited guest. While his stepsisters enjoyed outings with their mother and the necessities of life such as food and clean clothing, Gary was frequently hungry, frightened, and left alone for long periods while his stepmother and sisters disappeared for days at a time on trips to visit her family. On one occasion, Gary told his father about being left alone without anything to eat, and his father beat him senseless for telling "such a terrible lie". He reported that his stepmother stood and watched, smirking, while Gary's father beat him black and blue. Like many neglected children, Gary was hungry for affection and attention and was prey to those seeking to exploit vulnerable children. It did not take long for a predator to pick up on his scent. A teacher at his school began to pay "special" attention to Gary and he lapped it up, eager to do anything this teacher asked of him. Over a period of grooming, Gary was invited to go to this teacher's house after school and they began watching funny movies together. Gradually these movies changed to pornography, which then grew to include more and more violent sexual abuse. The sexual abuse was characterized by that damning mixture of arousal, pain, and terror. Gary described the teacher as being gentle with him, arousing Gary by stimulating him with his hands and mouth, gently lubricating his anus and rectum with gels in a way that was very stimulating, eventually bringing Gary to orgasm. However, as the abuse progressed it became aggressive, painful, and violent. The teacher began to forcefully rape Gary until his rectum was bloody, torn, and badly damaged. As an adult, Gary has had to have reconstructive surgery to allow some minimal bowel function. Anal sex is not an option for Gary as it would not only trigger terrifying traumatic memories, but also destroy the very vulnerable surgical repair. In spite of the increasingly violent abuse, Gary had a difficult time not returning to the teacher's home. The violent abuse was still tinged with some affectionate cuddling and was the only attention he received. Eventually, he was able to refuse to go home with the teacher. However, Gary paid a steep price for this; his teacher stalked him relentlessly until he moved to a different city at 16. Gary is a poor historian who struggled with severe dissociation in early sessions. It was very difficult for him to talk about his childhood and he appeared to come in and out of dissociative states, at times seeming to suddenly fall asleep in sessions. The information here was pieced together from tidbits gleaned over many months. He struggled to provide detail about his life, even things that happened the day before. Gary continued to experience trauma into adulthood, including physical and sexual assault. He had little access to education, social support, or even the capacity to engage with work due to such high levels of dissociation and traumatic symptoms. All of these conspired to force Gary into a life of poverty, often living on the streets, where he was revictimized physically and sexually assaulted.

Geoffrey is a person of colour who was adopted from Venezuela into a family of devout, born-again Christians. He was an only child and his parents separated when he was 7. His mother refused to allow his father to visit, which left Geoffrey without the one person to whom he had felt the closest. Over time, his father's visits diminished and by the time Geoffrey was a teenager, his father stopped trying to connect with him at all. Over the course of Geoffrey's childhood, his mother's behaviour became more and more erratic, and she was eventually diagnosed with bipolar disorder. When his mother was "up", she was amazing: they would go out for breakfast at an all-night diner at 2:00 in the morning, run through the park singing, and dance in the rain. When she was "down", Geoffrey had to hide. His mother would fly off the handle for any provocation and beat Geoffrey until he screamed at her to stop, he then locked himself in his room. Geoffrey struggled to acknowledge and accept his sexuality over the course of his teenage years, given his background in a conservative religious community. When Geoffrey came out at 22, his mother told him he was a disgusting aberration to nature and disowned him. Geoffrey has made several attempts to reunite with his mother, but she has rebuked all his efforts.

Gary and Geoffrey struggle with daily functioning, experiencing frequent fights and long periods when Gary is so dissociated and disconnected from his surroundings that Geoffrey is often left watching a non-communicative Gary rock back and forth in a corner. During these periods, Geoffrey's desperation to connect with Gary grows until he becomes unable to control his need for contact. At first, he approaches Gary tentatively but becomes increasingly more frantic when he does not respond until he finds himself screaming at Gary, in desperation, until he collapses in exhausted despair. By the time the couple began therapy, they were locked into an interminable cycle of distress.

In contrast to Anush and Amira, Gary and Geoffrey have not developed many of the vital developmental self-capacities that might assist them in managing their distress, either individually or as a couple. Their impoverished and abusive, early attachment relationships did not allow for, and in Gary's case actively hindered, the development of the capacity to regulate their emotional states, to develop and maintain basic attachments, and to mentalize well. In the absence of these essential developmental capacities, this couple is struggling to navigate the painful impact of their traumas on their relationship and, really, to navigate any challenges in their lives.

Camille and Chris

Camille and Chris are a young couple that has been together for 5 years, since they met in university. Camille is French Canadian and was raised in a small rural community, while Chris came to Montreal from England to go to university. When Camille and Chris met they were very attracted to one another but struggled to communicate. When they met, Camille spoke very little English and Chris spoke very little French. The couple has struggled with high levels of conflict from the beginning of their relationship. In the first session, they both reported that when it is good between them, it is very good, and when it is bad between them, it is very bad. The couple engages in verbal and physical interpersonal violence (IPV), which was a concern for the treatment team in considering them for the intervention. However, the couple indicated that these events were very infrequent and that there was a long lead-up to each incident. A decision was made to provide them with treatment and to monitor closely the potential for IPV in the hope that developing emotion regulation and mentalizing capacities would help the couple de-escalate their episodes of conflict.[1]

Camille grew up in a small community in northern Quebec where her father had been sent by a pulp and paper company to work as an engineer. She was the middle child, between two brothers, and their mother was devoted to her role as wife and stay-at-home mother. She had given up her career as a musician to stay home with her children. While her brothers were boisterous and always surrounded by friends and busy with activities, Camille was quieter and found it hard to connect with other children her age. She reported that she always felt somehow different or separate from others. She could see that her parents were trying hard, but she could not feel close to them, nor could she turn to them to talk about her feelings of ostracism and estrangement. Camille's memories are riddled with experiences of feeling overwhelmed and distressed and reaching out to her parents who seemed unable to tolerate, contain, or help her cope with her distress.

When Camille was 10, she was walking home from school one day and was grabbed by a man she knew from her community. He was very involved in local politics and she perceived him as powerful. He dragged her into the back of his car and raped her, viciously. After the rape, this man threw her out onto the pavement, clothes askew, bruised, and bloody. Camille went to the nearby woods and tried to clean herself up by washing in a stream. However, when she got home her mother could tell that something was very wrong and pressured Camille to disclose what had happened. The details had become confused in Camille's mind and her mother went to the police with a confusing story that was quickly dismissed. After this, Camille pushed the memory aside and continued to be socially withdrawn and disconnected. She remained lonely and unhappy, yet the memory of this violation that might help her make sense of some aspects of her life and relationships, albeit traumatic, was fuzzy and far away in her mind. When Camille was 16, she met a boy in a reading club to whom she felt close and attracted. One thing led to another and the two ended up kissing outside the youth centre where the club was held. As soon as his arms were around her, Camille reported that images of the rape came back to her; she struggled free from him and ran away. Since that time Camille has struggled with flashbacks, pervasive feelings of fear and anxiety, nightmares, and a desire to make the memories go away again. She moved to a large city in the hopes of getting away from reminders of the rape, but they continued to pursue her. When she met Chris, a young man so different from any she had known before, she hoped that he would be the solution to her desire for connection without reminders.

Chris grew up in the south of England in a middle-class family. He had one older brother and busy, professional parents. His parents were rarely at home, and he and his brother spent a lot of time roaming the countryside and playing sports with other neighbourhood kids. He was very close to his brother, who took care of him during the frequent absences of his parents. The family was distant from one another and Chris's parents frequently erupted into chaotic bursts of rage over seemingly unimportant issues with no predictable pattern, putting Chris in the middle as their go-between and confidant.

When Chris was 9 and his brother was 16, his parents left them alone for a weekend while they went away to a ski weekend in France. Chris and his brother were play-fighting and Chris pushed his brother to stop him from tickling him. Chris's brother slipped, tripped, and hit his head on the corner of a counter as he fell to the floor unconscious. Chris could not rouse his brother and called emergency services. Unfortunately, Chris's brother had a life-altering brain injury; although he recovered, he experienced significant long-term deficits in his cognitive functioning. Chris has never forgiven himself, and neither have his parents. Chris's brother is the only member of the family who does not blame Chris for the devastating injury. Chris decided to move to Canada for university to escape the constant guilt he feels when he sees his brother. Chris now struggles with shame and guilt, which interfere with his capacity to focus and concentrate on his studies, and he easily loses his temper with Camille.

Chris and Camille started out with the passion and determination of many new couples who have experienced childhood trauma. They struggled because of their language difference, but this was just one source of their difficulties. Camille longed for closeness with Chris, but their sexual relationship was fraught with turmoil and crisis. While Camille wanted to be sexually intimate, each time either of them would initiate sexual contact, she would become triggered and go straight into flashbacks. When Chris could not console her or help her become grounded, he would eventually storm away with feelings of hopelessness and helplessness, leaving Camille alone in her terror. After a few hours, the two would come back together, try to talk about it, come up with some plan for the next time, and then the cycle would be repeated. Over time, their disappointment and distress in their sexual relationship would spill over into the rest of their lives together as their bond deteriorated. By the time the couple found their way into my research study, they were fighting constantly and feeling despair about the possibility of healing their relationship.

Chris and Camille would fall in the middle between Anush and Amira and Gary and Geoffrey. Both Chris and Camille had some positive attachment experiences growing up and some moments of relative normalcy in their homes. While Camille found it difficult to connect to her parents and siblings, she did experience their love and desire to help her feel more connected. Camille experienced a violent trauma, but it was not within a primary attachment relationship; she was old enough to have developed some rudimentary self-capacities and coping skills with which to navigate the aftermath. Chris experienced the trauma of his brother's injury, and his own feelings of culpability continued to plague him, yet he also had experienced a sense of bonding and connection to his family prior to that trauma which provided a buffer against the severity of his guilt and shame. Neither had to deal with poverty or mental illness in their parents, but both felt disconnected from their families and supports following their traumas.

I have chosen to use these three couples to illustrate the issues facing couples with a history of childhood trauma because they are diverse and represent typical issues faced by childhood trauma couples. Heterosexual and LGBTQ couples, intrafamilial and extrafamilial abuse, diverse cultural and socioeconomic backgrounds, and single and dual trauma couples are all represented. Many childhood trauma survivors end up in relationships with other trauma survivors and with those with other mental health challenges (MacIntosh & Johnson, 2008; Putnam, 1989). Dual trauma couples face even greater challenges with mutuality of emotion dysregulation and attachment insecurity, and an even greater need for reliable treatment. Amira and Anush and Chris and Camille had some positive developmental experiences despite experiences of abuse. Gary and Geoffrey had few such developmentally beneficial experiences. These couples share certain common issues related to childhood trauma but also represent distinct poles of expression of functionality in terms of emotion regulation, attachment security, and impaired mentalizing (MacIntosh, 2013). It is always important to remember the context and social location of your couples. Race, class, culture, sexual orientation, and gender identity all intersect with developmental experiences and can pose increased risk for trauma occurring in the first place.

Establishing context

In your first session with the couple, you have the opportunity to introduce the couple to the treatment model and discuss the rationale for the approach. You will also be able to provide them with some guidelines about participating in treatment and make an initial assessment of their level of distress. Over the course of Stage One, make sure to focus consistently on the need to develop a strong therapeutic alliance and a feeling of safety. Therapeutic alliances with trauma survivors are, understandably, vital to the success of the therapeutic work and are hard earned. The first step in Stage One involves joining the couple in introducing and discussing the model of treatment and being responsive to any questions they might have. Provide the couple with the handouts included below and slowly review the stages and steps with them while remaining open to discussing their questions and concerns.

Introduction to the model

As you review the model, it will be important for the couple to understand the rationale for spending so much time and energy on skills building. In many cases, the level of individual and couple distress is so high that it can feel frustrating and painful to work on building skills instead of diving into the morass of pain and conflict. It is essential that the couple understand that these skills are vital to engagement in the deeper work of exploring conflict and trauma. I tell couples that it is important to find ways to contain conflict in the first stages of therapy so that we can all learn about each other, develop a strong working relationship, learn more about the impact of trauma on them and their couple relationship, and build the skills necessary to engage in therapy and build a stronger relationship. I also discuss with couples the importance of not divulging too much about their traumas until they feel safe, contained, and supported in the therapeutic milieu.

Over the first sessions, the basic process of getting to know your couple needs to be balanced with their introduction to the model and a focus on building a therapeutic relationship. As with any couple intervention, it is important to understand their current context: where they live and work, whether they have children, where they met, what first drew them to one another, where are the particular sources of pleasure and pain in the relationship, and why now – why have they felt that now is the time for therapy?

In the first session, I present the nature and process of the treatment with Chris and Camille. Chris and Camille approached me specifically for trauma-focused couple therapy, so I did not need to discover this; rather, we could dive directly into the rationale for the model after some initial discussion of their current context.

THERAPIST: So, let's talk about our goals for today and then we can talk a little more about what's going on with you guys right now. As we discussed on the phone, the therapy model that we will be working with has been developed with an understanding of the impact of trauma in childhood on adulthood and on couple relationships. Much of the focus of the therapy is on how those traumas affect your relationship, how we can work together to heal from those historical traumas, and to help you, as a couple, build a strong, healthy and loving relationship. Do you have any questions at this point, before we get started discussing the specifics of how this model works?

CHRIS AND CAMILLE: No, no.

THERAPIST: As we go along, I invite you to ask as many questions as you might have and to give me any feedback about what feels like it might be helpful or not. Sound okay?

CHRIS AND CAMILLE: Yup, so far. . .

THERAPIST: Okay, so let's dive in. You both know, because you've both had traumatic experiences and you are both struggling in different ways in your relationship, that trauma affects different people in different ways. However, there are some similarities that seem to cut across most people, and one of the biggies is relationships in adulthood. As you can imagine, if you are traumatized in childhood, especially by someone like a parent or a caregiver, then that's going to affect the way you feel about people you're supposed to be close to, people you're trying to build a family with. So, what we've seen with couples is that sometimes the early stages of the relationship go pretty well. Couples often feel like, this someone is different, a new relationship with someone who is completely different from the person that hurt them or, this is a new kind of experience, so it must be healthy and positive. And then, once they get deep into the relationship, they find themselves starting to fall into the same patterns as they have in other relationships from the past that didn't end up well or that even ended up being quite traumatic and destructive to them. Next thing, they find themselves filled with the kinds of patterns of mistrust and fear that they experienced early in their life around being able to feel connected and safe with people. And then we come to therapy and find that it is really hard. We need to be able to talk about things that are difficult but find that the trauma gets in the way of being able to talk about things that are difficult because emotions get in the way. For many trauma survivors, feelings become so overwhelming that they become flooded and don't feel safe or, even worse, they feel retraumatized. For other survivors, feelings just get shut down and the person kind of disappears from the room. In the end, then, it becomes really difficult to solve the problems in the relationship and people often feel really alone and ashamed. So, the way this approach goes, we are going to work together slowly and build up to looking at the harder things once we have worked on some of the issues that we struggle with after trauma and that will prepare for working on the harder, more painful struggles in the couple relationships. [distributes handout to the couple]

This approach is in four stages and where we are at now is right here at the beginning. This first stage then is to explore and build understanding about how trauma impacts us and our relationships. As we look at these different topics – trauma and individuals and couples, trauma and attachment, trauma and sexuality, shame, negative cycles and how trauma becomes embedded in them – and we learn about emotion regulation and mentalizing, we will also work on getting to know one another and building a relationship, in here, with me and you, that feels as safe as is possible for where you are right now. We are going to be talking about some of the most intimate, challenging, and painful parts of your selves and your relationship, so we need to take that time to build up some safety and connection between us. Part of what we're going to do in the first few sessions as we review the psychoeducation materials is to get to know each other, and we're going to move at whatever speed we need to for you to feel safe and not overwhelmed. And again, I really encourage you to ask lots of questions as you go along.

As the process moves along, our explorations will get more specific, more focused on the reason you've come: the deep inner workings of your selves and your relationship. So, we're going start with a lot of talking about how trauma impacts people without talking about the specifics of your trauma. As we get into the second stage, we will start to work on building skills that are really important for healthy relationships but that often don't develop in the context of trauma, or if they have developed, they get messed up by the traumas, especially when the perpetrator is someone you should have been able to trust. These skills are called emotion regulation and mentalizing. We'll talk a lot about what these are when we get into those sections but, basically, if we have trouble regulating our emotions, it can be really difficult to deal with the normal, day-to-day conflicts of being in a relationship. And, if we have trouble mentalizing, it can be really hard to see another person's perspective, to make sense of what is happening to you or even to know what you, yourself, might want and need. These are really important skills and, without them, survivors often feel lost, alone, overwhelmed, and hopeless. When we get to Stage Three, you'll see that we start talking more directly about your experiences and get into the processing around how trauma is living in your relationship now. Makes sense? Do you have any questions about that?

CHRIS AND CAMILLE: No.

THERAPIST: Okay. So, as I said, at the beginning we're going to talk a lot about safety and relationships and trauma. One of the things that happens is that trauma starts to get relived in the present like in a relationship. For example, I'm just going to make something up because I don't know how it works for you both, or if it works at all. Say someone was sexually abused by their father, and they also really loved their father, and their father gave them lots of special attention. On the one hand, you received all of that special attention from your father; on the other hand, your father was hurting you very badly. Imagine the conflict that creates in a child. And then, when you become an adult and you get into a couple relationship with someone, and you try to get close to them, a cycle of desire and longing alternating with fear and pain can start to happen. You can end up getting into a negative cycle with one another where one of you is maybe trying to get close to the other and the other is frightened by that and starts to run away. Over time, that can turn into a cycle where some of the dynamic of what happened with your dad starts to come alive in your couple relationship. Does that make sense?

CAMILLE: Yes, that makes a lot of sense and that feels like what is happening with Chris and I. I really want to get close to him but it's like some kind of force is tearing us apart no matter how hard we try.

THERAPIST: So those are the sort of things we're going to start to try to piece apart and resolve as we work together. The overall goals are to become more comfortable with your trauma as a part of your life as opposed to something you are working hard to keep separate and apart from yourself and your relationship because it's hard to cope with. It is a part of your life story, and without bringing it out of hiding and having a chance to work on it together, it will be hard for you to become comfortable with your emotional life, with each other, and even your interior self. We will learn more skills about managing emotions and traumatic states and experiences, and start to really identify those relationship patterns that get in your way. You know, that feeling you have when you're in the same fight you've had a hundred times and you think, why are we doing this thing again that we've already done before? To start to be able to piece that out, to notice it, and then to stop it, and to change it. So that, as you learn skills about that, but also as you become more comfortable with your emotional life, closeness and trust, those things will start to gradually shift. And also, to know how to support each other; you've both been through a lot. One of the first things that goes when there's conflict or distress in the relationship is that there isn't that sense of security because people end up turning away from each other instead of towards each other for support. Make sense?

CHRIS: Yes, we certainly have a fight we have over and over again! [both laugh]

As you can see, I reviewed the model using the handout, which provided the couple with the specifics of the stages and steps, and this was accompanied by a discussion of the rationale for the specific focus on trauma and its impacts.

Couple therapy guidelines

After this initial discussion about the approach, it is important also to outline for the couple what might be expected of them in terms of commitment, participation, and homework.

THERAPIST: Sessions will generally start with a brief check-in where you can tell me about your week and how you have been doing with whatever skill or issue we are working on. As we work our way through these stages and steps, there will sometimes be homework, so sessions will start by reviewing the homework that we've been doing. Sometimes it will be something that you'll do on your own. Sometimes it will be something that you do together as a couple. So, we'll review the homework, any questions you have, and move on to the goal for the session, which will change depending on the stage we are in.

[Chris and Camille both nod]

THERAPIST: Okay. So, all that I ask of you then, is to show up and to really try to listen to each other; to tell me, at any point if you have questions or concerns. I want to hear about it. And I mean that from the perspective of our relationship, but also if there are things that don't feel right or feel uncomfortable. It's important that this is a space where you feel you can express your doubt, worry, and fear, and it will be taken seriously.

This work is not for the faint of heart and there will be pain for all involved – you, the therapist included. It is really important, as you embark upon this challenging process with your survivor couples, to set the stage by beginning with respect, validation for their courage and commitment to improving their relationship, along with a clear statement that it is always darker before the dawn. Survivors have often been failed by some of the most important people in their lives – including, for many, therapists – so it is important that, as you establish context with them, you emphasize the importance of just showing up, coming even when it feels hard, and trying, against all the evidence against it, to trust the process. It is a slow process and one that will push up against all of the hard and crunchy spaces where trauma has rendered them scarred and yearning. It is a stance of clarity, confidence, and deep respect for their resilience in the face of horrors, to come and lay their pains bare in the hope that they might find deeper safety, love, and security in their relationship.

Note

1 A discussion on the issue of IPV and making decisions about whether to work with a couple in therapy is contained in Chapter 4: Containing Conflict.

Developmental Couple Therapy for Complex Trauma (DCTCT)

- DCTCT is a model of couple therapy that works from a developmental perspective to help couples cope with the long-term impacts of childhood trauma.
- This therapy was specifically designed for couples that have had traumatic experiences in childhood that have affected their relationships. In the couple context, childhood traumas can make it difficult for partners to engage with each other. Instead of turning to each other for support and comfort, people who have been traumatized in childhood often find that closeness feels frightening and dangerous.
- The overall focus of this therapeutic model is to help couples learn how to tolerate, understand, and manage their own and their partner's emotions, how to understand each other's perspectives, and how to be present and engaged to meet one another's emotional and attachment needs.
- Throughout the process of therapy, we will use exercises to help you develop the tools to develop the kind of close, loving, and supportive relationship you desire.
- The focus in the later stages of the therapy is on helping you to work with your partner to process some of the impact of your traumatic experiences on you and your relationship. Some of this will involve sharing the stories of your experiences and how they are living in your relationship in the present and slowly learning new ways of being together.
- Stage One – Establishing Context
    - Establishing safety, therapeutic alliance
    - Psychoeducation (creating a common goal)
        - Trauma and relationships
        - Trauma and attachment
        - Trauma and sexuality
        - Shame
        - The negative cycle and dyadic traumatic reenactment
        - What is mentalizing?
        - What is emotion regulation?
    - Containing conflict
- Stage Two – Capacity Building in the Attachment Relationship Context
    - Building mentalizing capacities
    - Building emotion regulation capacities
- Stage Three – Attachment-Focused Dyadic Processing
    - Attachment histories living in the present
    - Dyadic traumatic reenactment
    - Disclosure – telling the stories
    - Trauma processing in a dyadic context
    - Sex and sexuality
- Stage Four – Consolidation
    - Consolidation

Chapter 3

Stage One

Psychoeducation

Stage One of DCTCT involves engaging in a psychoeducational process with couples about the potential impacts of childhood developmental trauma on their adult lives and relationships. For many, there is a light bulb that turns on, and this can go a long way towards scaffolding containment and inciting motivation and hope as they move forward: *this explains everything and there's something we can do about it*! For others, this material fuels shame and hopelessness: *how can anything ever get better if I am all of these things*? Each of the modules involves the review of a handout and then an exploration of how the topic relates to this particular couple and the strategies they have attempted to resolve the issues related to this theme. The first area to explore is the potential impacts of childhood trauma on adults and on couple relationships.

This first topic will provide you, the therapist, with a lot of information about how the therapeutic process might unfold as you begin to see, first-hand, how the couple regulates their emotions, how they mentalize (or not), and how they approach guided, contained discussions about themselves and their relationship. Using your own empathic attunement as a guide, it is essential to help the couple manage their level of emotional distress through pacing and balancing closed- and open-ended emotional or cognitive questions. Asking more open-ended, emotionally charged questions heightens arousal, while more closed, cognitive questions shift the couple back towards regulation as emotional intensity decreases. Briere (2006) talks about the Therapeutic Window in work with trauma survivors, where the goal is to maintain a level of emotional engagement and arousal that allows for processing and resolution but avoids over- or under-regulation and dissociation; these are emotional areas where survivors are likely to either simply numb out and not process or – worse still – to be retraumatized within what is supposed to be a safe therapeutic space.

Remember, these are your first moments to engage in the therapeutic work and are therefore the first opportunities you have, as the therapist, to build safety and to demonstrate to the couple that you are paying close attention to what they need to be safe during therapy. As the educator in these first sessions, you demonstrate that you are listening to the couple, actively helping them to regulate their emotions, not judging, and empathizing with their struggles. These are your first opportunities to begin to establish yourself and the therapeutic space as a safe base and secure haven for this difficult work.

Trauma and relationships

In this first psychoeducational module, you set the stage for the modules to follow. As discussed in the introduction, the impacts of childhood trauma on adult couple relationships can be quite devastating. Couples may have significant difficulties developing and maintaining strong and safe relationships with partners. On the one hand, survivors are often directed inwards, towards managing their distress due to intrusive trauma symptoms, nightmares, and struggles with emotion regulation; this turns them away from their partner and can lead to a survivor seeking peace through avoidance and inward focus. On the other hand, many survivors have only had extremely negative and abusive models for relationships and have not had the nurturing "good enough" attachment experiences that would allow for the development of the basic capacities for fully engaging in a couple relationship in effective and emotionally rewarding ways. So, survivors may be directed inwards and away from their partners, and they may also struggle with the basic building blocks for developing and maintaining a strong couple relationship. And, when dealing with a couple where both partners have experienced trauma, the situation is even more compounded and challenging!

First, provide the couple with the psychoeducational handout, found below, to help survivors and their partners understand more thoroughly the impact of childhood trauma on adulthood and on adult couple relationships. The handout provides a launching pad to begin challenging discussions. It also provides something for the couple to take away with them to reflect upon and discuss. For those survivors who have a tendency towards dissociation, this may also allow them something to literally and psychically hang on to as they attempt to stay present in the sessions, or to process the material outside of sessions as they learn how to titrate their emotional response. Gary, for example, really struggles with dissociation and found it very difficult to stay present and engaged in sessions. After the session where we reviewed this handout, he pulled out a well-handled, folded-up wad of paper from his pocket and said: "like it says on this list, I have a lot of trouble trusting Geoffrey". In the session itself, Gary was very quiet and said very little, but he did fold up that piece of paper, take it away, and reflect upon it, and he had some thoughts to share at the next session. It is important to emphasize that it is not the "what" of the trauma that is vital to understand its impacts but the "who", "where", "when", and "why". What I mean by this is that it is not the title of the trauma (sexual abuse, physical abuse, neglect, etc.) but rather the relationship to the perpetrator, the "who"; the proximity to the trauma, the "where"; the age of onset, frequency, duration, and severity of the trauma, the "when"; and the nature of the experience of the trauma, the "why" that are important to these discussions. For instance, a child who from a stage of pre-verbal development is raped by a primary caregiver, in their own bed, over many years, will have a very different experience of sexual abuse than a 15-year-old adolescent, raped by a boy she just met on a date, who is able to go home and tell her parents about it and receive a loving, supportive response. Both are horrible and life-changing experiences, but their impacts are very different.

As this is the first session of "work", it is important to set the boundaries and frame around the work from the beginning. Emotion regulation and safety are the first order of the day and the role of therapists to both model and coach working on difficult material without becoming flooded or numbed out. I am a proponent of the "rule of thirds" (Kluft, 1993), where the first third of the session is spent checking in, planning the session, and discussing any potential concerns about the work to come; the second third is spent in the deeper work of exploration and trauma processing; and the final third is spent debriefing and grounding – getting the client ready to go out into the world.

The following transcript contains segments of a session with Chris and Camille, where we began to review the handout to explore the impact of trauma on their lives and relationship. Camille found the experience extremely painful and triggering, and it brought out her feelings of hopelessness, that nothing will ever change and no one will be able to help her. These feelings were overwhelming for Camille, and Chris found it difficult to understand how knowing more could cause anguish rather than hope.

The session starts with a brief outline of the contexts and characteristics of their traumatic histories. We begin with a short summary of the nature of their traumatic histories, very much the outline, not the details, to set the context and to look for similarities and differences in experiences and impacts. For dual trauma couples, this is the first opportunity to demonstrate holding, containing, and empathic attunement to both partners and to help them stop and listen to one another in spite of strong emotions. We do not explore the details of the traumas but rather their contexts – relationships to perpetrator, family situations, ages, sexual vs. non-sexual trauma, whether there was a disclosure and how this was responded to, and so on – along with characteristics about the abuse: whether it was sudden, violent, unpredictable, pleasurable or painful, chronic or episodic, and so on. This provides a framework for engaging with the handout and some avenues for the therapist to explore without going into detail about the abuse. Do not confuse the urgent desire to be unburdened of a story that has not previously been told with trust, safety, and alliance. Allowing for premature unloading of the details of a trauma story can lead a survivor to feel ashamed, alone, overwhelmed, retraumatized, and avoidant. Premature disclosures may mean that you may never see your client again. In sessions, I am quite explicit about this:

> I know that it might feel like you should tell me the story of what happened to you or, even, that you really would like to finally tell someone about what happened to you, but it is early days in our therapy relationship and you and I don't know each other very well. On the one hand, I want you to be in charge of how and what you share in here: you are the person who knows yourself the best. On the other hand, I want us together to really make sure that you feel safe here with me and that you have some new skills in place to deal with all of the feelings that might arise during and after telling a story that you have never fully told. How do you feel about that?

Following this initial framing of the trauma, I review the handout and consider the potential impacts on the individual. For some, this is just reading through the list and acknowledging "yes" or "no" about each item as though it were a grocery list. For others, this grows into a lengthy exploration of aspects of themselves and their adult lives that have previously been a confusing mystery to them. Simply follow along and make sure to include both partners in the discussion; this is not the place to allow a dynamic of the "sick" partner and the "well" partner, or the traumatized and non-traumatized partner, to take hold. Inevitably, if only one partner in the couple identifies with being "traumatized", the session may start to slant in this direction. However, my experience and that of others suggests that survivors tend to build relationships with others with similar histories or who struggle with other aspects of mental health challenges (Nordsletten et al., 2015), and so even without an identified trauma history, there is usually something that the "non-traumatized" partner can identify with in the handout. For many couples, these individual impacts can take up one full session.

THERAPIST: So, one of the things that we are exploring in this particular therapy is how trauma affects relationships and how that understanding will be an important part of the therapy process. The beginning phase is to just explore that a bit.

Last time you told me about how you met, a little bit about what goes well between you and the struggles you experience, but what I wanted to do today was just to talk about trauma and relationships and see where that brings up things for you in terms of – your backgrounds are different in the kinds of families you were in, the kinds of traumas you experienced – but there may be more commonalities than we know, in terms of how they affected you. So, we just want to explore that today, as a kind of a baseline for us in moving forward. Does that sound okay?

CHRIS: Okay.

CAMILLE: Yeah.

THERAPIST: [hands the handout to each partner] We'll go through this slowly and talk about where you see yourselves in these points. You can stop me whenever you need to and ask any questions or make any comments that come to you. And perhaps, over the next week, you can think about where you see yourself in this as you interact with each other.

For you, Camille, the main trauma you experienced was an incident that happened, suddenly, that was a completely overwhelming, terrifying incident, and then, you didn't have a lot of support around that.

CAMILLE: Yeah.

THERAPIST: So that trauma really accentuated or heightened some dysfunction that was already there in your family about how you guys talk to each other about difficult things and your parents' capacity to tolerate your distress.

CAMILLE: Yeah.

THERAPIST: And that kind of dynamic, it sounds like, is still there in your family.

CAMILLE: Yeah, it's made it worse.

THERAPIST: So, there's this horrible, sudden trauma, but it happened in the context of a family where you already felt unheard and that your feelings were too much for your parents.

CAMILLE: Yeah.

THERAPIST: But for you, Chris, you experienced the trauma of your brother's head injury and the unpredictable outbursts of your parents that occurred with a lot of regularity, yelling – a lot of drama, I guess. How would you describe it?

CHRIS: I don't know. After my brother's accident I didn't have any support either, so it was a bit like Camille except that everyone agreed that it was my fault, so I guess no one thought that I should have any help. But, always, even before my brother's accident, it was a lot of hot and cold, I guess. Sometimes we would go weeks with nothing, and then all of a sudden, just a big explosion, and then nobody would talk to each other, for like, forever, and then we would explode again.

THERAPIST: Was there any way of predicting what would set the trigger?

CHRIS: Yeah, you started to figure it out after a while but, like, it wasn't always obvious. Or sometimes it was unavoidable.

THERAPIST: Okay. So, the traumas you both experienced were different and the context was different, but let's look at how these traumas might have affected you both. If we look at this handout we start looking at the impact on the inside of yourself and in terms of your sense of self. Sometimes when people experience different kinds of traumas, they come into adulthood feeling helpless and unable to change things in their lives, a lot of shame and guilt or self-blame, or like there's something wrong with them, or even that they're much older than they are or that they're much younger than they are. Do any of those things fit for you?

CAMILLE: Yeah.

THERAPIST: You're nodding your head. Can you describe?

CAMILLE: Growing up, I always felt like I was much older, because I had to take care of myself, and my parents, and my family.

THERAPIST: And you were, sort of, accelerated, in growing up.

CAMILLE: And I didn't have much in common with kids my own age, because we didn't have the same expectation of what we were supposed to be doing.

THERAPIST: So, you didn't feel like you fit.

CAMILLE: No, I didn't feel like I fit. I was just way too mature for them.

THERAPIST: And what is that like for you now? Do you feel more like you fit in, or the same?

CAMILLE: No, I still feel like I'm older.

THERAPIST: Yes.

CAMILLE: And, it's tough. But, I mean, it's better now, because people my age are starting to mature. People are starting to get there, but they're not quite – I still feel like I'm much older than I am.

THERAPIST: Okay, so you still feel ahead of the people who are your own age. How about you, Chris?

CHRIS: I experienced the same thing, pretty much. I only got along with girls when I was younger, because they were the only ones who could actually keep up with me. And then, when I went to school, I had to like – it was weird, I had to discover this way of turning my maturity off so that I could hang out with the younger people, but then turning it back on again, and like, I still do this, it's really weird, it depends on who I hang out with, I have to dumb myself down.

THERAPIST: And what about with Camille?

CHRIS: With Camille, no. I don't know. I find with Camille that since I had to be mature for so long that, I'm trying to be a kid again sometimes too, and when I get anxious, I kind of do that. I don't know. When it's important I think that I can – I switch the adult on – but when it's not so important, I just kind of mess around.

THERAPIST: Is this something you recognized in each other when you met? This sort of difference?

CAMILLE: Yeah, definitely. I thought, you used to be less childish when we first met.

CHRIS: Well, that's because I was not comfortable with you, yet.

THERAPIST: His full, childish self was yet to emerge. [all laugh]

THERAPIST: So, if we look a little further on the list, another thing that happens for many people – and I know, Camille, that you mentioned you have some difficulty with memory and dissociation – that there are still aspects of the traumatic experience itself, that you – you've just sort of accepted that they're not clear, or a bit fuzzy. Do you have those feelings now? Do you have situations you fall into, where you feel a bit dissociated or where you have trouble remembering?

CAMILLE: Like, I'm talking to somebody, and I can't remember? Something like that?

THERAPIST: Just even now. So you're talking with someone and you start to feel a little bit fuzzy, or disconnected.

CAMILLE: I'd say, emotionally. I don't think memory-wise. I don't feel like I'm forgetting what I'm doing. It's more just I don't, I don't need to engage, like I decide on what level I want to engage?

THERAPIST: So, you can turn off parts of your emotional self.

CAMILLE: Oh yeah!

THERAPIST: In connection with others, pretty easily?

CAMILLE: Yeah, as soon as I don't feel comfortable, it's just, whsssht, gone.

THERAPIST: Okay, so that's something to be really aware of, in here. That we can find a way for you to signal that to me, so that I have a sense of when that happens – because my guess is that people don't necessarily know that you've done that.
CAMILLE: I'm good at hiding it.
THERAPIST: Right. So, it's important that I know.

Both Chris and Camille were able to talk about some of the contexts and characteristics of their traumas and to begin to discuss the potential impacts. However, while Chris was able to acknowledge a particular "style" in how he responded when triggered, using words, Camille "showed" me how she responds when triggered by suddenly shifting her emotional tone, physical posture, facial expressions, and language. At this point, Camille thrust the handouts back towards me and angrily indicated that she did not like the "lists". This was an opportunity for modelling emotion regulation, demonstrating non-defensive mentalizing, and striking the balance between avoidance/tolerance and approach/dysregulation.

CAMILLE: [sudden change in emotional tone from curious and playful to tense and fretful] Yeah. Actually, I just don't feel comfortable with this. [hands over set of papers] I don't like, I don't like the lists.
THERAPIST: Oh, you don't like lists at all?
CAMILLE: [arms folded] No, I just don't feel comfortable, with that, right now.
THERAPIST: This particular list? If it was a different kind of list would it be alright?
CAMILLE: Just this list is not working. [now sounding angry]
THERAPIST: And what about the conversation about what is on the list?
CAMILLE: The conversation is okay; I just don't want to list it now.
THERAPIST: You just don't want to have to see it. And what does it trigger for you? To see this itemized, bold list on your lap?
CAMILLE: Uncomfortable.
THERAPIST: Can you say more?

At this point I was wondering; how far can I explore without Camille becoming too dysregulated and shifting into flight mode? We had just been talking about dissociation and disconnection at the point that she rapidly shifted emotional states. On the one hand, it is important to model comfort with discomfort and to challenge automatic avoidance. On the other hand, it is important to model respect for the emotional boundaries and limits of regulatory tolerance, especially in an early session, to demonstrate that the therapy will be challenging but that the therapist will back off when it gets too hot in the kitchen. In this situation then, I decided to continue to ask about the trigger – what the list evoked – and to shift away from talking about the impacts of trauma on her.

CAMILLE: Um. When I was in high school, my teacher wanted us to all do research, on different science-y things, and we could all just do whatever we wanted, and it had to do with anatomy and physiology, and I researched PTSD, and was not happy with the things I found, so. . .
THERAPIST: About, yourself?
CAMILLE: Yes, and I just didn't want to have the list in front of me.
THERAPIST: And when you did that, did you know the things that you found out – like, did you have a sense of what PTSD was a little bit about, before?
CAMILLE: I had a sense, but I just didn't – I had to research damage on the brain, and, stuff, and it was just upsetting, so.

THERAPIST: So did you feel when, from the research that you did, that things were worse than you thought they were?

CAMILLE: Yup. It sounded more permanent.

THERAPIST: Oh-kay. Well that's something we can talk about, too, because that research is rather dire and terrifying, many of those neuroimaging studies are conducted with young children who experienced very severe early neglect and trauma that actually changes the shape and size of their brains.

CAMILLE: Yeah, I had picked the topic, and then, I had to stick with the topic, and then I got to the point where I decided I really didn't want to stick with the topic. . .

THERAPIST: So on the one hand, you sort of volunteer for a study like this, because you are aware of how trauma has affected you, and you really want to work on that. On the other hand, talking about it, and seeing these impacts written out so boldly, on a page, is pretty triggering.

CAMILLE: It's just, a reminder of, I don't know, it feels too set. You know what I'm saying? Like, too much black and white. It's here.

THERAPIST: Too permanent.

CAMILLE: It's too permanent. And I don't like that. I just, I personally believe – and I feel like some of the psychologists I've been to, that they feel like it's never going to change.

THERAPIST: That must have been really scary for you. Do you worry that I feel that way too, that you can never change?

CAMILLE: Yes, and I hate that. I hate that idea. I hate the idea that I'm never going to become 100% better, and I'm sorry, but I kind of believe that – I don't want to believe that just one thing in my life is forever going to impact me that way. I don't feel like it's fair.

THERAPIST: Well it's definitely not fair, for sure. My feeling is that, there is, a scar. Like, this thing happened, it can't ever not have happened. But there are ways in which your life, can in fact, learn to work around that scar. There are things that can't ever not have happened.

CAMILLE: Yeah, I get that.

THERAPIST: But that your life is gonna be shit forever? No.

CAMILLE: I get that it's still going to always be there. I mean, I don't care. I've got scars. I don't care, they're still there. I just care that – I don't want to believe that it's never going to work out.

THERAPIST: Well, I'm with you, there. I'm on board with that.

CAMILLE: Cool.

THERAPIST: Okay. How do you feel about continuing to talk about what is on the handout?

CAMILLE: It's okay, I just don't want to hold it or look at it.

And so, striking a compromise, we continued to discuss the impacts without Camille feeling the need to hold or look at the handout – a small concession to avoidance without backing away and running from the feelings and thoughts associated with examining the long-term consequences of her trauma.

THERAPIST: On the emotional level, there's many of the things we've already talked about, anxiety and sadness, feeling too much, feeling too little, and that's one of the things you've talked a lot about is that, in your childhood, people didn't really, what we would say, regulate your emotions. It was. . .

CHRIS: It was one or the other.

THERAPIST: It was more, explosions or nothing. And then, how do you learn how to regulate your emotions, or even to tolerate difficult emotions, if no one around you models how to solve the problem? When your parents would just avoid – how do you learn to talk about difficult things? And then you get into a couple relationship, and neither of you has that set of skills, for tolerating and managing your emotions, and talking about difficult things.

CHRIS: So I want to just go right into it, the conflict, and deal with it, because that's how we did it. It was always, push, push, like, deal with it fully. It would be, screaming matches, whatever, you know? Just get it out of the way. And she doesn't want to do it at all.

CAMILLE: And I don't do screaming matches.

CHRIS: She just wants to avoid it.

THERAPIST: [to Camille] Where you grew up with [makes hand gesture of blinders over eyes] nothing. Nothing. It's a perfect combo. Isn't it amazing, how you found each other. Lock and key. Puzzle pieces. And we've talked about this as well, how childhood trauma is different than adult trauma. When you're in childhood and you have a good enough growing up, your parents are reasonably supportive and responsive, and you grow up, and you have learned how to tolerate and manage your emotional distress, and you feel like a pretty solid person, and so when a really crappy thing comes along, you're already a fully grown human, so, while that crappy thing affects you, of course, you're already you, and you are equipped to deal with what comes your way. But when you're a kid, and a really bad thing happens, you're still developing, so you don't have a lot of the skills that you need to cope with something horrible, and if you're not in a situation where you have relationships that support you, then, as you say, you're all alone with it, and that can be really, really tough for kids. And that's one of the reasons why relationships can be so hard for childhood trauma survivors, that relationships weren't where you turned for support, so now, as an adult, you hope to turn to each other for support, but you really don't know how. One of our biggest goals here is to help you learn how to talk to each other about difficult things, how to turn to each other and feel safe and comfortable when things are difficult, as opposed to feeling that you have to – you [to Chris] pursue, and you [to Camille] get away as far as you can.

CHRIS: And we both want that, for ourselves.

THERAPIST: You want that for yourselves and for each other.

The session was intense and challenging for both Chris and Camille. Chris got a little goofy but was able to talk about it and explain that it is how he deals with difficult feelings. Camille pulled away and wanted to get rid of the psychoeducational handouts, but she was able to talk about her feelings of fear and hopelessness that this "list" might define her and that she might not ever change. This was good information for me about how Chris and Camille approach emotional challenges and it was a beginning opportunity for me to role model emotion regulation, responding to their distress without jumping into the desire to avoid. Through taking the role of educator and emotion regulation coach, the therapist begins to build a contained therapeutic relationship.

In the next session, we tackled the second half of the psychoeducational handout, the impact of trauma on couple relationships. Chris and Camille were drawn to the topics of safety, closeness, and how to manage communicating about difficult issues.

THERAPIST: Trust is a big thing, and trust connects to the idea of closeness. It sounds like sometimes you guys are quite close, and you are able to be close, and sometimes you're not.

CHRIS: I think it's weird, because sometimes I feel like we're close, but the trust is a little broken, but mostly I – I think, mostly on your side; I don't think I've ever not trusted you.

CAMILLE: Fair enough.

THERAPIST: Okay, trust has a big impact on your ability to feel close to each other. People often find that shame has a big impact on being close, like if you still feel. . .

CHRIS: That one would be more on my side, I think.

THERAPIST: Yes. If you still feel, like, what's the matter with me? Or who's gonna want to be with me, or, whatever that looks like for you.

CHRIS: I just feel guilty a lot, 'cause I feel like I, screwed up, or – 'cause I told you before, I know that I'm doing something wrong, and I can't stop myself. . .

THERAPIST: Can't stop yourself?

CHRIS: And so then I'm sitting there going, like, why am I doing this, you know?

THERAPIST: And that gets in the way.

CHRIS: Yeah, it's like what I told you, it's, like, getting in my way. I know it's there and I know I'm going to get through it, it's just in my way right now, and it's annoying.

THERAPIST: And these all feed into each other. We've talked already about, the challenges with tolerating or regulating your emotional distress, and how you [to Camille] have to shut off when you get upset, or you [to Chris] get so dysregulated or distressed that you pursue – fix it now, fix it now, fix it now – that those two things don't go very well together, that they really reinforce each other. They also make it hard to empathize, because you're so distressed, that it's hard to really think, wow, he or she is really struggling right now, you know, let's just take a breath.

CHRIS: We talked about that this week, actually.

THERAPIST: Did you?

CAMILLE: Yeah, it just. . .

CHRIS: 'Cause she felt like I wasn't listening to her, and I was listening to her, but I wasn't doing it, the right way.

CAMILLE: [angrily] Well, you weren't. . .

CHRIS: I was just hearing what I needed to hear, to revalidate what I needed out of it.

CAMILLE: Yeah, and too, you just kept on pushing. I'm listening to you, I'm listening to you, and, it's just like, you're not! You keep on, like, you just. . .

CHRIS: Yeah, I was, I was just stressed out.

CAMILLE: The thing is, is that when I'm upset, I need a lot of room, to just feel comfortable, and I don't – as soon as I feel like I'm being pushed, or somebody's expecting something out of me, I can't be there. When I get upset, I just need to feel very comfortable, in that moment, and actually allow myself to feel upset. So, it's not, it's not easy for you to be chasing me and I just want to stay put, and I don't want to have to run away, but yet you're overwhelming me, so I need to run away, because I can't feel this. I can't – I can't, both, feel, and let myself feel, if you're running after me, and it's just too much.

THERAPIST: So you need to be able to really stay steady and breathe, to be able to let yourself feel your feelings.

CAMILLE: Yeah. Which is why I'm more comfortable being upset, in a situation like this, than if I feel like somebody's mad at me or yelling at me. I can't do that. I can't let myself be upset.

THERAPIST: It sounds like you will easily interpret Chris's anxiety as him being upset with you.

We were able to have a good exploration of the struggles the couple had with engaging with one another when either or both of them is emotionally dysregulated and how this impacted their capacity to be present for one another. While we had yet to explore the modules on emotion regulation and mentalizing, I began to sow the seeds of these future discussions as we explored their challenges with tolerating and modulating their own emotions and being able to imagine or understand their partner's perspective as they attempt to resolve whatever issue is facing them. This appeared to affect the couples regardless of whether the issue at play related directly to their relationship. For instance, both Camille and Chris discussed issues that arose for them in their work and how these struggles caused them significant distress that had nothing to do with each other. Due to the high levels of dysregulation, though, neither found themselves able to turn to the other for support and solace, resulting in conflict between them instead of an opportunity to develop the capacity to support one another in their daily lives. This represents an opening to discuss the impact of emotion dysregulation and mentalizing on communication between partners in trauma survivor couples.

THERAPIST: Yes, that really connects with something else that we've already talked about: communication. When you have these patterns where you're [to Camille] anxious and that anxiety kind of triggers a shutdown, and your shutdown triggers anxiety [to Chris] and you push and push to get close to her, and around and around you go, that makes it hard to communicate. But other things can make it hard to communicate, like not knowing what you're feeling. Like, I know I'm feeling something, but I don't know what it is.

CHRIS: That's like a constant, every day, for me.

THERAPIST: And, sometimes, we are triggered by things that don't seem to be a big deal but feel like a big deal, like if you are communicating about something like, the dishes, sometimes the dishes can take on the power of, a bigger thing, because, if you don't really know what you're feeling, or your feelings are too much or too little, or, like the dishes become. . .

CHRIS: Well, it does, because I get angry when I do that, and she always gets worried about me.

CAMILLE: When you do the dishes? [everyone laughs]

CHRIS: And a lot of times that's just all you're doing, you're just trying to help me, but I just lash out at everyone, because I'm pissed off at something else and I'm too anxious to confront people about things and then it explodes all over Camille.

THERAPIST: Well, it's another example of trauma and communication, like, you feel too fearful, maybe even you don't trust to try to have that kind of conversation, because you're afraid. . .

CHRIS: I'm afraid I'm going to explode on them and then I explode on Camille, and then that's not fair, you know, like. . .

THERAPIST: Right. So, that's important.

The session continued as we explored attachment in greater detail. Chris was more engaged in this exploration and, as the more preoccupied partner who tends to anxiously pursue or is preoccupied with fears of abandonment, it made sense that he would be more vocal and eager to share his anxieties and his awareness of how his current strategies were not working for either partner. It is important at this early stage in the treatment to be tracking how attachment styles are beginning to express themselves in the therapy. As Chris was more preoccupied, it was important to provide a lot of containment and "marking and parking" for him, validating his concerns without becoming mired in them. If I dove into every rabbit hole with him, I would neither be modelling for him that his concerns were valid but manageable nor demonstrating to Camille how to tolerate high levels of emotional dysregulation without either falling in and drowning or running as fast and as far as she can. I would also run the risk of losing Camille, the more avoidant partner; balance between partners within sessions is essential for building a strong alliance. We ended the session with a quick wrap-up and discussion of what will come next. Camille tried to throw a small grenade into the therapy room as I moved towards ending the session. For an avoidantly attached person who really struggles with emotion regulation, it is quite common to hold things in all session and then try to thrust them out into the room before leaving so that they can both express their distress and escape at the same time.

THERAPIST: So that is an overview, and it sounds like a lot of those things speak to you, they kind of make sense to you. Do you have any thoughts, or questions, about what we've been talking about?

CAMILLE: Uhm. [Shakes head no]

CHRIS: Well, I'm kind of happy, like this is validating that we have been working, in the right direction, like the whole time, it's just – we didn't really realize it until, you actually brought it out, now. It's nice to know that, like, coming here wasn't, a waste of time.

THERAPIST: Oh, well. I'm glad to hear that. [all laugh]

CAMILLE: There was one thing, though, like about. . .

CHRIS: [getting flustered] Oh, well, she's going to say that all our arguments have the same theme, all the time. It's always the same, like, whenever we argue, the root cause is generally the same.

CAMILLE: I feel that it's like I, I care about something. Chris has a different opinion. . .

CHRIS: But my opinion is right and hers is not, hers is not valid.

CAMILLE: And then that just pisses me off, and then we argue about it. It's like. . .

CHRIS: We solve it then, but then – it comes back up again.

THERAPIST: I'm aware that we are near the end of the session and it sounds as though this is a really important aspect of what we have been talking about. It also sounds as though when things feel out of control neither of you fully understand what you are *really* fighting about. I would encourage you then, over the next week, to write down examples of when this happens between you, or reflect on it, so that we can really have a fleshed-out example, lots of muscle on the bone so that I can really get inside that with you, because it sounds like that's very complex. Does that sound manageable? [both nod]

It is important to acknowledge the validity of their concerns while also framing the need to bring up issues at earlier points in the session and wrap up the session on time. While one might imagine that a survivor would feel special or understood by a therapist who allows sessions to go overtime when these kinds of issues come up at the end of sessions, really, it is the opposite. For survivors, boundaries have often been violated in ways that made them feel special but then had horrible consequences; the abuser that groomed a child with candy or special time alone from the other children before raping her is but one example. So, I always end on time but always wrap up any late disclosures in an accepting way that invites exploration in the next session.

How trauma impacts individuals and couples

INDIVIDUALS

What is trauma?

- A traumatic event is an overwhelming or uncontrollable experience that can happen to anyone at any age.
- It may be a life-threatening experience or may involve witnessing something that causes you to feel horrified, helpless, or intensely fearful for your life or the lives of others.
- Traumatic events can include child abuse, domestic violence/partner violence, combat violence, sudden/unexpected loss of a loved one, car accident, sexual abuse/violence, and natural disasters (e.g., hurricane).

How might trauma impact you?

- **Sense of self**: helplessness, shame, guilt, self-blame, feeling "not normal", altered sense of age.
- **Memory and perception**: memory problems, dissociation (feeling outside of your body, losing time, not feeling real).
- **Sense of meaning**: loss of faith, despair, feeling that you don't have a future, hopelessness.
- **Relationships**: tendency to be revictimized, isolation, difficulty having close relationships due to mistrust, difficulties with resolving conflicts, secrets, tendency to view others as rescuers/victims/aggressors, repeating problematic relationship patterns.
- **Physical well-being**: sleep problems, eating problems, substance abuse, other health problems.
- **Emotional well-being**: difficulty tolerating and experiencing difficult emotions, including anxiety, sadness, and anger; alternating between numbness (no feelings) and out of control (too much feeling).

How is childhood trauma different?

- It occurs during periods of important development of social, emotional, cognitive, and physical growth.
- It is an overwhelming or uncontrollable traumatic experience that can happen to anyone at any age; however, when trauma occurs in childhood, the impacts can be more severe and long-lasting because the trauma has an impact on your overall development.
- It often happens in the context of relationships where the person who hurts you is also the person who is supposed to take care of you.

How have you coped with these challenges?

- How effective were these strategies?
- Did these behaviours work long-term?

COUPLES

How might childhood trauma affect your couple relationships?

- **Trust**: When people are traumatized in childhood, especially by people close to them, this can impact their ability to trust their partners in adulthood.
- **Closeness**: Because you may feel that being close to others has been the source of pain and trauma, being close to your partner in adulthood may feel frightening and dangerous. Often, childhood trauma survivors avoid closeness and, in so doing, become alienated and isolated from their partners. It may seem cliché, but there is research supporting that adage that you cannot love someone else until you can love yourself. Different researchers have found that childhood trauma can lead to long-lasting feelings of shame, self-doubt, insecurity, and high levels of self-criticism, all of which can, in turn, make it very difficult for childhood trauma survivors to share with and feel close to their partners.
- **Sexuality**: Because childhood trauma occurs during periods of developmental growth, including sexual development, trauma can impact a person's capacity to feel comfortable in their sexuality. In particular, sexual abuse, especially when perpetrated by someone close to you, can make it difficult to enjoy sex and sexuality in your couple relationship. Certain sexual positions, feelings, and states of arousal may bring up intense feelings of fear and anxiety and provoke flashbacks or vivid reminders of your abuse experiences.
- **Emotion regulation and empathy**: Childhood trauma can make it very difficult to understand, feel, and tolerate your emotions and those of your partner. This can mean that when you or your partner are feeling upset and need one another, it may be very difficult for you to tolerate these feelings, to understand the feelings of your partner, and sometimes, to even think in the presence of your own or your partner's distress.
- **Communication**: Childhood trauma survivors often have significant difficulties with communication. As a child, being assertive, clear, and honest may have been dangerous or the information you shared might have been used against you. This may make it very difficult for you to talk to your partner about challenges and conflicts, and sometimes, even everyday things like domestic tasks and childcare become a challenge.

How have these challenges affected your relationship?

- What was it like at the beginning?
- Have things changed over time?

How have you coped with these challenges?

- How effective were these strategies?
- Did these strategies work long-term?

Recommended readings for the therapist before beginning this topic

Impact of childhood trauma

Briere, J., Kaltman, S., & Green, B.L. (2008). Accumulated childhood trauma and symptom complexity. *Journal of Trauma Stress*, *21*(2), 223–226. https://doi.org/10.1002/jts.20317

van der Kolk, B.A. (1994). The body keeps the score: Memory and the evolving psychobiology of post traumatic stress. *Harvard Review of Psychiatry*, *1*(5), 253–265.

van der Kolk, B.A. (2007). The developmental impact of childhood trauma understanding trauma. In L.J. Kirmayer, R. Lemelson, & M. Barad (Eds.), *Integrating biological, clinical, and cultural perspectives* (pp. 224–241). New York: Cambridge University Press.

Whiffen, V.E., & MacIntosh, H.B. (2005). Mediators of the link between childhood sexual abuse and emotional distress: A critical review. *Trauma, Violence, & Abuse*, *6*(1), 24–39. https://doi.org/10.1177/1524838004272543

Trauma and relationships

Godbout, N., Runtz, M.G., MacIntosh, H.B., & Briere, J. (2013). Childhood trauma and couple relationships. *Integrating Science and Practice*, *3*(2), 14–17.

MacIntosh, H. B. (2017a). Couple therapy with male survivors of childhood sexual abuse. In R. Gartner (Ed.), *Healing sexually betrayed men and boys: Treatment for sexual abuse, assault, and trauma* (pp. 233–260). New York: Routledge.

MacIntosh, H. B. (2017b). Developmental trauma, couple relationships and the process of couple therapy. In J. Fitzgerald (Ed.), *Foundations for couples therapy: Research for the real world* (pp. 426–437). New York: Taylor & Francis Group.

Psychoeducation

Trauma and attachment

One of the most devastating impacts of early developmental trauma is the struggle that survivors face to building and maintain loving, safe, and resilient relationships in adulthood. One primary factor associated with these challenges is the damaging effect of childhood trauma, especially in an attachment context, on the capacity for secure attachment with others.

When working with survivor couples, building safer attachments is always at the forefront of my mind. I work to build conscious knowledge and understanding among survivors and their partners of what it means to experience attachment traumas, and how these translate into adult relationships, as well as to help the couple find new ways of being together that will allow them to unfurl their vulnerable attachment needs and find safety in their relationship. The first step is understanding, a conscious, cognitive process. And so, the second psychoeducational module focuses on helping each couple to understand and articulate to one another the impact of their particular experiences on the attachment relationship between them.

While trauma creates the conditions for a child to feel the need to move closer to an attachment figure for safety and comfort, that attachment figure may at the same time be violating the child. A vicious cycle can develop as the child develops an ever-greater need for proximity to the (potentially dangerous) attachment figure, which can end up leading to further abuse and, eventually, a continuous fear of retraumatization. Or, a child filled with unfulfilled longing for an unavailable or unpredictable attachment figure may develop a kind of vulnerability that can mark a child for further abuse. This child is so eager for love and connection that they become fodder for lurking paedophiles and abusers. Over time, through seeking and finding only woundedness in relationships with caregivers, a child can become deeply fearful of connecting with others.

As therapists, we have learned about attachment theory in our training and perhaps use the clinical applications of these ideas in our work. For trauma survivors it is essential that, as attachment figures within the therapy, we embody security, safety, and the capacity to regulate our own attachment anxieties in the context of our relationships with our survivor couple patients. This psychoeducational module uses the handout to provide the couple with a short lesson in the basics of attachment theory and help them articulate their own preliminary understanding of the impact of trauma on their attachment relationships and sense of security. Different couples allow for a more superficial or a deeper discussion of this topic, depending on their level of prior knowledge of these ideas, their comfort with discussing attachment at this early stage in their therapy, and their ease exploring the impacts of their trauma.

When they hear about attachment, most people think about mothers and infants, or caregivers and children. However, studies have begun to examine the ways those early relationships form an imprint inside of us for the kinds of attachments we may have in adulthood. Even more recently, the recognition has dawned that couple relationships constitute a form of attachment where the emotional bond in adult romantic relationships serves a similar function to the infant-caregiver bond. As researchers have looked at the continuity of attachment from childhood to adult couple relationships, they have suggested that these relationships were driven by the same motivational system – the attachment behavioural system – and that both have similar characteristics (Hazan & Shaver, 1994).

Researchers have determined that the majority of childhood trauma survivors, especially those who have experienced intrafamilial sexual abuse, evidence insecure attachment styles in their relationships in adulthood. One of the important foundations of a strong and vital couple relationship is secure attachment and, for many survivors, this is elusive, if not impossible. When trauma occurs in our families, especially the kinds of traumas that betray our trust and vulnerability, a child learns that attachment figures are not safe even as they experience overwhelming feelings of longing and desire for connection. And so, what is that vulnerable child to do when, as an adult, they long for closeness and connection with their lover? Well, often, they end up in relationships characterized by what I call the approach-avoid tango: they move forward, longing for connection; they get close; they get terrified; they run. When both partners in a relationship have attachment traumas, this tango can be devastating, chaotic, and in some cases, even dangerous, as the vulnerability caused by unmet attachment needs interacts with emotion regulation difficulties and violence ensues.

Researchers looking at attachment in adult couple relationships have identified two dimensions that can help therapists understand how survivors orient themselves towards others. Anxiety about attachment can be conceptualized in terms of a model of self in relation to attachment figures. Avoidance of attachment can be conceptualized in terms of a model of other, or the view of others in relation to attachment. Assessing attachment in various ways, the therapist emerges with a sense of how clients feel about themselves in relationships and how they feel about others – or how fearful they are about being abandoned and how much they view connecting with others as something to avoid (Bartholomew & Horowitz, 1991; Brennan, Clark, & Shaver, 1998). Different combinations of levels along the anxiety/self dimension, and the avoidance/other dimension, result in different adult attachment styles. For instance, someone who has had a "good enough" childhood with fairly reliable responsiveness from their caregivers and pretty consistent love and care would likely grow up to have a secure attachment style. They would feel that they are worthy of being loved and cared for (positive view of self) and not feel worried about others abandoning them (low anxiety). They would also likely feel that others are pretty reliable and that they could be counted on (positive view of other) and they would not feel afraid of connecting with others and getting close to intimate partners (low avoidance). Partners that are securely attached within a strong couple relationship can turn to one another in distress, find comfort and soothing in their partner, and feel as though they can rely on them as a safe haven. For survivors, the very place they long for love and comfort is also a place of terror and isolation – as their childhood echoes on.

What, on the other hand, might this look like for someone who was abused by a caregiver who should have protected and cared for them? If we take the example of Gary, a young man who was sexually abused by his mother at a young age, physically abused by his father, neglected physically and emotionally in the blended family with his stepmother, and later sexually abused by a trusted teacher, we can see the devastating impacts of violence on attachment. Gary has developed a very negative view of others (negative other) and feels fairly certain that humans should be avoided at all costs (high avoidance). He has also developed a negative view of himself, feeling that he is not worthy of love and care and, consequently, has a high level of anxiety about the potential for being betrayed and abandoned (high anxiety). And, as a result of repeated trauma at the hands of people who should have cared for him, he has a very negative view of others (negative other), which results in a fearful avoidant attachment style where, despite a deep inner longing for connection, other people are felt to be emotionally terrifying and he does not feel that himself worthy of love anyway. This is the approach-avoid tango: the adult survivor in a couple relationship alternates between longing for attachment and becoming consumed with terror about attachment; I approach, out of a desire to get close to someone who may be able to love and care for me; then I run away when I realize that they are just like every other person who has hurt me and I am a loser who cannot get anything right anyway. The fearful avoidant style, which is present in 92% of childhood sexual abuse survivors (Alexander, 1992) is a confusing and painful back and forth, in and out, near and far, kind of chaotic relationship. Add another trauma survivor to the mix and you can only imagine the attachment chaos.

However, many trauma survivors live an alternative narrative of their attachment trauma: that, in fact, they themselves were horrible people who deserved to be abused, while the people who were abusing them could not possibly be blamed – the victim is bad, the abuser is good. This really messes with a little person's head. This can lead to an attachment style where a negative view of self (high anxiety) is paired with a positive view of other (low avoidance): a preoccupied attachment style. For instance, Chris has learned that he is a pretty bad person who cannot be trusted and is very dangerous to those he loves. He also came to believe others – his parents, his brother, and others – to be innocent victims of his badness. For Chris, this combination resulted in a negative view of self (high anxiety) and a positive view of others (low avoidance).

One last attachment style, the dismissing style, arises from the development of very little anxiety about being abandoned (low anxiety) and a negative view of others (high avoidance). This is a less prevalent attachment style among survivors: most childhood trauma survivors feel pretty lousy about themselves, and this is the least likely attachment style for couple therapists to see. Dismissing partners rarely seek out therapy, as they typically believe that the problems in their relationships rest solely with their partners. When individuals with dismissing attachment styles do show in couple therapy, it is often to "present" their partner and hand them off for treatment. It is often a surprise to them that I want to see both of them together.

Working through this module with a couple, it is essential to provide them with psychoeducational information (found in the following handout), to help both survivors and their partners better understand the impact of childhood trauma on their adult attachment relationship. Facilitate an initial discussion with the couple about the impact of trauma on their attachments throughout their lives with a focus on how trauma has impacted the primacy of their couple attachment. This conversation is a prelude to more profound conversations about attachment that will be undertaken as the couple goes deeper into the therapeutic process.

The following transcript is a short sequence from a session with Gary and Geoffrey, talking about how their experiences in childhood have primed them to feel fearful and easily disconnected in their relationship.

THERAPIST: So, it sounds as though when things are calm and the two of you are doing okay, the two of you can do it, can really be supportive and loving of one another. But that at other times it becomes really difficult for you to be with each other and also to have both of your needs met, for both of you to feel like you are safe, cared for, and loved. There's a delicate balance that sometimes you're able to really pull it off under these optimal circumstances and then there are times when that's really hard for the two of you.

GEOFFREY: Yeah.

THERAPIST: So, it's good to hear that you have these kinds of pockets of memories of times that were really good that you can remind yourself, "okay this is what we're capable of at these good times", and this is where we would like to get back to. But right now, you're really struggling. It sounds as though there has never been a question of love, desire, or commitment between you. It's been a question of what falls apart when you are both struggling and can't seem to find ways to be close and caring and even kind to one another. Last week we spent some time talking about the impact of trauma on relationships and individuals and we went through some of the different things through the handouts and through your own descriptions of what it's like for the two of you to be together. There's another really important area that we're starting to talk about that is attachment and the impact of trauma on attachment and the idea of the safe space. When you grow up in a loving family, it's a natural thing to go home to your nest, recharge yourself, and go out into the world, knowing that there's a safe nest for you back at home. And you might not have grown up with that. The nest was dangerous, it was not safe.

GARY: That's for sure.

GEOFFREY: Yeah, my nest wasn't perfect either.

GARY: Yeah.

THERAPIST: There's no such thing as a perfect childhood, we all escape childhood with some scars, there's no way out of that. However, statistically speaking about 70% of the time, even when there are challenges here and there in childhood, people come out feeling as though other people are pretty reliable and that it's okay to turn to others for comfort when you need them. These adults feel as though they are worthy of other people responding to them and being there for them. So, it's both how you see yourself and how you feel about others. And different combinations of that results in different ways of being with other people. If you think other people were pretty great but you yourself were pretty awful that will cause you to chase after people and never feel like you really deserve the people that you get. Or you might think that other people are pretty horrible, you're just fine and then you just ignore people altogether and try to stay away from them and that's just another way of being.

Let's take a look at this handout. [gives the couple time to read through the first few sections]

So, when you read this, what stands out for you, what comes to mind?

GARY: I guess I feel like I must be a train wreck, like what's the point of even trying?

THERAPIST: So, when you read about how challenging attachments can be for survivors you kind of feel like giving up?

GARY: Yeah, we are always in such chaos and I feel like I can't do anything else.

THERAPIST: It sounds as though you have a really negative view of yourself in this relationship, does that sound right?

GARY: Yes, I really don't feel like I can do it. I can see how hard we are trying, but it's like we're just banging up against each other.

THERAPIST: We talked a bit about the different styles of attachment a little earlier. One of the ways that survivors of sexual abuse often feel in relationships is that they don't feel that they are worthy of love, that they can be loved and cared for in a relationship. They also often feel as though others aren't safe and capable of not annihilating or abandoning them, emotionally, in a relationship. So, in other words, they can feel really anxious in relationships at the same time as tending to avoid others. Does that sound a bit like what you are saying here?

GARY: Yes . . . that's it. I just can't imagine it ever being any different.

THERAPIST: What about you Geoffrey? You seem to have gotten quite quiet in the last few minutes.

GEOFFREY: Well, I guess I feel kind of the same way about the chaos. I know that we are always trying and that I really love Gary, I'm just not sure it's going to work. Every time I try to get close to him, he just shuts down and, I guess [crying] I feel like he's just pushing me away when I need him the most.

THERAPIST: That must be very painful for both of you, to feel as though you need each other so much but just can't find a way to feel safe in being close and vulnerable together. Geoffrey, in terms of your own attachment style, it sounds as though you are saying to me, Heather, I feel like Gary is a good guy, but I don't know if he loves me and, well, I don't think I'm worth being loved. It sounds like you are telling me that you feel like others are okay, you don't avoid trying to get close to others but, you feel really badly about yourself and feel quite anxious about being abandoned or let down. Does that sound right?

GEOFFREY: [crying – long pause] Yes, I guess so, I guess I do feel like if I was a better person this could work better and maybe it would be easier for me to figure out how to be with Gary in a way that he could love me.

THERAPIST: That must be so painful for you, Geoffrey, to feel as though if there was just something you could figure out how to do differently, or be differently, you might be able to make it work.

GEOFFREY: [still crying] Yes.

THERAPIST: But, here's the thing, there are two of you in this relationship and both of you are here, showing me how committed you are to fixing this relationship and telling me how much you love each other. It's really easy, at this point in therapy, where we are just digging in to understanding the impact of your traumas on yourselves and your relationship, to feel like you are facing a mountainous, impossible goal, fixing your relationship. But it is important to remember that we are just gathering up important information that is going to help us understand your struggles in new ways that are going to give us what we need to start working together to rebuild your relationship so that you both feel safe and secure with each other. We talk about the "earned secure" attachment style – you didn't have what you needed when you were growing up, to become securely attached without a little help but, with some help and hard work, lots of love and perseverance, you can "earn" a secure attachment, with each other.

HOW ARE YOU FEELING NOW?

GEOFFREY: I'm just holding on to that and trying to believe you.

GARY: I guess we'll see.

As outlined above, Gary has the classic fearful avoidant attachment style of the majority of childhood sexual abuse survivors – negative view of self (high anxiety) along with negative view of others (high avoidance). Geoffrey carries the preoccupied attachment style, with a positive view of others (low avoidance) but a very negative view of himself (high anxiety); he is filled with shame that was seeded over the years of his childhood rejections. So, when we see the preoccupied with the fearful avoidant, we know that a couple will likely struggle with the approach-avoid tango: one partner seeks proximity and closeness while the other runs away and then – switch – the other turns and desperately seeks out their partner who is now cowering in a corner filled with the shame of repeated rejection. This was the story of Gary and Geoffrey's tumultuous relationship.

Trauma and attachment

What do we mean by attachment?

- The term "attachment" relates to the relationships we have with significant others in our lives. In particular, we are referring to the relationship between an infant and their primary caregiver and the relationship between romantic partners.
- There are different ways of being attached. The majority of people (70%) have mostly positive experiences of closeness with their primary caregivers in infancy and childhood and these people, called securely attached, come to believe that people would be there for them in their distress and that they, themselves, were worthy of care and comfort from others. A smaller percentage of people experience relationships with their primary caregivers that cause them to feel insecure about whether they, themselves, are worthy of consistent care and whether people would be there for them.
- Research with couples has demonstrated that attachment security/insecurity is quite consistent from childhood to adulthood. This research also indicates that the needs for closeness, safety, and a "secure base" are lifelong needs. This tells us that if someone has a secure attachment in childhood, they will likely have a secure attachment also with their romantic partner.

How does childhood trauma impact attachment?

- Childhood trauma may have a significant impact on attachment. The earlier in your life the trauma happens and the closer the relationship with your abuser, the more significant the impact of the trauma is on your attachment security.
- The majority of childhood trauma survivors do experience some insecurity in their attachment relationships.
- For those who have experienced sexual abuse, attachment insecurity can be even more complicated. For instance, while you may really long for connection and closeness with others, that very same closeness and connection may feel dangerous. This can lead to difficulties with maintaining close relationships and a tendency to jump into relationships quickly, becoming overwhelmed and frightened, and then running away.

Where do you see yourself in these descriptions?

- Do you tend to be anxious about whether others will let you down or abandon you?
- Do you tend to avoid closeness with others and fear that they will hurt you if you let yourself get close?
- How has this affected your relationship?
- How do you understand the origins of these feelings?

Recommended readings for the therapist before beginning this topic

Alexander, P.C. (2009). Childhood trauma, attachment, and abuse by multiple partners. *Psychological Trauma: Theory, Research, Practice, and Policy*, *1*(1), 78–88. https://doi.org/10.1037/a0015254

Allen, J.G. (2013). Treating attachment trauma with plain old therapy. *Journal of Trauma & Dissociation*, *14*(4), 367–374. https://doi.org/10.1080/15299732.2013.769400

Hazan, C., & Shaver, P.R. (1994). Attachment as an organizational framework for research on close relationships. *Psychological Inquiry*, *5*(1), 1–22. https://doi.org/10.1207/s15327965pli0501_1

Muller, R. (2010). *Trauma and the avoidant client: Attachment based strategies for healing*. New York: W.W. Norton & Co.

Whiffen, V.E. (2003). What attachment theory can offer marital and family therapists. In S.M. Johnson & V.E. Whiffen (Eds.), *Attachment processes in couple and family therapy* (pp. 389–398). New York: Guilford Press.

Psychoeducation

Sex and sexuality

In Stage One, a key topic for psychoeducation and initial exploration is sex and sexuality. Where avoidance is one of the biggest struggles of survivors in their lives and relationships, therapists must bravely move forward to overcome the silent but strong injunction against exploring such vulnerable topics. Psychoeducation can be the first step in breaking down avoidance and opening up dialogue in excruciatingly painful and shameful areas.

The first step in engaging in this psychoeducational process is preparing yourself to be open to hear whatever you hear, to remember that childhood trauma, especially sexual trauma, can impact the nature and process of sexual desires and responses of survivors. Our job is to hold the reins steady as we create a non-shaming, non-judgemental environment of exploration. One of the best tools in a therapist's arsenal as you delve into this topic is your own education and understanding, your own desensitization, and the work you have done on your own traumatic experiences. Before diving in with instructions on to how to work with a couple, the impact of childhood trauma on sexuality in adulthood must first be explained.

For most couples, the sexual relationship is a large part of the glue that binds them together. For couple therapists, sex and the multitude of potential struggles a couple might experience in this domain is an important element of the work of therapy. For some couples, the sexual arena is the only place they feel safe and close, while for others, it is a source of great conflict and pain. Regardless, sex and sexuality are important areas to be explored, and issues resolved, in couple therapy. Most of what we know about the challenges that childhood trauma survivors experience in their sexual relationships and personal sexual identities comes from research and clinical practice with cisgendered, female, childhood sexual abuse survivors in heterosexual relationships (Beitchman et al., 1992; Chauncey, 1994; Colman & Widom, 2004; Kendall-Tackett, 2002; Kinzl, Traweger, & Biebl, 1995; Loeb et al., 2002; Testa, VanZile-Tamsen, & Livingston, 2005; Vaillancourt-Morel et al., 2015, 2016; Wilson & James, 1992). However, while sexual abuse can have devastating impacts on sexuality, any form of childhood trauma may make the intimacy and vulnerability of sex tremendously painful and challenging, especially for those who were betrayed in childhood attachment relationships. Also, for many survivors, discussing sex and sexuality can feel impossibly vulnerable and shameful. That said, survivors of childhood trauma that includes sexual violation are more likely to have significant and pervasive sexual challenges than do other survivors. Conflict can arise in couples over the frequency of sex and in negotiating a sexual relationship where sexual touch and intimacy can be a trauma trigger for flashbacks and intrusive symptoms, bodily reactivity, and negative or shameful thoughts about sexuality.

Background

Research and practice in the area of sex and sexuality shows significant gender differences in the long-term impacts of childhood sexual trauma. For women, the most common strategy to manage overwhelming feelings about sex is to suppress their sexuality. For some women, the impacts of sexual abuse can be quite concrete, resulting in sexual pain with penetration or genital stimulation or even painful responses to sexual arousal itself. For other women, the impacts are more indirect, such as sexual avoidance and fear, low sexual desire, and flashbacks and nightmares in response to such triggers as specific sexual positions, means of stimulation, or activities that are reminiscent of past trauma. Sexual conditioning within the abuse can lead the survivor to experience sexual arousal in response to stimuli that can feel disturbing to either partner. In female survivor couples, most partners described imposed periods of celibacy as painful but necessary to decrease the conflict and pressure associated with sex (Bacon & Lein, 1996; Chauncey, 1994; Feinauer, Callahan, & Hilton, 1996; Firth, 1997; Harway & Faulk, 2005; Reid, Taylor, & Wampler, 1995; Reid et al., 1996).

The limited research that does consider the impact of sexual abuse on male survivors' sexuality suggests, unsurprisingly, that when sexual abuse involves more force and is more invasive, the sexual challenges in adulthood for male survivors are more severe (Banyard, Williams, & Siegel, 2004). Male survivors often struggle with the impacts of being sexually conditioned at a young age. For instance, a young boy who is frequently masturbated and fellated by an older male perpetrator and, in spite of his feelings of shame and terror, becomes erect and has an orgasm during the abuse, can become a man who feels sexually aroused by the fantasy of sex with older men, while identifying as heterosexual. While this man may consciously desire a strong, loving, and vital sexual relationship with his female partner, he may also, on another level, crave sexual stimulation by another man. This is one of the factors that may lead to a splitting or bifurcation of sexual desires and actions, which is a primary strategy for male survivors to deal with their overwhelming feelings in relation to sex (MacIntosh, 2017b; Crawford & O'Dougherty Wright, 2007; DiLillo et al., 2009; Zala, 2012). This splitting apart or bifurcation can lead to hyperactivation and trauma reenactments "outside" of intimate relationships, and hypoactivation and sexual suppression within intimate relationships (MacIntosh, 2017b). In the end, the survivor and his partner are disconnected and alienated sexually, and he is left experiencing painful and shameful disavowal of the other branch of his sexuality that is held away, secret, and separate.

Very little research has investigated the dynamics of male, queer, and trans-identified survivors, so I draw on my clinical work to inform my understanding of how these impacts affect a diversity of survivors in their couple relationships. Working with childhood trauma survivors in couple therapy, certain themes typically emerged as they discussed and explored their sexual relationships and the impact of trauma on their sexuality. These themes may appear in your work with survivors, so I will outline them here and provide some examples of survivors discussing these themes in DCTCT sessions, so that you may be able to identify, explore, and shift these struggles with couples.

Boundaries

In their sexual relationships, survivors often struggle with boundaries in relation to sex. In my clinical experience, most survivors raised this issue whether or not their personal history included sexual abuse. Survivors described finding it difficult to say no to sex, and when they did say no they became overwhelmed and emotionally dysregulated. Additionally, regardless of the nature of their traumas, survivors described feeling confused about boundaries around sex, how to get close to their partner sexually, and how to tolerate their emotional and physical responses to sex without dissociating or disconnecting from their partner. Survivors described finding it easier to feel sexual when not emotionally or even physically close to their partner, as though a certain distance was required to allow for closeness.

Survivors reported feeling confused about boundaries around family, love, and sex as they struggled to allow these to be compatible with one another. Survivors described feeling confused, and that they felt like parents instead of girlfriends, and family instead of lovers – fundamentally, family members cannot be lovers in this confusing existence where those who should protect and care for us are also those who violate us.

Survivors also often report having sex when they do not want to. While having unwanted sex was framed in the context of their desire to meet their partner's needs and an effort to be affectionate with partners, it was also described as something that survivors felt they had to do to maintain the attachment with their partner. This leaves survivors feeling resentful, revictimized, and triggered, despite acquiescing and even initiating these sexual contacts. Upon hearing about this in sessions, partners reported feeling dumbstruck, angry, hurt, and deeply sad when they realized that their partners were engaging in sex with them when they did not want to. In the following transcript, Camille describes her experience of engaging in sex when she did not want to because she felt as though she had to hold on to Chris.

CAMILLE: Yeah, there's a few occasions that we had sex that I didn't wanna have. But I didn't feel that I could end it, or that I could say anything about it.

CHRIS: Which I was told recently, and it was just a complete shock to me.

THERAPIST: You didn't know?

CHRIS: No, I had no idea.

THERAPIST: What made it hard for you to say something?

CAMILLE: In the past, when I refused to cuddle or hug he would be upset and then slam the door, and that's one of my triggers. I can't take sudden sounds. They just put me on edge. I mean that sometimes even if I don't feel like it, if I don't feel like being intimate I'll do it anyway, just because I feel like, because I'm in a relationship, you do have some obligation to, right? Like, it's a need in a relationship, so sometimes I have . . . actually, many times . . . put my own needs aside, to meet his.

Sex is triggering

For survivors, sex can be experienced as a trigger for traumatic emotional states and memories of sexual violation. These emotional states can evoke discomfort with arousal, sexual flashbacks, dissociation, regression to childlike states, and generally being overwhelmed. This can reduce sexual pleasure and create challenges with reciprocating their partner's attempts to provide them with sexual pleasuring. When triggered in these ways, survivors can become confused and even associate their partner with their perpetrator. This can be terrifying for survivors and extremely upsetting for their partners. For many couples, this kind of confusion can lead to real conflict. In the next transcript segment, Gary describes his experience of sexual touch being triggering and how this impedes his capacity to engage with and enjoy the couple's sexual relationship.

GARY: I have issues with intimacy. I don't know if it's because sometimes sex makes me feel like a kid, and like mentally I'm not able to, like, be an adult, it's very – it's a very odd thing. But it is very difficult for me to enjoy sex. I don't know why; it's always been like that.

THERAPIST: It's always been difficult for you to enjoy sex?

GARY: It's physical, it's difficult for me to enjoy any part of it, but also, I just get freaked out and, I can't do it, the sex, I. . .

THERAPIST: Okay. There's a lot of physical and emotional distress related to sex for you.

GARY: Exactly. I can't tell you why, I just know that I get really freaked out and I start to feel like a kid and I just need him to stop. It's not fun for me. I just get so triggered and I remember all of these things, the abuse things, and I just have to get him off of me.

Couples may try to deal with these triggers by controlling aspects of their sexual relationship including prescribing the time, negotiating forms of touch, and identifying tolerable ways of being close including non-sexual touch. Most couples, however, simply avoid the possibility of triggers in the sexual relationship, rather than actively exploring, understanding, and strategizing, which results in an absence of sexual closeness.

Avoidance of intimacy

Avoiding sexual intimacy to steer away from distress and conflict is a strategy that couples often try for managing these reminders of trauma and feelings of terror and vulnerability. Maintaining consistent sexual closeness with partners is a real challenge for survivors. Sexual abuse survivors, in particular, may feel terrified of the touch and physical closeness that accompanies sexual activity with their partners, and also fear the emotional closeness that they hoped would accompany sexual closeness. This deadly combination of traumatic triggers and feelings of mistrust and fear, an interpersonal residue survivors face, can lead to more mistrust, shame about their sexualities, and being triggered by sex, and growing avoidance of sexual activity and stimulation. This painful dance of avoidance of desire and closeness can go on and on. For most survivors, avoidance feels like the only way to manage their distress, in spite of the shame and sadness it may engender. For Anush, his inability to engage with Amira sexually was shameful and painful.

ANUSH: I want to satisfy her in every way, it's not that. . .

THERAPIST: And how does it feel that you have not been able to?

ANUSH: It hurts.

THERAPIST: It's painful. . .

ANUSH: It hurts even before she started saying that she's having these problems, that she's not happy.

Avoidance strategies often include attempts to cope with distress through dissociation and sexual disconnection from their partners, being there in body but not in spirit. Strategies for titrating sexual closeness can include initiating sexual contact while the partner is asleep or while in an altered state such as dissociation or intoxication. Avoidance of sexual engagement within the couple relationship seems to increase as the relationship continues over time, leading to overall gradual reductions in sexual desire and frequency.

Gradual reductions in sexual desire and frequency

Survivor couples may experience a gradual but sustained decrease in the frequency of sexual interactions over time. Sexual abuse survivors often appear to be the "drivers" of the reduction of sexual desire and frequency of sexual contact. For some couples, other mental health issues such as depression, anxiety, and intrusive trauma symptoms, as well as the medications taken to manage these symptoms, also get in the way of sexual engagement.

Many couples talk about a period of intense sex at the beginning of the relationship. While this is common among couples in general, many survivor couples describe the early burst of sexual activity as distressing, even overwhelming, and that this experience was followed by a dramatic decline until sexual intimacy was virtually eliminated. Over time, survivors describe themselves as suppressing their desire and pleasure, with this suppression increasing as feelings of attachment, emotional intimacy, and sense of family connection increase. Many survivors describe deep feelings of shame and distress as they become aware that their sexual relationship with their partners had faltered and, in some cases, disappeared.

Issues with decreasing sexual engagement in the relationship have a significant impact on partners. Partners describe feeling sadness about the loss of their sexual relationship, blaming themselves for their perceived failures in protecting sexual connection, and longing for intimacy, cravings for sexual closeness with their partners. Partners report feeling that the survivor's lack of sexual engagement with them is a reflection of their self-worth, sexual desirability, and trustworthiness as a partner. In response, partners describe feeling losses of self-esteem, declining self-image, and unbearable feelings of aloneness. In the following segment, Amira describes her feelings as she slowly realized that her partner, Anush, appeared to be uninterested in her sexually. Since he did not disclose his childhood sexual abuse to her until more than 10 years into their relationship, she had come to believe that his apparent lack of desire for her must mean that something was wrong with one or both of them.

AMIRA: I was totally infatuated with him. Eventually that died, I did my own thing, but even then, I just, it was. . .

THERAPIST: So disappointing?

AMIRA: It was sad, I used to cry about it and confide in friends, they'd say all these things about how great and beautiful I am, and I wondered what the hell is wrong with him, what must be wrong with me. And it used to make me feel even worse to hear those things. . .

THERAPIST: So it didn't help that they were. . .

AMIRA: No, I mean it helped that they were there to listen to me, but it made me think, well it's weird, what can it be? I didn't know then. So for me, for a long time, I felt like it was me. It's like either you are gay or it's me. I couldn't see any other reason for him being that way. So I never in a million years thought it was something else, I feel bad that I didn't think that it was something else. . .

THERAPIST: Hmm.

AMIRA: I used to cry at night a lot. I really would.

THERAPIST: Could he hear you cry?
AMIRA: He'd be asleep. I don't think he did.

In the next transcript segment, Chris, a non-sexually traumatized partner, describes his confusion as his relationship with Camille shifted from a high initial level of sexual engagement to unpredictability and then the virtual absence of any sexual contact in his relationship with Camille.

CHRIS: From my perspective, sex is always unpredictable. She's not as into sex as I would like, as what I would perceive as the average, and it's not like it was at the beginning. I do notice that sometimes she works at it, as though she doesn't really seem like she wants to do it. She's like, okay, fine, we can do it. She has ups and downs. Like, sometimes she would be super into it; we would go to sex shops, and buy toys, and we'll be super into it for a month. When we first met, we had sex seven times in one weekend, which was insane. I was like, holy shit, I can't do this anymore. We used to have so much more sex. But, I didn't pay attention to it, in the beginning. I didn't even notice the difference, it was gradual but, now I would definitely like to have sex more often than we do.

To cope, partners protect themselves through withdrawal, avoidance, and in some cases, turning towards alternative sexual activities and relationships to meet their sexual needs. This was the case when Amira turned outside of her marriage for sexual solace.

AMIRA: So, for me, I think I am at a place in our marriage where I feel like we're great friends, we are great roommates, great parents, I don't feel like we have anything else . . . I just feel like as a couple, as a married couple, we don't know how to differentiate a friendship family bond from being a couple.
THERAPIST: And how would you describe the things that are missing?
AMIRA: Well there is no sex, for one.
THERAPIST: For how long?
AMIRA: Well, now, it will be 2 years in June.
THERAPIST: That's a long time.
AMIRA: Shortly after marriage. It started with me feeling like I was not wanted in that way and that there was something wrong, so I did voice that back then. For him it was like, he didn't really have an answer. I just felt like I was always the initiator. I can't think of one time, not even one time, where he has initiated sex and it never bothered me in the beginning, I didn't think it was an issue. Over time, it has become an issue and I tried from my side to do different things to change myself, maybe make things more exciting, but I just never felt like there was any interest. I tried at one point, a reverse psychology, so I stopped initiating. I thought if I stopped, if I pulled back and stopped showing attention or interest in that area, that he would show interest or feel threatened, and think maybe there was someone else. He's not interested. I thought it would bring out something, but it didn't really change. I am not happy this way. I can continue to live the way we do, but something is missing fundamentally, and I don't want to go outside of the marriage as I have already done that and I don't feel comfortable doing that.
THERAPIST: You've already done that?
AMIRA: Yes, and I don't feel any more desire to work on it with us. Like it's just, I wish there was, there isn't, I feel stuck.

Eventually, for most couples, a bifurcation of sexuality begins to emerge as the gulf between the desires and compulsive urges and the fearful, avoidant, even protective sexual relationship with the partner grows.

Bifurcation of sexuality

A growing separation or bifurcation of sexuality and intimacy often appears in survivor couples. In many cases the tension between unintentional and non-consensual celibacy and unmet sexual needs comes to be met through experiences and relationships outside of the couple. These may be discussed and agreed upon by the couple or kept secret. This bifurcation of sexuality appears to be a division between a suppression of sexual engagement within the primary relationship and an activation of sexual arousal outside of the relationship in forms about which survivors often feel ashamed and distressed and feel a need to keep secret. Infidelities were often disclosed within individual sessions (the relevance of individual sessions in addressing sexual bifurcation will be discussed in Chapter 6 on "Working With Sex and Sexuality"). Affairs were often described as a way to cope with sexual rejection, even when the partners continue to feel ambivalent about turning away from their primary relationship. In the following segment, Amira describes her realization that she did not feel any guilt or remorse about her affair. Anush, meanwhile, reports feeling as though he has no right to be anything but accepting and acknowledging of the context in which this infidelity occurred.

AMIRA: The first time I went (to individual therapy), it was when I started to feel a shift in my feelings. I was really confused as to why I was feeling that. I was starting to have less interest in trying to fix us, I felt drawn to somebody else. I questioned that a lot. Like how am I able to feel that and feel like it's okay, why is it not bothering me? I don't feel guilt and remorse about that and that's the issue I went to see somebody with.

THERAPIST: And how much does Anush know about this?

ANUSH: I had a strong idea . . . I had a feeling, I never questioned it, I never outright asked her. I can't blame her. I don't feel like I hold that against her. I don't think I've ever had the feeling that she shouldn't have done this, that it's wrong. I feel as though she was put in a place where she didn't need to be, a place where she's lost, she's not getting something, and she doesn't know where to find it, it's not coming from me, and everybody deals with things in different ways. I had asked her, at some point or another, I brought it up and you know, asked, have you been with anybody else? She paused for a second or two and said yes, and I believe I told her right there and then that I didn't hold that against her.

AMIRA: He did.

ANUSH: You know that I can look past that, it's not something I've ever held against you because, doesn't matter what it is, we have to work, we have to work through it. My love does not tell me otherwise.

Further on in this transcript segment, Amira describes the feeling of being sexually aroused, feeling attractive, desired, and wanted by her affair partner.

THERAPIST: So things crossed a line to kissing and how did it go from there?

AMIRA: Kissing became making out, like first it was this kiss, just blew me away, and his reaction was always like, very blown away too.

THERAPIST: So it was both of you?
AMIRA: So it was very new and it was very good, he made me feel very special.
THERAPIST: And you hadn't felt special for so long.
AMIRA: Yeah, I felt special. I put more effort into looking good. When we did end up having sex, it was really good; it was very good, actually. I kind of felt relieved, like it felt like I had something, scratching an itch, it just felt, a relief.

For Amira, the loneliness and longing she felt in her marriage and her feelings of rejection and hurt were momentarily dulled as she was swept up in a scintillating, stimulating affair with someone who was able to openly lust for her, be with her, and enjoy her sexuality. For Geoffrey and Gary, this unacknowledged bifurcation challenged the intentional and thoughtful polyamory that was a part of the way they envisioned their relationship from the beginning. Trust was broken when the "rules" of the open sexual relationship were not respected.

GEOFFREY: He said he wanted to talk about other people that he was dating and I didn't really want to hear about it and he was like don't worry I didn't break our agreement but it was already broken 6 months ago so why does it matter now?
THERAPIST: So your relationship has been open?
GARY: Yeah, we were supposed to be poly.
THERAPIST: Okay.
GEOFFREY: Our agreement was that we wouldn't have sex with somebody else without having a talk together.
THERAPIST: Is that why he wanted to talk to you about these other people?
GEOFFREY: Maybe but . . . he's already had sex with somebody before we talked about it so why does it matter now I wouldn't believe him anyway?

Eventually, this bifurcation resulted in secrecy around engaging in sexual activities that they felt ashamed about, which included conditioned sexual responses to abuse-related stimuli, compulsive masturbation, use of pornography, autoerotic self-injury, and sexual reenactment of traumatic experiences.

Sex and emotional connection

Trauma survivors, especially sexual abuse survivors, feel that the abuse they experienced in childhood is directly related to the challenges they experience in their sexual lives as adults. For many survivors, this is characterized by struggles in being able to combine sexual and emotional intimacy. However, in the context of therapy sessions, some couples described how they have explored sexuality as a way to renew their emotional connection. These apparent contradictions make sense in their specific context. For survivors whose attachment figures violated sexual boundaries, the combination of loving family attachments and sex can be tormenting and must be avoided at all costs. For other survivors, often those whose abuse involved isolation and rejection, the connection of emotional and sexual intimacy can feel deeply healing of attachment loss and disconnection. As with all of these issues, the cues come from the particular couples with whom each therapist is working. Survivors and partners describe how intimacy can help repair conflict and enhance feelings of emotional safety, connection, and closeness – when they are able to be sexual without ending up triggered and dysregulated. In the following segment, Gary and Geoffrey talk about how sex is almost the only way they know how to resolve conflict and that, as a corollary, without conflict they might have no sex.

THERAPIST: It sounds as though you started to feel a bit out of control and you ended up saying things that are hurtful and that are hard to take back?

GARY: Yeah . . . we can be mean to each other and we say things that are hurtful I'm sure.

THERAPIST: And when you are in a conflict, are you able to touch each other, to comfort each other at all or is it every man to himself?

GARY: He is a lot better at that like this morning he was holding me, touching my back and trying to connect with me even though we were fighting and I was still angry. He initiated.

THERAPIST: You are very motivated to find a way to end the conflict, which is very positive.

GEOFFREY: Yeah, I don't think we . . . yeah, we wouldn't have sex otherwise.

THERAPIST: It's like make-up sex?

GEOFFREY: Yeah.

GARY: It's so good. The make-up sex is so fabulous.

THERAPIST: You come so close to losing each other and that energy, for you [to both] I think, when you feel that he is gone for a short time, it's like you need to smack him up against a tree so that you get him back.

GEOFFREY: Yeah, I mean it doesn't feel like that to me, it's just I can't handle this, his distance and the conflict, I guess it's the only way we have figured out how to stop the fight.

These are some of the themes that you may see arise in early sessions with survivor couples, as you begin to explore the dynamics of their sexual relationship with them. The best way to understand these issues is by working with these couples, delving into the issues together.

Psychoeducation with childhood survivors around sex and sexuality

This specific module aims to help therapists as they explore the impact of childhood trauma on the development of healthy sexuality. The module explores the impact of childhood trauma on the couples' sexual relationships including the nature of conditioned sexual responses, how to identify and handle triggers, and how to communicate about sex. The goal of this psychoeducational process, then, is to shine a light on this vital aspect of the couple relationship that may be avoided and even hidden away beneath shame, guilt, or overwhelming emotional distress.

For therapists, it is essential to check their assumptions and biases at the door when discussing sex and sexuality with childhood trauma survivors. For many, conditioned sexual responses to stimuli, such as experiencing sexual arousal in response to violent imagery or pain or being aroused by fantasies about the gender that is opposite of the orientation to which they identify, may evoke deeply painful feelings of shame and guilt. For instance, a cisgendered male survivor who identifies as homosexual but finds himself aroused watching heterosexual porn and imagining performing oral sex on a woman might find himself feeling ashamed, embarrassed, and confused about his sexuality. However, many survivors also find ways to reclaim their sexuality by taking control of certain conditioned responses. These survivors may engage in various sexual fantasies, activities, and relationships that could be construed as "kinky" or alternative, such as BDSM. Our task is not to try to change a survivor's conditioned sexual responses – this would not likely be successful or productive – but rather to ensure that they engage in their chosen sexual activities safely and consensually. One element of healing is to help survivors shift out of compulsive sexual reenactments that are highly ritualized and controlled by forces related to the traumatic unconscious, and empower the couple to negotiate ways to integrate hived off sexual desires, fantasies, and responses into the couple relationship in a way that is consensual and positive for both partners. It may also be necessary to negotiate how survivors can safely satisfy sexual needs with which their partner is not comfortable, in non-compulsive ways. Engaging in negotiation based on an open discussion of needs and values, aiming at a mutually satisfying agreement that does not result in betrayal or cause either partner to fall back into secrecy and isolation is an excellent first step in learning how to resolve other couple conflicts.

Depending on each therapist's own personal, familial, and educational background, your ideas about what constitutes the ideal context for a couple will differ. The field of couple and family therapy was built up from a fairly conservative, Christian framework of marriage preparation and counselling to become the robust and diverse field that it is today. The vast majority of writing in the field has historically been based on the model of the cisgendered, heterosexual, middle-class, white, monogamous couple. Most therapists work with couples where those descriptors are not applicable and navigate difference with fluidity and ease. However, in some cases, internalized ideas about what makes a good marriage can get in the way of working for the best interests of a particular couple. In my supervision and teaching experiences, the two areas I have found to be the most challenging to move through are related to kinky sexual practices or BDSM and couples who choose a non-monogamous model for their relationship.

There is a heated debate about kink and BDSM in couples where there is a history of childhood trauma, especially childhood sexual abuse. Many practitioners suspect any form of dominance, submission, or arousal in the context of pain and control to be a dangerous reenactment of trauma histories that should instead be processed and worked through in therapy. From another perspective, these forms of sexual engagement are about survivors taking back power, leaning into conditioned arousal rather than fighting against it and feeling in control of things that were once out of their control. From my perspective, it is not my role, as therapist, to decide whether kinky sexual practices are good, bad, or otherwise for any given couple. However, I will wade into the fray when I see signs of high levels of dissociation, more literal or concrete enactments of trauma scenes that appear to be accompanied by compulsion or dissociation, or disclosures prompting concerns about lack of consent and safety. Therapists cannot decide what is right or wrong for any given couple, but that does not obviate the need to engage fully with the couple in exploration and understanding aspects of their sexual life that may be connected to their trauma, to ensure that their sexual world is safe, satisfying, and pleasurable (however that is defined), and not retraumatizing or dissociogenic. Because these topics can be triggering for some survivors, I have not included a section on BDSM and kink in the psychoeducation handout. I do make reference to sexual conditioning and sexual pain, but I do not refer directly to couples who make the choice to include kink/BDSM in their sexual relationship. I would encourage you to ask questions about the couple's sexual repertoire and to be open to explore wherever the discussion goes.

The same can be said about monogamy. For those of us raised in a heteronormative society, even those who are queer ourselves tend to make restrictive assumptions about what makes the ideal couple composition. Additionally, for couple therapists raised on attachment theory and the primacy of the attachment bond for the safety and security of the couple, we might make an automatic, pathologizing assumption about what it means when a couple opts for non-monogamy or polyamory. While infant attachment theory has been expanded by researchers like Karlen Lyons-Ruth and colleagues (2006) to include more than one attachment figure, couple therapists predominantly retain the belief that a happy and healthy couple can include only two partners in its attachment system. It has been suggested that those who resort to non-monogamy do so because of insecurity in the primary attachment system or their inability to nest safely with one partner due to a history of attachment trauma. I have worked with couples where attachment feels so dangerous to trauma survivors that they need to spread it around a bit. It is as though the survivor needs to park all of their attachment needs in different people to tolerate being attached at all. However, there are couples who make a conscious decision to have a non-monogamous or polyamorous relationship, and, as therapists, we need to examine our biases to ensure that our exploration of their decisions around these primary attachment themes aims to understand the couple relationship with them without assuming anything pathological. Again, I wade in if the decision appears to be coercive, where perhaps one partner wants monogamy and the other partner does not, if there are high levels of dissociation in relation to the connections between partners, if there is no clearly outlined agreement about how the couple engages in relationships and/or sex outside of the couple, and if there are experiences of ongoing betrayal and insecurity arising from polyamory or non-monogamy. If I am honest, my own bias is to see the couple that has decided to come to me for therapy as having primacy of attachment. However, I do not believe that that primacy is necessarily threatened by a consensual and well-considered decision to engage in non-monogamy or a polyamorous relationship. I am aware of my bias and the role that my own traumas and attachment history play in my desire to be in a monogamous relationship. With this knowledge I hold myself open to understanding how the couple in front of me works out the parameters of their relationships. Each couple must be understood within their own context and histories.

To introduce this topic, the handout *Sex and Sexuality After Childhood Trauma* is provided to the couple. Handing over the piece of paper and seeing how the couple reacts will usually reveal a great deal about how they feel on this topic. Some survivors will fold the paper up in a million little pieces or actually drop it to the floor as though it were on fire, while others will pore over it voraciously, looking for answers. No matter the response, it is important to be as deeply empathically attuned as you are able, as you track and respond to signals of emotion dysregulation and shame. As with all of the psychoeducational topics, the stage is set for a deep dive into vulnerable topics and shameful emotions; in practice, the goal is to seek the Therapeutic Window (Briere, 2006) that allows us to keep our therapeutic foot on the gas while monitoring for emotional over- or under- regulation and dissociation. The handout gives us a frame for the discussion, like talking to a teenager about using condoms while driving in the car, side by side – everyone has the option to look out the window at the scenery rather than looking at each other. Reviewing the handout may bring up a bundle of responses, each element of which can be explored and the couple supported to reflect on them individually or together.

Some of the topics that might arise concern what "normal" sexual development looks like. In the following transcript segment, I am talking to Anush about how his sexuality might have developed had it not been derailed by sexual abuse.

ANUSH: It's overwhelming. I've got somebody here. That attraction, there is that physical attraction. It's there, she may not think it's there, but it's there. . .

THERAPIST: But you don't know how to do it. . .

ANUSH: No, I just don't know how.

THERAPIST: So that's something that we can work on. When someone is traumatized in the way you were, pardon my expression, it fucks up the natural development of a boy. You were at that age when you were just getting to learning about what an erection is, a wet dream, it's surprising but it's natural and it feels good, it's pleasant, and you fantasize about the girl that you like and you think you are going to ask her out and you want to kiss her. Over time that evolution gets you feeling like, I know how to do this thing, and I feel she's attractive, I am kind of attractive and you learn how to approach a woman. But when something interferes with that development, this violent act, you go [shows hands closing up] and you protect yourself and your desire, your erection, your arousal, it may be dangerous and maybe it's not a good thing, and maybe your desire isn't a good thing, maybe your arousal is not a good thing and then it's all so confused. We have to work that back a few steps, so that healthy development gets restarted. And, for you [to Amira], we also have to help you heal from the hurt of feeling rejected, and not wanted and not desired and how that's caused you to close up. It makes sense that's what happens when you feel that your man does not want you, doesn't desire you, you protect yourself. So we have to help both of you heal together and develop a sexual relationship that can feel intimate, safe, close, loving and passionate, exciting, and vibrant. That can take a little time but it's an entirely doable thing.

Through this process of psychoeducation, the therapist begins to help the couple identify their dynamic of avoidance and develop strategies to reduce it, understand triggers and manage dissociation and emotion dysregulation in the context of sex, and develop a strategy for re-engaging healthy sexual contact within the couple relationship. This involves helping the couple communicate openly about triggers and their origins and developing the skills to communicate directly about sexual needs and preferences.

In exploring sex and sexuality in the psychoeducational process, it will be important for the therapist to be both open and direct in establishing the frame for the couple to engage in future discussions about sex and sexuality. At the same time, the therapist must also give thought to the risk of premature disclosures. At this point in the process, facilitating disclosures that may result in major ruptures in the relationship is premature. You do not know enough about them yet, and they are just getting the feel of you. The challenges posed by sexual secrets are to be held off and navigated in Stage Three. Therefore, therapists need to open the door to an ongoing conversation about sex and sexuality while holding the couple back from exposing sexual secrets. Should it become evident from this psychoeducational exploration that there are significant sexual issues in the couple, it would be wise to ask the couple to come in for individual sessions. These are framed as a normal part of the process, to allow each partner a dedicated space to discuss more of his or her history. However, it is important for the therapist to know what they are dealing with in terms of sexual secrets. Survivors may experience high levels of shame and avoid disclosing their sexual challenges, and so we are always walking the tightrope of balancing emotion regulation with disclosure and processing and knowing when it is the right time to bring a partner in to discussions about sexual secrets. This will be explored in-depth in the chapter on working with sexuality.

Sex and sexuality after childhood trauma

How does childhood trauma impact sex and sexuality in adults?

- Childhood trauma comes in many forms, including sexual and non-sexual abuse.
- For survivors of non-sexual abuse, childhood trauma may lead to difficulties with trust, self-image, or identity, such that they do not feel that it is safe to be close to another person or even to know themselves well enough to feel that they know who they might be attracted to or what they might enjoy, sexually.
- For survivors of sexual abuse, the consequences for adult sex and sexuality can be very complicated both directly and indirectly. These impacts might be different depending on the age when the abuse occurred, your sex or gender identity, or if the abuser was a same-sex or opposite-sex perpetrator.

How might sexual abuse impact an adult survivor?

- Childhood sexual abuse can make it hard for you to feel safe sexually and to feel like you can be fully open to your sexual feelings and desires.
- Childhood sexual abuse often happens before puberty, before the full development of your adult sexual body. Stimulating a body sexually, through force or through attempts to sexually arouse a child, can throw off the gradual and slow development of sexual responses and lead to problems with sexual pain, or difficulties with becoming aroused and having orgasms in adulthood.
- Childhood sexual abuse can cause some survivors to experience certain kinds of sexual activities or stimulation as triggering of flashbacks or nightmares.
- Some survivors find it hard to know what they do and do not find sexually pleasurable, and this can lead them to engage in sexual activities that end up feeling retraumatizing.
- Some survivors find that their sexual responses become "conditioned" to things connected to their abuse. That can often happen if the abuse itself was both arousing and painful or exciting and frightening. This can mean that survivors might be really turned on by things that, as an adult, now confuse, disgust, or frighten them. This can mean that they feel very turned on by things that are painful or involve harm to themselves or someone else.
- For some people, especially boys abused by men, this can mean that they are turned on sexually by adult men but identify as straight. This can cause people to feel anxious or confused about their sexual orientation.

How can the sexual impacts of trauma affect relationships?

- Being triggered by certain sexual positions or kinds of stimulation can make feeling close and safe in your sexual relationship with your partner very difficult and feel frustrating and painful.

- Being triggered by certain sexual positions or kinds of stimulation can leave your partner feeling as though they are hurting you or feeling like they are getting it wrong with you, especially if you can't talk about it.
- Having sexual pain can make it difficult to fully enjoy your sexual relationship with your partner.
- If the things that turn you on are things that you feel bad about, it can be hard to share these things with your partner, which may lead you to keep those parts of your sexual life a secret.

How have these sexual impacts affected your relationship?

- Have you been able to make a list of triggers and share and discuss these with your partner?
- How do you cope with feelings of fear or avoidance in your sexual relationship?
- Have you been able to talk together about what turns you on and what you would like more of and less of?
- Do you have sexual pain and, if so, have you been able to find appropriate resources to help you manage and treat this pain?

Recommended readings for the therapist before beginning this topic

Bacon, B., & Lein, L. (1996). Living with a female sexual abuse survivor: Male partners' perspectives. *Journal of Child Sexual Abuse: Research, Treatment, & Program Innovations for Victims, Survivors, & Offenders*, *5*(2), 1–16.

Finkelhor, D., Hotaling, G.T., Lewis, I., & Smith, C. (1989). Sexual abuse and its relationship to later sexual satisfaction, marital status, religion, and attitudes. *Journal of Interpersonal Violence*, *4*(4), 379–399.

Kinzl, J.F., Traweger, C., & Biebl, W. (1995). Sexual dysfunctions: Relationship to childhood sexual abuse and early family experiences in a nonclinical sample. *Child Abuse & Neglect*, *19*(7), 785–792.

MacIntosh, H. B. (2017). Couple therapy with male survivors of childhood sexual abuse. In R. Gartner (Ed.), *Healing sexually betrayed men and boys: Treatment for sexual abuse, assault, and trauma* (pp. 233–260). London: Routledge.

Maltz, W. (2002). Treating the sexual intimacy concerns of sexual abuse survivors. *Sexual and Relationship Therapy*, *17*(4), 321–327.

Maltz, W., & Arian, C. (2001). *The sexual healing journey: A guide for survivors of sexual abuse.* New York: HarperCollins.

Maltz, W., & Maltz, L. (2009). *The porn trap: The essential guide to overcoming problems caused by pornography*. New York: HarperCollins.

Reid, K.S., Wampler, R.S., & Taylor, D.K. (1996). The "alienated" partner: Responses to traditional therapies for adult sex abuse survivors. *Journal of Marital and Family Therapy*, *22*(4), 443–453.

Psychoeducation

Shame

Shame is the emotional dance of healing from trauma: one step forward, two steps back. When shame is triggered, it can eat away and dissolve any tendrils of feeling that might have been slowly growing through hard work and perseverance, like the feeling that one is an okay human being. For many survivors, shame is simply a part of the furniture, as much a part of themselves as the colour of their eyes; the story of their "badness" is older than their earliest memories. The couple therapy process can be a rich space to explore and heal shame as the survivor is seen, accepted, and heard within the primacy of the attachment relationship with their partner. And yet, it can also be one of the most challenging arenas in which to explore shame. The attachment context "ups the ante" as partners are encouraged to share their needs, hurts, and injuries with one another, and survivors are faced with the evidence of the negative impacts of their trauma on themselves and their partners. The caustic burn of shame is at its most painful when the person one loves the most in the world says that we have hurt them, are letting them down, or are not meeting their needs. It is an affirmation that one's inner conviction is true and that we really are a horrible person who does not deserve love, safety, and happiness. So one fundamental aspect to the beginning of a couple's healing process is working with the pervasive impacts of shame in the adult relationships formed by childhood trauma survivors. Shame gets in the way of closeness, intimacy, and the ability to deal with conflict, leading to distance, detachment, and dissatisfaction in couple relationships.

Couple therapy is one place where male survivors in particular may be more likely to engage in the therapeutic process. Left to their own devices, many male survivors avoid therapy like the plague. However, it is often the case that a male survivor will tell me in couple therapy, "she told me if we didn't come, she was going to leave me". It may be that the context of couple therapy is the only space where many male survivors have the opportunity to work on their healing from trauma. Gender norms around sex, sexuality, and masculinity can reinforce male survivors' tendency to blame themselves and feel ashamed about the abuse, which can impact their feelings of confidence and clarity around their sexuality, and their ability to tolerate feelings of vulnerability and tenderness. For male survivors like Anush – who waited until Amira threatened to leave him before he disclosed – shame also leads to avoiding disclosures, even with their sexual partners. Living in constant fear of being found out, many male survivors isolate themselves in their lives and relationships, drifting apart from their partners. Women are conditioned to internalize their shame, and many female survivors engage in such self-abusive behaviours as cutting, binge-purging and self-talk filled with self-loathing, but men are typically conditioned to externalize. This can mean that male survivors will turn their shame outwards. Men who have been sexually abused are more likely to engage in interpersonal violence in relationships and protect themselves from feelings of vulnerability and shame through high levels of defensiveness, contempt, anger, reactivity, and suspicion and control directed at their partners. These responses to shame and secrecy can accentuate the distance between partners even further and reduce the potential for intimacy.

For all survivors, shame can really get in the way of the unfolding therapeutic process, shutting down capacities for emotion regulation and possibly leading the session to shut down entirely, as the therapeutic energy in the room is displaced from exploration and processing to containment and grounding. In some cases, shame eradicates the capacity for empathy and perspective taking: when overcome by shame, survivors are unable to tolerate the needs, feelings, and hurts of their partner. In these cases, it is necessary to slow the process down and help survivors regulate their distress so couple therapy can continue. For survivors who tend to internalize their distress, shame can cause them to become flooded and shut down in sessions. For other survivors, however – those who tend to externalize their shame – the triggering of shame in sessions can lead to agitation, anger, and at times even aggression. The effect on therapy is the same: the process shuts down as the therapist shifts their focus to dealing with the mounting, shame-fuelled dysregulation. The work of exploration and building new skills for improving their relationship is necessarily left behind.

It is important to prepare survivors, at least cognitively, for how shame might creep into the therapeutic process. Of course, we can only really work with shame when it is alive and lurking in the session; at that point, we can help survivors with the emotion dysregulation that often accompanies the toxic impact of shame, as they attempt to balance the needs of their partner with their own need for self-protection. To work with survivors steeped in shame, and their partners, it is necessary to contextualize their responses, to help partners understand that agitation and aggression reflect an underlying shame and vulnerability – an emotional state that is much easier to empathize with than anger and aggression. To begin from a perspective at least of intellectual understanding offers the partners a support to lean on as shame is explored as it emerges in therapy.

Using the handout as a starting place, begin a conversation with the couple about how shame might pervade their senses of self and their relationship. Many couples will find it challenging to point to where they experience shame, because it is an emotional state that is quickly smothered and hidden away under layers of self-protection. However, partners are often keen observers and can help identify where they see their partner struggling with shame, especially around conflict and negotiation. After all, it is pretty much impossible to manage conflict if every expression of hurt or dissatisfaction triggers off a wave of shame that seems exponentially larger than the event in question. How can you accept responsibility for hurting your partner or not being a full participant in the life of your home and family if you are using all of your psychological resources to avoid being annihilated by the shame of your very self?

As an example, Amira and Anush struggled with the impact of Anush's sexual abuse on his sexuality and his emotional availability in the marriage. Many of their struggles are rooted in how shame paralyzed Anush and made it impossible for him to disclose his abuse to Amira, to provide her with a story, a context, for his difficulties with sex and sexuality. This couple would be seen as a single trauma couple. While Amira's upbringing was far from easy, she emerged from it with a strong sense of self, and strong self-capacities, both for emotion regulation and mentalizing. In these cases, reviewing the handouts is often a real eye-opener for the partner who has not experienced developmental traumas. For the survivor, it is often a first conversation with their partner about these impacts, while for the partner it is often the first time they have been let into the vault of trauma that has felt like a vast void separating them.

In the transcript that follows, Anush is talking about how shame has isolated him from some aspects of family life: in particular, intimate contact with his young daughter. He further discussed the impact of feeling that he is not the husband he "should be" and how this shame fuels even more isolation and disconnection. This was surprising to Amira and helped her to understand more about Anush's avoidance of certain aspects of parenting. It was the beginning of a larger and longer conversation between the couple of all of the ways in which shame had infiltrated their lives together and pulled them apart.

THERAPIST: As we look at this handout, I'm reminded of what you told me about how long it took you to disclose your abuse, Anush, to Amira and that you were really only able to do it when Amira threatened to leave. I wonder what you are thinking about that as we review these points?

ANUSH: I see it; I definitely see it. I also see how it [shame] gets in the way of so many things. Like I feel I have spent our whole marriage trying hard to do other things right, to compensate for what a fuck up I've been. You know, I can't go back now and change it so it just didn't make sense to talk about it.

THERAPIST: No, you can't change the abuse or make it like it didn't happen. And, you can't go back and change how long it took you to disclose to Amira, but it seems as though that shame is still inside of you, compelling you to put it all away – I can't change it so why should I have to talk about it?

ANUSH: I can't erase it and since starting to talk about it, it's all I can think about.

THERAPIST: There are, however things we can do, things we CAN change, and some of those things are the shame, the guilt, the avoidance, the strong desire to keep people at a certain distance even when you want Amira to come close to you. Anush, can you give me an example of some of the ways you were trying to, as you said, "compensate", for the struggles you were having being fully in the relationship emotionally and sexually?

ANUSH: Well, you know, I tried to be a friend, a supportive husband. Taking care of things around the house so she didn't need to, the finances, all the regular everyday stuff that's normal, the husband stuff.

THERAPIST: But you tried to do these things the best way you could, to make up for the ways you felt you weren't shaping up as a husband.

ANUSH: The best way I could, to show her appreciation for everything else, that she does as a wife, as a daughter, and a daughter-in-law, as a sister, as a sister-in-law, to show her that, this is all known and appreciated.

THERAPIST: Being a good husband, you hoped that would be enough to cover up or compensate for the areas inside of you that you were struggling so much inside of you, your struggles with being close to Amira.

ANUSH: And I always thought that it would be something that, it would fix itself.

THERAPIST: Hmmmm.

ANUSH: But it just felt like, it's going to iron out, this will work itself out. So much is working. I felt, everything in our marriage was working, that this is one element (sex) that will kind of, although it's damn huge, damn huge, but it will, iron itself out. I figured I would be able to get past it with my strength of will.

THERAPIST: With sheer will?

ANUSH: That's it, that's what I hoped, but things just kept slipping away and never really resolved and I, I don't know, I just couldn't seem to do it.

THERAPIST: That deep, deep shame that you hid away inside of yourself, it is incredibly lonely and, in a way, it's leaving Amira out of the conversation about how you can work on your relationship and sexual challenges together.

AMIRA: Yes, I had no idea he was going through all of that. I had no idea he felt that way.

We went on to discuss how shame isolated Anush from his family and from any supports that might have been available to him. It was impossible for Anush to imagine that he could tell; he truly believed that disclosure would destroy his family. Some of this grew out of his cultural training in what it means to be a man, what is required of a man in a family and how fragile he imagined his parents to be. In discussing his shame in more detail, Anush was then able to disclose his fears about being a parent and how he might, inadvertently, do something wrong and hurt his children. His shame was so pervasive that he could not consciously place it alongside his adult sexuality and confirm that he has no paedophiliac tendencies. In his mind, his sexuality was tainted by abuse and therefore no aspect of his masculinity could be trusted.

ANUSH: For years, I don't know what it was that kept bringing back that past. The trauma that I went through, it was just making it difficult to do even simple things I want to do. I am trying to get past this shame, this fear but, after we had our children, I have never felt comfortable giving them a bath. I've told Amira, I don't feel that I can feel like I can touch them, but I guess I couldn't really tell her why.

THERAPIST: You didn't trust yourself. You were afraid of yourself, of your sexual trauma self seeping into your father self?

ANUSH: I was afraid, maybe I wasn't doing the right thing, I know I am their father, but you know like it's just never felt right and now you know, you [to Amira] should be the one giving them a bath. I don't want something wrong to happen.

THERAPIST: You mean something wrong between. . .

ANUSH: What happened to me . . . you know. I don't want anything to trigger . . . I don't want to touch them in the wrong way. If they've got to go to the bathroom, I just tell them, "mom's taught you how to clean yourself".

THERAPIST: So it's just that you are afraid that something will happen outside of your control?

ANUSH: I guess so. The emotional attachment that they share, the way they cuddle, it's such a wonderful feeling. You can't explain it. I know the love that they have, you don't know what can happen. The bad things, you know they're young. They're going to be growing up and I look at them and, I'm terrified that they will have to go through what I went through.

THERAPIST: Have you ever had any sexual feelings towards your children or have you felt aroused when you were caring for them?

ANUSH: No! Never! I have never, ever felt anything like that towards any child. I would kill myself!

THERAPIST: So what you are saying then, is that there is a way in which your trauma has imprinted on you a fear that even though you don't have desire, you don't have sexual desires for your children, you are afraid you might accidentally touch them in the wrong place or hurt them in some way?

ANUSH: I am afraid for them, I don't want to do the wrong thing. It's just gotten even worse as they have started growing up.

THERAPIST: So you are very afraid and that shame is eating you up from all angles – it is keeping you from confiding in Amira and getting the support that she might be able to offer – it is keeping you from feeling safe and confident in being close to your children – and it is keeping you from sharing your story with anyone else in your close friend or family circle who might be a useful resource in your healing. It sounds incredibly lonely.

ANUSH: You know I have never even thought about it.

In situations where disclosure has been avoided, the psychoeducation modules also serve as a first foray into sharing stories of the impact of their traumas. In this case, Amira really had no idea how devastated Anush had been by his trauma and how shame was ruling all of his relationships: with her, with their children, and with their friends and family. It was a first step to help Amira shift out of her anger at being left to blame herself for the couple's long-term sexual difficulties into empathy for her husband, who was doing everything he could to navigate the shame, pain, and avoidance he lived with every moment of every day.

Shame

What is shame, and how is it connected to trauma?

- Shame is an emotion that involves negative beliefs about yourself that can be pervasive and destructive to your sense of self. These feelings are strongly associated with experiences of childhood trauma.
- Shame is an emotion that can feel like it defines who you are as damaged, bad, helpless, and a failure. Shame is different from guilt. Guilt is a feeling of doing something bad. Shame is a feeling of being bad.
- Shame can be a response to secrecy, such as secrecy about sexual abuse or trauma and can lead to feelings of disconnection, detachment, and distress in relationships.
- Shame is a common response to trauma because it is sometimes easier to believe that there is something wrong with you than to believe that your abuser, often a parent or loved one, could hurt you for no reason.
- When childhood trauma includes sexual abuse, when abuse happens at earlier ages or when a survivor believes that they were at fault for the abuse or even enjoyed aspects of the abuse, shame can be far worse and very painful.
- When boys are sexually abused they can come to feel that they have failed as "men", failed to protect themselves and be strong as men should. This can lead to high levels of shame as sexual abuse of boys is still something that people think does not happen or, even that a boy is "lucky" to be abused by an older person who "initiates" them.

How might shame impact you?

- Shame can cause you to believe that you do not deserve to be in a happy, healthy relationship or that you are at fault when things go wrong in your life.
- Shame can cause you to feel that you are unable to take action in your life and relationships to make them better.
- Shame can cause you to feel so terrible about yourself that you hurt yourself through eating, drinking, drugs, sexual behaviours that feel shameful, or self-injury in the hopes that these things will soothe you or help you feel better. It is more common for female trauma survivors to respond to feelings of shame by "internalizing" those feelings and turning their shame inwards through hurting themselves.
- For some people, when they feel ashamed, like they are bad and have done something that makes them feel even worse, they can react by becoming aggressive, angry, or even violent. It is more common for male trauma survivors to "externalize", or react in these ways, and for them to find it unbearable to instead share how bad and vulnerable they feel, with their partners.

- Shame can cause you to feel the need to keep parts of yourself separate from other people, including important parts of your history of trauma and your intimate self that exists in your couple relationship.
- Shame keeps people from fully engaging in life and relationships.

How can shame impact relationships?

- Shame can make people feel that they are unlovable and damaged, and this can lead them to believe that they do not deserve to be in a healthy, loving relationship or that they do not have the right to stand up for themselves in their relationships.
- Shame may lead people to avoid disclosing their traumatic experiences, which can keep you feeling separate and alienated from your partner.
- Shame can lead to people keeping other kinds of secrets, secrets about their sexuality, their feelings of hurt and pain, or secrets about things that need to be discussed and resolved for the relationship to be healthy.
- Shame can cause you to believe that you deserve to be in relationships where you might be hurt or treated poorly, and so shame can lead people to stay in relationships where it might be safer or healthier to separate.
- When someone feels strong feelings of shame it can make it very difficult for them to empathize with their partner, especially if their partner is upset about something that they themselves have done. It can cause them to be unable to hear their partner's concerns and to responding without being overwhelmed.
- When someone feels strong feelings of shame, this can cause them to protect themselves from the pain and vulnerability of these feelings. How they protect themselves might not be something that is healthy for them or their relationship. This includes the issues discussed above, such as self-injury or addictions that the trauma survivor might hide from their partner, or becoming aggressive or violent towards their partner.

How has shame affected your life?

- How have you been aware of the impact of shame on how you feel about yourself?
- How does shame impact your life and relationships?
- How do you cope or respond to feelings of shame?
- How does shame affect your ability to be close and sharing in your relationship?

Recommended readings for the therapist before beginning this topic

Dorahy, M.J. (2010). The impact of dissociation, shame, and guilt on interpersonal relationships in chronically traumatized individuals: A pilot study. *Journal of Traumatic Stress*, *23*(5), 653–656.

Dorahy, M. J., & Clearwater, K. (2012). Shame and guilt in men exposed to childhood sexual abuse: A qualitative investigation. *Journal of Child Sexual Abuse*, *21*(2), 155–175.

Hlavka, H.R. (2016). Speaking of stigma and the silence of shame young men and sexual victimization. *Men and Masculinities*, *20*(4), 482–505.

MacIntosh, H.B., Fletcher, K., & Collin-Vézina, D. (2016). "I Was Like Damaged, Used Goods": Thematic analysis of disclosures of childhood sexual abuse to romantic partners. *Marriage & Family Review*, *52*(6), 598–611.

Platt, M.G., & Freyd, J.J. (2015). Betray my trust, shame on me: Shame, dissociation, fear, and betrayal trauma. *Psychological Trauma: Theory, Research, Practice, and Policy*, *7*(4), 398.

Talbot, J.A., Talbot, N.L., & Tu, X. (2004). Shame-proneness as a diathesis for dissociation in women with histories of childhood sexual abuse. *Journal of Traumatic Stress*, *17*(5), 445–448.

Psychoeducation

Negative cycle – Dyadic Traumatic Reenactment

Most models of couple therapy provide theoretical frameworks for understanding how couples end up in cycles of repetitive, painful negativity that lead to relationship ruptures and dissatisfaction. These models also provide strategies for how these repetitive negative interactions might be addressed through treatment. Two of the most established models of couple treatment, which have received the most consistent support from research to date, are Emotionally Focused Therapy for Couples (EFT, Johnson, 1992) and Cognitive Behavioural Marital Therapy (CBMT, Dattilio, 2009). These models provide an important basis for work with couples to build stronger, more loving relationships where interactions between partners meet their needs for closeness, comfort, and support. However, for couples where one or both partners have experienced extensive childhood trauma, the strategies suggested by these models to address challenging negative cycles often only address the first step in a more complex struggle, the struggle to break free from the entrenched effects of childhood trauma within their complex interaction cycles. While these strategies bring insight and understanding for many trauma couples, they are often stalled as they try to make the leap from insight to change. The couple can get stuck as trauma cyclically echoes between them, over and over again, in what I have termed a Dyadic Traumatic Reenactment (DTR; MacIntosh, 2013). The next section will review those strategies and then discuss the challenges of addressing the DTR cycles in trauma couples, as we go deeper and engage with the trauma that is both consciously and unconsciously living in the couple cycle.

Emotionally Focused Therapy for Couples (EFT) is based on the premise that rigid cycles of interaction, such as blame/defend or pursue/withdraw, are primary factors that maintain dysfunctional interactions in couples, fuelled by such negative emotions as anger or fear. EFT posits that unveiling shrouded emotional needs and identifying negative cycles that maintain each partner's interactional stance is the path forward to changing these negative cycles. The first step in this process is to delineate the conflict between the couple and to identify these negative cycles of interaction. This process expands to explore unacknowledged emotions that underlie the self-reinforcing cycle. Over the course of this process, couples come to gain insight into their cycle, identify it when it is happening, change it, and begin to build some flexibility into their response to one another. As therapy continues, couples learn more positive, healthier ways to respond and to communicate their underlying needs and emotional states, so as to prime new cycles of interaction (Johnson, 2003).

Cognitive Behavioural Marital Therapy (CBMT) considers that a number of factors, including early experiences, core beliefs, assumptions, emotions, and negative automatic thoughts, fuel the potential to trigger destructive behaviours and prime negative cycles of persistence or withdrawal. CBMT approaches this challenge by first identifying these triggers and then working to understand how they are involved with the development of the couple's negative cycles of behaviour. Once these have been identified, the CBMT clinician works to help the couple develop new strategies, involving cognitive and behavioural changes, to respond to the triggers in ways resulting in better listening and mutual support, and the development of new cycles of greater flexibility and resilience (Baucom, Epstein, Kirby, & LaTaillade, 2015).

Given the success demonstrated by EFT and CBMT therapies in shifting these negative cycles, how can therapists understand the challenges that couples dealing with a history of childhood trauma often experience as they try to shift from new insights into their negative cycles to begin to move away from these and into new patterns of interaction? All couples carry with them historical injuries and relational pain that might find their way into their reactions to one another, and certainly these historic experiences condition the patterns of response within each couple. Why is it that couples not dealing with the ravages of childhood trauma appear more able to use that insight and awareness and to make vital changes in their relationships? One way of thinking about this is that their historical traumatic experiences, relational and otherwise, are less likely to be embedded outside of their conscious minds, within the unconscious and unsymbolized realm of experience deep inside. What this means is that for someone who has experienced trauma in adulthood or injuries in the context of romantic relationships after adolescence, these traumas are held in their autobiographical memory, along with all of the emotions and reactions reminders of them might bring. For childhood trauma survivors, many traumas – especially those occurring at early developmental stages – are embedded in the unsymbolic realms of the mind; they live in a more dissociated space of embodied sensory states, smell, touch, sounds, physical postures, and bodily feelings. Traumatic memories from childhood are often known and not known; the words of the story are often separated from the sensations and feelings of the story. And so, even when childhood trauma survivors develop insight into their negative cycles – possibly even insight into how their own histories of trauma are being triggered by the cycle or fuelling the cycle – these insights are, in a way, separated from the guts of the story, the part of the story that must be accessed to allow for change. It would be like a singer running through their recital pieces in their head without ever singing them. They might do pretty well at memorizing the words, but they would never wrap their body around how the lyrics and the melody embrace and dance with one another and where in their body the song resonates; they would know the mind of the song, but they would never know the body of the song.

Given these challenges, it makes sense then that couples not dealing with the aftereffects of major childhood trauma translate insights into their negative cycle, and the triggers that fuel it, more easily into a growing capacity to change their patterns of interaction and develop more emotionally satisfying and intimacy-enhancing ways of being with one another. It also follows that, for survivors of childhood trauma, this process is going to be much more challenging. Trying to make changes based on intellectual insights, when the unsymbolized or dissociated aspects of their trauma story are not yet available to them as a coherent symbolized narrative of experience leaves survivors profoundly challenged to shift these cycles when they are triggered. Many survivors have talked about how frustrated and ashamed they felt when they found themselves back in an entrenched negative cycle, voraciously clinging to their insight and understanding as it slipped between their fingers and sucked them into a traumatic abyss of old sensations and feelings. These sensations and feelings quickly overrode any conscious, cognitive framework that they might have hoped would help them escape the void of trauma and allow them to respond to their partner in ways that were more about the new relationship they were trying to build and less about the reenactment of their trauma. Unsymbolized and unprocessed trauma has a powerful pull on relationships and on the therapeutic process itself. Insight, emotional engagement, and attempts at in-session behavioural change are frequently not sufficient to make a dent in trauma-embedded negative cycles.

In my research and practice with couples dealing with the ravaging impacts of childhood trauma, the strategies suggested by CBMT and EFT succeeded in assisting the couple to gain valuable insight into their cycles and, over time, helped couples identify triggers and underlying emotional states. They even began to identify the cycle in the moment when it was occurring. However, a key difference between the negative cycles of these couples dealing with significant childhood trauma and other couples is that the trauma "story" was concretely and rigidly embedded in the cycle – the themes, feelings, and actual behaviours of partners were experienced as reflecting aspects of historical traumatic experiences (MacIntosh, 2013; MacIntosh & Johnson, 2008). In couples where both partners experienced childhood trauma, these cycles were even more rigidly fixed in past traumatic experiences and were tightly and reciprocally reinforced.

For example, with Geoffrey and Gary, their cycle was often triggered by Geoffrey seeking out Gary for sex. Gary would become triggered and dissociate in response to Geoffrey's approach, which led him to withdraw both physically and emotionally as he became mute and physically rigid. Geoffrey would usually respond by becoming highly anxious and continue to poke at Gary to find a response. Finally, Gary would explode in rage and say horrible things to Geoffrey, confirming all of his worst fears. At the first level, the cognitive or intellectual level, there is a clear pursuit-withdrawal cycle, now fixed and rigid, resulting in major relational ruptures that repeated themselves over and over again. At a second level – incorporating insight into historical trauma and how it is currently influencing the couple – Gary's trauma was all about people initiating sex with him and then going on to hurt him; he knew this in a cognitive sense. Geoffrey also understood, intellectually, that these were triggers for Gary and that he "shouldn't" feel so insecure about Gary's withdrawal. Then, at a third level – the unsymbolized level outside of awareness – Gary's withdrawal and near-catatonia was fuelled by a deeply dissociated, traumatic reliving within his emotional, sensory, and physical being, of being pursued for sex, within his emotional and physical being, and all of the ways in which he had responded to unwanted pursuit. Geoffrey and Gary came in to treatment knowing and understanding, at the first level, how this cycle was being triggered – the knowledge; they quickly grasped the second level of how this cycle was being triggered; the insight into why, and even how; but it took many months of treatment for the deeper, unsymbolized, embodied aspect of the triggers (the DTR) to come into awareness and become available to work with (the unsymbolized coming to life within the treatment).

When traumatic affects and unconscious, unsymbolized, dissociated traumas continue to be alive in the unconscious underworld of couples, more than insight is required to change these relational patterns.

> In fact, that which the couple needs to know is exactly that which the couple cannot know. That which would allow the couple to break free of their tyrannical repetitions is locked away in the unsymbolized, dissociative unknown; simply not available for thinking, feeling and knowing.
>
> (MacIntosh, 2017b, p. 345)

To achieve change in these trauma-embedded cycles, these DTRs, we need to help those unsymbolized, dissociated affect states and memories come alive, safely, within the therapeutic context to help the couple gain more than insight: a deeper knowing of themselves, their partner, and how their trauma has become entrenched between them.

The only way for a couple to really engage with this challenging work is for them to work together, to externalize the trauma as a mutual enemy that is triggered by the cycle (Johnson, 2002). Moving past the first two levels of identification and insight and into the deeper realm of the unsymbolized entrenched between them, therapists must work with the couple to explore how the trauma has become embedded in the cycle and how couple interactions trigger old traumatic states of reliving.

This psychoeducational module is oriented to help couples begin to understand these negative cycles and the role trauma plays in their rigidity and persistence. You will have an opportunity to learn more about the couple and their relationship struggles. As always, you are straddling the line between assessment and treatment. Ask the couple to reflect on their negative cycles. Couples are frequently able to identify trauma triggers together and talk about them, as this is work that they may have been engaged in with individual therapists or as a couple struggling to get out of the grip of the DTR on their own, unsuccessfully. How do they see these being enacted between them? Does either partner easily acknowledge being a pursuer or a withdrawer? Does either one quickly reject the idea of a cycle? This is both psychoeducation for the couple and assessment for you. You will get a glimpse of both partner's approaches to solving problems, capacities for mentalizing about themselves and their partners, and capacities for emotion regulation and managing any shame that might arise as they discuss the challenges they are having in their relationship. If the couple readily "buys in" to the idea of the cycle, ask them to map it out for you. Once mapped out, ask the couple to start noticing the cycle in their day-to-day lives. If the couple balks, struggles, and rejects the idea of any kind of repetitive interaction cycle between them, you can let it go, but ask them if they would try to begin to notice how their interactions "usually" unfold. This may be a way to allow them to bring their cycle back to you without feeling embarrassed or ashamed.

The process of disentangling, acknowledging, and exploring negative cycles may take a couple of sessions. I typically start the discussion by looking at the first two levels to understand the cycle, what happens, and perhaps why it happens: the knowledge and insight levels. During this process, it is very important to track emotion regulation strategies consciously and verbally. For example, "it seems as though when your partner tells you that he feels pursued by you, you start to feel really overwhelmed with shame". Simply saying such things out loud is the first step as you begin to identify and build insight into the cycle approach. Do not try to work with the cycles or emotion dysregulation yet; instead, try to "mark and park": noticing patterns, acknowledging them, and marking them to be addressed in the next phase of work.

Moving to the deeper level of the DTR, our psychoeducational goal is to explore how the couple experiences the trauma to have become embedded in their cycle. This embedding may be quite concrete, such as someone who was sexually abused and then locked away in their room to prevent them from telling anyone, who then becomes overwhelmed with anxiety and distress when their partner withdraws from them or hides him- or herself away. However, trauma may be embedded in a less concrete way that has more to do with emotions, sensations, thoughts, and expectations that are embedded in cycles, such as being unable to tolerate attempts at any kind of intimacy. If the survivor develops the expectation that any kind of intimacy is dangerous, this can result in active (albeit potentially unconscious) withdrawal that will not shift even in response to insight. The survivor is so terrified of being close to someone, at a deep level outside of their awareness, that they are completely embedded in the withdrawal. Do they find that particular concrete or symbolic aspects of their trauma experience are being relived in the negative interactions between them? Do they feel that they get pulled into a spiral that terrifies them but which they cannot yet understand, or even see? All of these are okay; it is really about enabling the couple to understand, acknowledge, and begin to explore these new ideas.

In the next transcript segment, I was exploring the negative interaction cycles in which Camille and Chris were stuck. They easily articulated an awareness that Chris tends to pursue Camille and that Camille's go-to response is to withdraw. Her withdrawal is often framed around the justification that Chris has done something hurtful and that she needs to take some time away to recover. Camille does not think about the possibility that she could use Chris as a resource for her distress or talk to Chris directly about her hurt. Camille learned in childhood that it is best to keep feelings, especially feelings of hurt and disappointment, to yourself: nothing good could ever come of sharing these kinds of feelings. Chris, as we have already learned, was particularly primed to feel anxious and fearful in response to someone withdrawing from him out of disappointment. From here we were easily able to wander into the DTR domain. Both Chris and Camille had thought a lot about the negative interactions between them, but neither had considered the role of the traumas they relived within their interactions.

When asked for an example of their negative interaction pattern, the couple was able to discuss a recent incident involving a water bottle. Camille described having recently been sick and Chris bringing her a water bottle to her bedside. Because things had been messy around their home, Chris placed the water bottle on the floor next to the bed, and the next time Camille got up to go to the bathroom she stepped on the water bottle and water went all over the floor. Camille was able to describe her fury with Chris for leaving the bottle on the floor and how she completely shut herself down and pulled away from him. Chris was also easily able to describe his feelings of anxiety at Camille's withdrawal and his immediate feelings of failure and self-doubt. With a little jolt, it was very easy to get the couple to move into discussing the deeper embedded trauma in this particular incident of their negative interaction cycle. Camille was able to call up memories of her internal chaos after the assault, her need for care, and being berated and humiliated for making a mess. This humiliation followed hot on the heels of her experience of sexual abuse and a disclosure that resulted in her parents failing to provide her with the help that she really needed. So for Camille, in this situation, the DTR triggered a traumatic state of experience.

CAMILLE: It doesn't help me if there's a constant threat of mess, it feels as though it's this huge ever-present threat like there's a landmine waiting to explode, as though there's something about this threat that's really big and it's unchangeable and really hurtful in some way.

CHRIS: I agree and it's hard for me because I'm always under threat too, the threat of her getting angry and going completely silent on me, it drives me insane, and it's just like what it was like with my father after the accident, he was always just silent and then he would explode all over the place.

THERAPIST: When the two of you get pulled into this explosive dance, you are like the perfect puzzle pieces that fit together. You both are living with a sense of threat in relation to each other: something bad is going to happen, something explosive, and that really sucks you both into a vortex of re-experiencing your early traumatic experiences.

CHRIS: It's hard for me. How Camille deals with things is that literally anything anytime anywhere, even if it's on a table or on the floor or anywhere, any kind of tiny mess, can be a threat at all times.

During this session, I was aware that the work we are doing was psychoeducational. I was concerned that Chris was becoming emotionally engaged in a way that could have pulled him back into his traumatic emotional states and led to both dysregulation and a lack of safety for both partners in the session. While I was very interested in their thoughts and feelings about their DTR, I wanted to focus mostly on identification, awareness, and acknowledgement of how the trauma is living in their interaction cycle, so I pulled the session back from Chris's emotional response to a focus on understanding what is happening between them.

THERAPIST: Okay, let's just take a breath and try to put this stuff together and see if it works to help us make sense of what is happening between you in these moments. If it doesn't work, we'll start again. There's a feeling that's currently taking over. The name of it is "mess", currently, but it could be named something else another time, it's a feeling. Do you feel a dread or an anxiety or. . . ?

CAMILLE: I don't know it until that happens . . . and then . . . it's, it's too much. I just don't feel comfortable and I just can't deal with it.

THERAPIST: Okay, so it's like you're just walking along in your life and something happens, like the mess of the spilled water bottle and – and snap [snaps fingers] you're into some other feeling state that's really uncomfortable?

CAMILLE: Yeah.

THERAPIST: And in the ideal world of your hopes for your relationships, these "messes" wouldn't happen, you could avoid them. And, you feel as though, if Chris really cared about you, those things wouldn't happen because, well, he just wouldn't ever make a "mess" like leaving a water bottle on the floor.

CAMILLE: Yeah.

CHRIS: But, well that's not true. . .

Remaining very aware of the goal – articulating and understanding the DTR, not starting to work on or with it – I pulled back again and tried to create a more cognitive picture of the DTR.

THERAPIST: Let's just hold on to these ideas and try to put these thoughts together. There's a sense of dread versus what you hope for – that this could be avoided, I shouldn't have to feel this way?

CAMILLE: Yeah.

THERAPIST: First, it sounds like you are thinking, "I shouldn't have to feel this way", and, then, in your [to Chris] "real" relational world, there is a feeling of "What am I going to do wrong? What landmine am I going to step on? What mistake am I going to make? How am I going to get into trouble?" And so, Chris, you are sent into a spiral of trying to figure out how to avoid making a "mess" and frantically trying to remember all of the rules you have come up with to avoid triggering Camille.

CHRIS: Yeah, like all of my energy all of the time is focused on not stepping on the landmine, but I don't always know what the landmine is.

THERAPIST: That sounds just like how you have described living life in your family growing up.

CHRIS: Yes. [sighs]

CAMILLE: Sometimes one little thing drops and I feel like my entire world is in danger.

THERAPIST: If we go back to your childhood experiences, you find the trauma, and the unpredictability and the trauma, as you described, Chris. Life would be going on, and suddenly someone would explode. The unpredictability and the sense of not being able to get anything right, or even, "I'm trying as hard as I can but I made this one mistake and everything goes to hell" feeling from your childhood gets activated in these interactions. It sounds like you're listening, you're trying, but then this thing happens. So, again, it's like perfect puzzle pieces. Camille, your dread and fear and feelings of threat that the "mess" triggers brings up inside of you, beyond your consciousness in the moment: this old traumatic memory of being really shamed and humiliated for making a mess, and all of the ways your parents continued to fail to help you in the ways you needed them to, meshes perfectly with Chris's experience of being humiliated and berated for any small error.

CHRIS: Yes, that's it, we really do just completely trigger each other in the worst ways.

CAMILLE: Yes, but if you didn't do those things, if you really understood why I hate mess so much, you would stop, you wouldn't do it anymore.

In this moment, Camille was being drawn into the emotional experience of the DTR and was starting to be triggered into the repetitive cycle as she concretized the "actual" interaction with Chris rather than remaining aware of the deeper trauma-related triggers. In this moment, Camille was experiencing a concrete, subjective "reality" – if Chris would stop making messes, we would be fine, and he would be showing me that he really does love me. It is important, given the stage of the therapy that we were in, given the limited emotion regulation and mentalizing capacities that these two were showing at this point, and given that we were near the end of a session, to return to the conscious level of understanding and insight, to try to help Camille see the connection between the past and the present.

THERAPIST: Yes, that feeling of frustration and fear and dread gets triggered, a lot, and it's so easy to get pulled back into experiencing your interactions as though they ARE the trauma, as opposed to reminders of the trauma. In those terrifying moments, you really long to find a way to just avoid them rather than to have to feel them and work through what is keeping you guys stuck. I think we would talk about it being like when you drop something in a glass of water and it disperses, it's like that memory hasn't had that opportunity to disperse, it is still living there, almost as if it was yesterday, poof, *there it is* [hand gestures of "poof"] and then you're [to Chris] walking on tiptoes trying to get everything right, and, it's inevitable that sometimes things are going to happen. This is a really good example, because something like making a mess is a normal, everyday thing that happens in life. You [to Chris] brought her the water bottle because she was feeling pretty sick. You put the water bottle down and you both forgot that it was there. The next thing that happens is that you both end up back in a traumatic place of reliving feelings of hurt, fear, dread, and loneliness. The worst part about it is that you are both so triggered. Camille, you just shut down and withdraw, and Chris, you get so fearful and pokey, that you can't be there for each other in ways that would feel safe, comforting and soothing and around and around you go again, reliving the past in the present.

DYADIC TRAUMATIC REENACTMENT

What do we mean by a negative cycle?

- Many couples who come to couple therapy say that they have the same argument over and over again and that they just cannot escape the pattern that they get stuck in no matter how hard they try.
- In couple relationships, especially when there is a history of childhood trauma, attempts to get our attachment needs and longings met by our partners sometimes result in disappointment, hurt feelings, and discouragement. When partners are feeling angry, discouraged, and hurt, they can often turn to "secondary emotions" as a way of protecting themselves from further hurt. For example, instead of showing our partner how hurt and sad we feel, we may lash out in anger. In response, our partner may simply withdraw from our angry or critical approach, and these types of interactions lead the couple into a repetitive cycle of hide-and-seek, where one partner is longing for connection and the other is running. In couples where there is a history of trauma, shame and fear about connection can be a big factor in this negative interaction cycle.
- Often, how one partner responds to a distressing interaction results in an almost opposite response from their partner, such as: I seek you out and you move away from me. Frequently, the response is exactly the opposite to what we feel we need in that moment and, often, we end up feeling more hurt and alone than we did before the interaction.

What do we mean by a Dyadic Traumatic Reenactment (DTR)?

- Childhood trauma frequently occurs in the context of relationships with people who should have cared for and protected a child. The traumas often have a significant impact on the survivor's capacity to trust and feel safe in adult relationships.
- When we experience these kinds of traumas, our memories, feelings, expectations, and fears follow us into our important relationships. When looking at the patterns and cycles of couples where one or both partners have experienced childhood trauma, we see that the past has gotten stuck in there and clings to the cycle that unfolds between them with a lot of force.
- In therapy, survivors can often identify and articulate what happens between them, understand it and sometimes even begin to stop it. However, when it comes to really getting to the bottom of it and changing it, many childhood trauma survivors get stuck at this point in therapy and keep repeating the patterns over and over again with increasing frustration: they keep sliding back into the chaos and pain of their early traumas as they are relived with each other.
- Part of the process of understanding the DTR is to externalize the trauma as a force that you and your partner are fighting together, a force that makes it very difficult to shift out of these negative cycles. It is very difficult to make the shift from insight and understanding to real change, when the thing we are trying to change is not something we are even aware of.

- For many couples, this powerful pull of unprocessed trauma happens because the trauma has not been "symbolized", or made conscious and put into words. Being able to think and know our traumas, not just the details, but the feelings and sensations of those deeply embedded experiences, allows someone to talk about their traumas as a part of their life story and to really "get" how these traumas have impacted their relationships. These unsymbolized traumas typically remain stubbornly stuck in their cycle. When traumatic emotions and memories or feelings continue to be unconscious and dissociated, they continue to be alive in the underworld of the couple's interactions. To help you with these trauma cycles, we have to work at a deeper level. We have to find ways to bring those stuck traumas into our minds and bodies so they can be talked about and explored. This can be a real challenge, because it involves paying attention to the ways in which we "find" the trauma being relived in our couple relationship; these can be hard and painful. However, your therapist will help you learn to pay attention to these parts of the cycle so you can start to really pull those stuck traumatic relivings out of your cycle and begin to build a new relationship where your interactions with your partner are not based on reliving traumas from the past.

Where do you see this in your relationship?

- Can you identify a repeating argument or negative cycle in your relationship?
- How does this feel when it is happening?
- Can you identify aspects of your trauma that get triggered when this happens?
- What strategies have you tried to work on this?

Recommended readings for the therapist before beginning this topic

Bromberg, P. (2009). *Multiple self-states, the relational mind, and dissociation: A psychoanalytic perspective Dissociation and the dissociative disorders*: DSM-V and beyond (pp. 637–652). New York: Routledge, Taylor & Francis Group.

Ginot, E. (2007). Intersubjectivity and neuroscience: Understanding enactments and their therapeutic significance within emerging paradigms. *Psychoanalytic Psychology*, *24*(2), 317–332. https://doi.org/10.1037/0736-9735.24.2.317

MacIntosh, H. B. (2016). Dyadic traumatic reenactment: An integration of repetition and enactment into the understanding of negative interaction cycles in childhood trauma survivors and their partners in couple therapy. *Clinical Social Work*, *45*(4), 345–353.

Stern, D. B. (2007). Opening what has been closed, relaxing what has been clenched: Dissociation and enactment over time in committed relationships. *Psychoanalytic Dialogues*, *16*(6), 747–761. https://doi.org/10.1080/10481880701357444

Psychoeducation

Mentalizing

The previous sections have worked through psychoeducational modules to help couples understand more about the impact of childhood trauma on their lives and relationships. The two modules that remain shift focus to the two main developmental self-capacities that underline much of the work of the second stage of treatment and beyond: mentalizing and emotion regulation.

Mentalizing can most easily be defined as a way of thinking about thinking (Fonagy, 1991). This simplified definition may help survivors “get” the concept as we begin to delve into their mentalizing capacities and to consider how we might work together to develop and strengthen this skill set. Where a person is able to reflect on themselves and others and be flexible in their exploration of their own mind and emotional states, they are also often capable of understanding and empathizing with others. In each developmental stage, optimal responsiveness from a caregiver allows for the slowly unfolding growth of mentalizing capacities (Bateman, Fonagy, & Allen, 2009). The child grows, through this responsive attachment relationship, to believe that they are knowable, tolerable, and loveable, and that others are also knowable, safe, and understandable. The child learns that the minds of others are not frightening and that their own feelings are important, as are the feelings of others (Fonagy & Target, 2006). When a caregiver provides what is known as contingent mirroring, they are both mirroring the child’s current state but they also feed back to the child the emotional state seen through the eyes of the caregiver. This is demonstrated through changing vocal tone, facial expressions, and ways of communicating with the child while heightening or dampening the mirrored emotional state back to the child (Soderstrom & Skarderud, 2009).

At the other end of the spectrum, a misattuned, traumatized, or dissociated caregiver, through confusing and incongruent mirroring of their own distressed state, sends the message to the child that their internal world is bad, unknowable, and not understandable; the child may even come to believe their internal world to be dangerous. These messages leave the child feeling disoriented, confused, and bad about themselves and their own inner world (Fonagy & Target, 1998, 2006; Stein & Allen, 2007). Fear and abuse are the enemies of the development of strong mentalizing capacities: sometimes you just do not want to know what the other is thinking or feeling because it would be too traumatic. Imagine being a child who is sexually abused by the same person who feeds them cereal and juice in the morning: to know the mind and feelings of that person would be so confusing and terrorizing as to be destructive to the child's developing mind. However, strong mentalizing capacities are essential in developing and maintaining healthy social relationships.

When a person's developmental experiences have allowed for strong mentalizing capacities to develop, they tend to be comfortable with exploring the mental world, curious about themselves and others, and able to imagine the perspective and emotional experience of another person. Such a person is able to reflect upon themselves as they go through their life and relationships and can tolerate uncertainty and the changing nature of minds. They are often able to be flexible and playful in their mental and emotional life and their life with others, and to understand that they cannot ever completely understand the experience of another person, but they can empathize with them through their own imagining of it. Ways of describing "good" mentalizing include openness to mental exploration, interest in the mental states of self and others, comfort when exploring even difficult memories and experiences, and an integrated sense of one's own cognitive and emotional states and those of others. A person who mentalizes well can be relaxed and flexible and not stuck in their perspective; they can solve problems by using others as a resource; they are curious about others and learn from them; and they can tolerate uncertainty and the ways various aspects, like perspectives, change over time and between people. They are interested in understanding how they impact others, are capable of forgiveness, and tolerate conflict and conflict resolution (Luyten, Fonagy, Lowyck, & Vermote, 2012). You can see how vital these kinds of capacities are for the development and maintenance of a strong, loving couple relationship.

When a person has not had developmental experiences conducive to the growth of strong mentalizing capacities, they may struggle with being able to reflect on their own or others' experience, become rigid and inflexible about their own perspective and interpretations, develop certainty about themselves or others, and tend to make automatic and distorted interpretations about others. These individuals may become defensive in response to the diversity and changeability of the minds of others, especially where they may have a very strong and clear assumption about how something "is". Individuals who struggle with mentalizing often find that they lose their capacity to regulate their emotional distress in relation to others: mentalizing and emotion regulation are highly interconnected. A list of phrases descriptive of "bad" mentalizing include an overall lack of reflection, a tendency to make automatic assumptions, an inability to regulate emotional distress in relation to others, certainty when it comes to their assumptions about their own internal states and others, rigidity and lack of flexibility about their own perspective, a focus on the external features of self and others (or even a complete lack of awareness of the mental states of others), difficulty tolerating more than their own perspective, a tendency to focus on behavioural characteristics rather than deeper motivations, and a general lack of interest in and defensiveness about mental states. In general, a poor mentalizer is someone who tends to avoid mentalizing and can become angry, defensive, avoidant, or uncooperative when challenged to expand their mental view (Luyten et al., 2012). You can see how challenging it might be for someone with poor mentalizing capacities to be fully engaged in a reciprocal, empathic, and evolving couple relationship. One can also imagine the challenges faced by someone with weak mentalizing capacities engaging in the couple therapy process with openness and flexibility.

Trauma has been found to impede the development of strong mentalizing capacities (Fonagy, 2010; Stein & Allen, 2007). Among trauma survivors, those who demonstrate higher levels of mentalizing experience less distress and fewer struggles in their adult lives. For trauma survivors, then, developing these vital self-capacities is potentially challenging, but when survivors are able to mentalize well, they do better in their lives and relationships. Peter Fonagy et al. (1996) suggests that mentalizing is a buffer against many of the difficulties trauma survivors may experience in their mental health, interpersonal relationships, and overall functioning, in response to trauma. This would suggest that building strong mentalizing capacities would promote resiliency in young children who are exposed to maltreatment. For some survivors, especially those who experienced abuse and neglect at very early stages in their lives, mentalizing capacities may simply never have emerged due to the caustic impact of mentally dangerous caregivers. For others, perhaps those whose early development unfolded reasonably well but who experienced severe trauma at later developmental stages, the development of mentalizing capacities may have begun to unfold but have been cut short or damaged by an abrupt end to mental, emotional, and physical safety.

In my research with couples, poor mentalizing capacities strongly influence the development of distress in the couple and make the therapeutic process extremely challenging. In sessions, survivors often become severely emotionally dysregulated in response to a partner having a different perspective, challenging their rigid assumptions, or not understanding their point of view. Adding in the significant challenges that survivors often experience with empathy and perspective taking, both related to poor mentalizing, the resulting therapeutic process may leave one or both partners severely dysregulated in response to the other and significantly challenged in empathizing or understanding the experience of the other. It can end up looking like a therapist putting out fires, and containing and explaining, but never getting anywhere.

A number of individually focused treatment interventions have been developed that focus on the development of strong and flexible mentalizing capacities. Mentalizing-Based Treatment (MBT) for Borderline Personality Disorder (note that 86% of BPD patients have a history of childhood trauma; Herman, 1992) has been found to help patients diagnosed with BPD with their trauma symptoms and emotional distress and has helped them build increased stability in their interpersonal relationships (Bales et al., 2012; Bateman & Fonagy, 2008). These individual interventions focus on working with trauma survivors to rebuild shattered mentalizing capacities or to help the survivor develop these from scratch where opportunities for safe mental exploration had never before existed. Interventions are focused on helping clients learn how to mentalize about themselves and others, and also to apply this ability in the context of relationships (Bateman et al., 2009, p. 767).

As with the other psychoeducational modules, you will provide the couple with the psychoeducational handout on mentalizing. One of the trickiest aspects of this conversation is, if the survivor does not mentalize well, they may not be able to see that they are not mentalizing well. For instance, Camille would often rush very quickly to make assumptions about the meaning of some aspect of Chris's responses to her. She was highly certain of the truth of these assumptions and would cling to them with fortitude. As you can imagine, that kind of certainty and rigidity is not going to be easily made flexible by a psychoeducational handout and a short discussion. Remember, then, that the goal of these modules is to introduce couples to new ideas about factors that may relate to the struggles they are having and to start a discussion about how they, in this moment, see and understand these new ideas. The therapist is really just opening up a conversation. Sessions during Stage Two will allow ample opportunity to break down rigidity and build mentalizing capacities that are flexible, open, and responsive. For now, open the dialogue and engage in ongoing assessment by listening and really hearing how survivors receive these ideas. It is important to remember that mentalizing capacities are vulnerable to break down in the context of stress, especially in attachment relationships, so while the success of the couple therapy will be impacted by the budding capacity to develop and hold on to these skills in future sessions, it is also essential that survivors feel contained and regulated during these discussions.

Unlike the discussion of other psychoeducational topics, where I shared a transcript to demonstrate the process of engaging with a couple on that topic, this discussion will include snippets of different transcripts to demonstrate what it looks like when a couple is struggling around mentalizing and how you might identify some key difficulties in early sessions.

THERAPIST: So you just used a few words there: "correctly", "as I expected", and "the right way". In that, I hear a statement of fact, that there is a right way and there is a wrong way.
CAMILLE: Yes.
THERAPIST: And I also hear that he is not measuring up to the "right way".
CAMILLE: Yes.
THERAPIST: Who decides what the right way is?
CAMILLE: Me.
THERAPIST: Why do you get to be the person who decides what constitutes the right way?
CAMILLE: Me.
THERAPIST: [to Chris] Do you agree?
CAMILLE: Obviously not.
CHRIS: [nods a no]

When exploring challenging, potentially shameful areas in the couple relationship, attempt to be light and curious, where appropriate. This will tell you a lot about the degree of flexibility and insight available within the survivor's current mentalizing capacities. An interesting challenge when it comes to mentalizing is that things that might appear hilarious from an outside perspective just are not funny in context. In this snippet, I was trying to expose Camille's rigidity, automaticity, and lack of mental flexibility and curiosity, employing some humour to inflate the one-sided character of the decision about "right" and "wrong". This attempt fell flat. It fell flat because, as far as Camille was concerned, she was "right", and this was not something that was even on the table for discussion. In this early session, I saw that this rigidity and automaticity of seeing one's own perspective as the only valid one was going to be really important in my work to build this couple's mentalizing capacities.

Continuing that same conversation, Chris described his frustration at not being able to get it right with Camille and how he simply does not share her perspective about the right way or the wrong way – in this case, about how to unpack a suitcase.

CHRIS: Yeah, as far as I knew, everything was unpacked.
CAMILLE: Yes, but you didn't make sure.

CHRIS: Yes, but it's no big deal; I'll just get it tonight.

THERAPIST: So from your perspective [to Chris] "I did my best, if there is something missing, I will find it later, it's not a big deal, it's not the end of the world".

CHRIS: Yeah.

At this moment I was talking to Chris, but I was really talking to Camille. I was trying to get a sense of whether Camille could tolerate me speaking Chris's perspective, when Chris is in an emotionally dysregulated state such that he is not able to articulate it for himself.

THERAPIST: What is it like for you when Camille tells you, "this is the way it is supposed to be" and you hear the message, you aren't getting it right?

CHRIS: Well, I hate it.

CAMILLE: But he had the chance of doing it, he had to have a chance to unpack his things correctly, but things like this happen constantly and I am constantly having to fix things because he can't get his shit together.

Camille was evidently struggling to tolerate Chris's perspective and to tolerate my speaking his perspective. The emotional tone of her responses was angry and indignant. She was showing signs of rigidity, lack of flexibility, automaticity, inability to tolerate differing perspectives, and inability to regulate her emotions in relation to others. On another occasion, we were discussing another conflict between the couple over a similar issue: Camille's belief that if Chris really loved her he would not do things "his" way, he would do things the "right" way and, if he did things the "right" way, he would not lose things like a key. I was pushing the narrative envelope a bit by suggesting that everyone loses things and wondering whether she could expand her perspective to acknowledge that she too loses things, perhaps contextualizing her interpretation of Chris as betraying her. This is very much about assessment – how much flexibility, curiosity, and openness is there in their responses to one another?

THERAPIST: So you gave me an example of losing something, which is something we all do, we all lose things. When you lose things, what is it like for you?

CAMILLE: Well, sure, I lose things, but really compared to him, very rarely.

THERAPIST: What do you think it means to lose something?

CAMILLE: It means to lose control over something, and I can't lose control.

THERAPIST: Tell me more.

CAMILLE: It makes me panic if I'm not in control.

THERAPIST: So something like a key, which can be replaced, even losing a key would make you feel out of control?

CAMILLE: It's not easy to replace and it costs money!

You can see Camille's struggle to regulate her emotions and to tolerate the narrative being expanded to include her in the class of people who might lose things. Going a little deeper, it was also clear that this mentalizing rigidity was tied to a traumatic need to maintain control over the people and things around her: without control, everything was terrifying for her. This means that there must be a right way and a wrong way, and people who care about her must adhere to her right way. It simply would be too terrifying to live in a world where there were multiple perspectives.

THERAPIST: Something like that makes you very anxious, you start to panic, something is out of control. It sounds like being out of control is the worst thing for you, so something that Chris might think of as a little thing, losing a key that can be easily replaced, each of these little moments can send you into a panic. Can you help me understand where that comes from?

CAMILLE: I know where it comes from, from my childhood. Everything was out of control and I never felt safe but, at the same time, there were rules for everything and everything had to be done a certain way or my Dad would flip out. So, if things were done right, he would be fine, and if they weren't, it was kind of chaos.

THERAPIST: It was one or the other, or both at the same time?

CAMILLE: Both at the same time.

THERAPIST: That must have been very confusing for you; there was no sense that life can just wend its merry way along and everyone will be fine.

CAMILLE: No.

THERAPIST: It was like everything is catastrophic and everything is in control at the same time. That's a very strange message for a child to get. How did you integrate that message? How did you make sense of it?

CAMILLE: Now, well, I have to have everything under control.

THERAPIST: Like your dad. So when things are out of control around you, you get really scared.

CAMILLE: Yeah.

THERAPIST: And you carry that around you, inside of you. And you feel like Chris knows this and he should respond differently. If he knows how scary this is for me, he should be different.

CAMILLE: He should at least try to. I mean, I wouldn't scare a person on purpose. If a person knows this insecurity that comes with all this chaos around me about not unpacking things correctly – if a person knows this is happening for my partner, I would never do it, I would try to keep things in order so that my partner doesn't panic.

THERAPIST: I see, so what you are saying is: he knows this, so he shouldn't do any of these things, because he knows that they upset me. That's making the assumption that it is intentional, what he does is intentional.

CAMILLE: No, he is just not mindful about what he is doing and how that will affect me. If he was being mindful these things wouldn't happen.

In this segment, Camille was focused on Chris's external behaviour, imbuing it with intentionality and meaning. She was making the automatic assumption that Chris intended to cause her fear and pain by losing the key, that he was intentionally not doing things her way because, if he loved her, he would never do anything to cause her to feel this way. Camille was demonstrating rigidity and automaticity and was equating an external behaviour with a psychic reality: this behaviour equals this thought or feeling. And, at the end of the day, Camille's struggle with flexibility and tolerating that others' mental states might be different from her own left her in a state of deep despair and isolation. For her, this was the "truth", Chris really did not care for her or he simply would not do these things. Poor mentalizing often results in loneliness and isolation because the survivor cannot tolerate conflict or differing perspectives, and they become so upset by others as a result of their assumptions of intentionality or malignance that they end relationships due to conflicts that they feel cannot be resolved.

Moving to Gary and Geoffrey, similar themes emerged in their discussion about managing conflict. Here was another example of mental rigidity, a lack of capacity to see the other's mind because there was only one possible "right" answer.

GARY: He's going to say that all of our arguments have the same theme all the time, so it's the same . . . like whenever we argue the root cause is generally the same. I get angry about something, I don't know how to express myself, so then we get into an argument about something small and then it turns into the same argument, basically like I'm not going to bed with him and then he gets annoyed with me.

GEOFFREY: I feel like it's like if I care about something, Gary has a different opinion.

GARY: But my opinion is right, and his is not. His is not valid [laughs] . . . well, you know I know it is. . .

GEOFFREY: And then that pisses me off, and then we argue about it and then it's the same argument about everything and anything.

GARY: We solve it in the end but then it comes back up again.

GEOFFREY: It's just differences, like it's every time we've got a difference about something, we're not arguing about that difference, we're arguing about the fact that. . .

GARY: That there is a difference.

GEOFFREY: I have a different opinion, I'm trying to be calm and resolve this and Gary feels like I'm wrong and then he just loses it.

GARY: It's actually not that you're wrong, it's just actually that . . . I feel like . . . my idea is different than yours and it's more important I guess . . . and I think it swings back to the whole thing where it's like I'll try to solve my own problem instead of working with him to solve the problem in general for both of us.

You can see in this snippet that Gary and Geoffrey are tied up in a similar mentalizing struggle: who's "right" and who's "wrong". However, you can also see that they are a little further along. Both can tolerate that while they believe very strongly that the other is wrong, they can see that it is probably true that both perspectives have value. This was a big stretch from their initial conflicts, where it was very clear that both were stuck in the rigid place of believing that only their "truth" was the "right" one. Additionally, I saw a little flexibility, a little bit of humour and playfulness, and some self-awareness that their struggle to tolerate the other's perspective is playing a role in their repetitive negative cycle. There was also some awareness that these problems were not going to be solved in the isolation of their own minds.

Mentalizing

What is mentalizing?

- Mentalizing is a term used to describe a form of imaginative mental activity involved in how we perceive and understand others and ourselves. It is a mental process of making sense of others and ourselves through understanding the states and mental processes that can be seen and heard, and those that are more hidden or subtle.
- Mentalizing is a capacity that one develops throughout infancy and early childhood. This happens in the context of your relationships with the people who closely care for you. Caregivers who are responsive and make an effort to understand your needs and distress will help you develop the capacity to mentalize. When a caregiver "gets it" or seems to be responding to your feelings, needs, and distress, you learn that your emotions, bodily signals, and even your "self" are important and understandable. As early as in infancy, you also learn to understand that caregiver through their vocal tone, facial expressions, ways of communicating with you, and how they help you to regulate your emotions. Essentially, this means they understand when it is time to help you become calm, soothed, and settled and when it is time to play, roughhouse, and laugh. Through all of these experiences, the child learns that their feelings, thoughts, and even they themselves are okay and understandable.
- When you learn how to mentalize well, you can then think about, reflect on, hold, and explore emotions, thoughts, and mental states. Strong mentalizing capacities are fundamental to a person's ability to have positive relationships and manage in social environments.
- Strong mentalizing can be seen when someone is easily able to explore their own mental states and has interest in the mental states of others. These individuals understand how mental states change and can integrate thoughts and emotional aspects of themselves and others. They have the ability to regulate their own and other's distress and to be playful and solve problems through give and take. People who can mentalize well are able to take responsibility and acknowledge their own behaviour. They are curious about other people's perspectives and are comfortable with uncertainty. As you might imagine, these capacities are essential for a healthy and happy couple relationship.
- Poor mentalizing can be seen when someone is unable to reflect on their own thoughts and feelings and makes automatic assumptions about others that may not be accurate. These people find it very difficult to tolerate and regulate their own or others' distress, and they tend to be rather rigid and certain about what they and others might be thinking, feeling, and understanding, often without any exploration or discussion. Those who find mentalizing to be difficult tend to become overly focused on the internal or external aspects of themselves and others and find it hard to think about their own and someone else's perspective at the same

time. For instance, a survivor of childhood trauma might assume that their partner is really angry with them because they are not talking to them. However, instead of asking their partner what is going on or thinking of ways to engage with their partner, they make this assumption based on their partner's external behaviour and then act "accordingly", perhaps by shutting down, becoming afraid of being rejected, or angrily shutting out their partner. However, the partner might in fact be thinking about something that is quite worrisome, like an upcoming mortgage payment, and actually be worried about talking to their partner about it out of a desire to protect them or a fear of getting into a fight. When their partner responds to their silence with silence, this might then "prove" to them that they were right to be silent and avoid the conversation. And in the end, they were both "wrong", and now the couple is further apart and struggling to regulate their emotional distress without being able to talk to one another about the distressing event. Had the couple been able to imagine that there was more than one possible reason for the silence, and had they been able to talk about it, explore together, and solve problems together – both emotion regulation and mentalizing – they would have felt closer to one another instead of feeling so far apart and distressed.

How does trauma impact mentalizing?

- At its most simple, studies suggest that those who have experienced abuse have lower mentalizing capacities.
- This relationship goes two ways:
    - First, trauma can make it very difficult for a child to develop the capacity to mentalize well. For instance, a traumatized or dissociated caregiver sends the message to the child that their internal world is bad or dangerous, through their lack of understanding of their own distressed state and that of the child. This leaves the child feeling disoriented and confused. Also, when traumas occur, a child should be able to turn to their caregiver for soothing, support, and comfort. What then does a child do when the caregiver is the person who inflicts the trauma? Getting closer to the caregiver might lead to more abuse, more distress, and more need.
    - Second, it can also be dangerous for an abused child to mentalize. Not only can it be more dangerous to turn to an abusing caregiver in terms of the potential for more abuse, but mentalizing can also be dangerous for the developing mind of the abused child. Imagine being able to think about what is going on in the mind of the abuser, someone who is intentionally hurting a child physically, sexually, or emotionally. This could be incredibly terrifying and emotionally dangerous for a child. The best defence against this is to avoid thinking about the mind of the abuser altogether. However, this then means that the child never develops these essential skills to build and maintain relationships.

How is mentalizing relevant to couple therapy?

- Mentalizing is an essential capacity for being able to get into and then nurture a healthy romantic relationship. Without being able to reflect upon and tolerate your own thoughts, feelings, and behaviours and those of your partner, a couple relationship would be very difficult. Mentalizing makes it possible to acknowledge and take responsibility for ourselves in relationships, to have empathy and compassion for each other, to be vulnerable and open, and to have safe and clear boundaries with your partner.
- When people experience trauma in childhood, their mentalizing capacities can either not develop or be damaged. This means that it can be hard for a trauma survivor to think about and understand their own feelings, thoughts, and behaviours as well as those of their partner. If you combine this with difficulties in emotion regulation, it can be very difficult to talk about or navigate difficult or painful issues. At the beginning of a relationship, when things are fresh and there has not been an accumulation of painful hurts or conflicts, things may be somewhat manageable, but as relationships move along, it is inevitable that conflicts will arise, one partner will hurt the other's feelings, and difficult life events will crop up that require the use of these mentalizing and emotion regulation skills.
- Couples that have experienced trauma may find it very difficult to do some of the things that couples need to do to repair hurts and conflicts and just to function day by day. These include being able to help each other feel better and safe with each other, take responsibility for how they impact and affect each other, tolerate that they may not know everything about their partner and their feelings, be curious and playful with and about one another, avoid becoming defensive when important discussions arise, correct and repair misunderstandings, not get stuck when misunderstandings arise, trust one another, and be responsive to one another.

Can mentalizing capacities be developed in adulthood?

- In adulthood, if one has not learned how to mentalize or one's capacity to mentalize was damaged by trauma, it is important to work actively to develop these capacities. Practice is the most important approach to learning these skills.
- With your partner, you can practice these skills in everyday normal situations:
    - You can ask questions of your partner about their thoughts, feelings, and behaviours.
    - You can take a moment to share your assumptions about what is happening in that moment, listen actively, and work on changing your assumptions in response to what your partner tells you.
    - You can be curious about what is happening in your own and your partner's mind in response to situations that might have gotten you into conflict in the past, by slowing down, listening, not making assumptions, taking a moment to step away and calm down, coming back together and reflecting on what has just happened, and trying to understand and empathize with your partner even when it is painful or difficult to do so.

Recommended readings for the therapist before starting this topic

Alexander, P. C. (2009). Childhood trauma, attachment, and abuse by multiple partners. *Psychological Trauma: Theory, Research, Practice, and Policy*, *1*(1), 78–88. https://doi.org/10.1037/a0015254

Bateman, A., & Fonagy, P. (2008). Mentalization-based treatment for BPD. *Social Work in Mental Health*, *6*(1–2), 187–201. https://doi.org/10.1300/J200v06n01_15

Bateman, A., Fonagy, P., & Allen, J. G. (2009). *Theory and practice of mentalization-based therapy textbook of psychotherapeutic treatments* (pp. 757–780). Arlington, VA: American Psychiatric Publishing, Inc.

Luyten, P., Fonagy, P., Lowyck, B., & Vermote, R. (2012). Assessment of mentalization in A. Bateman & P. Fonagy (Eds.), Handbook of mentalizing in mental health practice (pp. 43–65). Arlington, VA: American Psychiatric Publishing, Inc.

MacIntosh, H. B. (2013). Mentalizing: An exploration of its potential contribution to understanding the challenges faced by childhood sexual abuse survivors in couple therapy. *Journal of Couple and Family Psychoanalysis*, *3*(2), 188–207.

Psychoeducation

Emotion regulation

The final psychoeducational module is focused on emotion regulation. Emotion regulation is, in essence, the ability to tolerate and modulate emotional states. The majority of childhood trauma survivors have difficulties regulating their emotions – many severely – and these difficulties tend to be much more challenging than those faced by survivors of trauma in adulthood (Pelcovitz et al., 1997). It is important to remember both emotional poles when thinking about difficulties with emotion regulation. There are survivors who respond to overwhelming feelings by becoming flooded and overtly distressed, often turning to external behaviours to stifle the overflowing emotions, and there are survivors who resort to numbing and dissociation in response to overwhelming feelings. Just because one looks calmer than the other does not mean that they are not both distressed.

Emotion regulation and mentalizing are deeply interconnected. Like mentalizing, a child develops the capacity for emotion regulation through the mutually regulating experience of the attachment relationship. Essentially, emotion regulation begins "outside" of the infant and young child. As a caregiver responds to signals of distress and arousal, both positive and negative, and makes efforts to figure out the distress and provide soothing and containment, a child is regulated by the attachment figure, outside of themselves. Over time, the capacity to regulate emotions becomes internalized "within" the child, and that child grows into an adult that can tolerate strong emotions and regulate both their internal experience and their external expression (Sroufe, 1996). Emotion regulation strategies function to soothe and contain an infant or young child in their distress. They also function to help the infant or young child learn about the pleasures and joys of emotional arousal and stimulation. A caregiver who is responsive and empathic will excite and arouse a young child through play, within the limits of the child's tolerance for excitation – like the parent who tickles and stops when the child asks them to stop versus the parent who keeps tickling well beyond the point where the child's laughter has turned to tears. We need to learn how to experience both positive and negative emotions from our early attachment figures. Without these containing and soothing experiences, distress can become unbearable and regulation of emotions becomes impossible. In adulthood, survivors often become overwhelmed, unable to think and tolerate their overwhelming feelings, and they end up turning outwards to external behaviours to turn off the emotional noise. Self-injury, addictions, sexual compulsions, eating disorders, and other self-destructive behaviours become the best strategy a survivor can find to distract, soothe, and numb themselves, where internal emotion regulation capacities fail or are simply absent (Briere, 2006; Cloitre et al., 2006; Linehan, 1993; van der Kolk, 1996; Zlotnick et al., 1999). On the other hand, many survivors learn at an early age that expressions of distress are futile, and they develop finely honed capacities for numbing and dissociation. Think of the infant in an orphanage whose cries of distress are not heeded and who, eventually, simply stops crying. This child is likely to turn to dissociation in their future when they become distressed because mechanisms for emotion regulation, in their earliest experiences, were not internalized from responsive and consistent caregivers. Rather, shutting down and dissociating into a state of nothingness was the only option for psychic survival. All efforts at managing emotions are focused on reducing emotional arousal. Unfortunately, you do not get to choose which emotions to experience or express, so when emotions are shut down or denied, all emotions shut down. If the "negative" emotions like anger, fear, and jealousy are shut down, so are the "positive" ones like love, joy, and pleasure, as well as the potential to move towards emotional engagement and intimacy.

Many childhood trauma survivors who struggle with emotion regulation believe that they cannot control their emotions. They may say things like "It just happens" or "I can't control it; it just builds up and I explode". This is how it feels to them, but it also represents a strong belief in the impossibility of changing something that has plagued them most of their lives, along with helplessness to do anything about it. Many survivors do not have the ability to use their emotions as useful gauges to understand themselves and others, learn about their experience of the world, and guide their approach to interpersonal situations. Instead, survivors often leap immediately from the hint of a feeling to some strategy of avoidance or behavioural response to get rid of the feeling.

One of the most significant challenges in therapy with trauma survivors is avoidance. For many survivors, frantic and determined attempts to regulate overwhelming emotions can lead to a constant state of avoiding emotions through numbing and dissociation (Hayes, Wilson, Gifford, Follette, & Strosahl, 1996). This works, in the short term, to keep emotions under wraps, but in the long term this kind of chronic avoidance of emotions can lead to feeling isolated, being unhappy in relationships, and having even higher levels of trauma symptoms and distress. If you are not aware of feeling anything, nothing is particularly satisfying or pleasurable, even if this protects you from being overwhelmed by threatening negative emotions. And, if you spend all of your energy holding back a tidal wave of emotion, after a while, the pressure is going to build up and it is going to blow. There is no shortcut past feeling what needs to be felt, but we can help survivors build emotion regulation capacities to learn how to tolerate their feelings and manage them in ways that are not destructive.

In a couple relationship, these challenges can get in the way of successfully navigating the normal ups and downs of couple life: handling small conflicts, discussing important decisions, even sharing one's emotional life with a partner. If a survivor cannot tolerate their own emotional states, they will avoid them and, as a consequence, avoid sharing them with their partner. This can lead to a relationship that is devoid of comfortable and intimate emotional connection. There might be voluminous emotional reservoirs hidden away outside of expression, or even awareness, but they are not shared. Couples may come to therapy describing emotional isolation from one another. They may just as likely come in and describe a chaotic relationship where there are outbursts of overwhelming feelings, which can even result in interpersonal violence.

Our early research on couple therapy with childhood sexual abuse survivors identified a number of key themes related to emotion regulation difficulties that appeared to impact not only the level of distress of the couples but also the process of therapy itself (MacIntosh & Johnson, 2008; MacIntosh, 2017a). When emotions were dysregulated in sessions, the therapeutic process slowed down to a standstill, while the therapist shifted focus away from working with the couple and onto helping the survivor contain the flooding of overwhelming emotion or recover from dissociative moments. Many survivors reported feeling flooded with feelings, that they experienced their feelings as dangerous and overwhelming. Acceptance, tolerance, and regulation of emotions was another dominant theme. Survivors felt easily triggered by their partners' discussions of issues in their relationship, and the ensuing emotional dysregulation derailed the therapy process due to the necessity to stop processing work to contain the survivor's distress. These survivors were particularly challenged to regulate their emotions when their partner was seeking them out for support or emotional closeness and intimacy in sessions. Many survivors described becoming so overwhelmed that their capacity to think became clouded – another reminder of the important interconnection of emotion regulation and mentalizing. For many survivors, numbing is an automatic strategy to deal with overwhelming emotions that the survivor is afraid will overwhelm them and result in loss of control. Many survivors turn to dissociation in sessions, seeming to disappear in front of your eyes as their emotions become too overwhelming. Some survivors are very direct about their unwillingness or inability to stay present in emotionally challenging moments of therapy. Frequently, the dissociation of the partner is nothing new and has been woven into the thread of the relationship and has become intricately tied into the couple's negative interaction cycle.

Another aspect of emotion regulation difficulties is the impact of a constricted range of emotions arising from years of avoidance, suppression, and/or dissociation. In sessions, when a survivor who struggles with emotion regulation difficulties is confronted with conflict, and with their partner's dissatisfaction, needs, and emotional triggers, there is often one emotional state that predominates even if that state appears disconnected from or inappropriate to what is happening in the session. For instance, Geoffrey's dominant emotional state was shame. When he was in any emotionally arousing situation in therapy, shame would be triggered even if the tone of that moment in the session was sadness, pride, joy, and so forth. For Gary, on the other hand, since dissociation was his primary strategy for managing his emotions, regardless of the context of the emotional tone of the session, he went off to dissociation land. Such dominant emotional states – often shame or anger – do not match the current context of the session and can result in a major empathic rupture between partners. When one partner needs the other to acknowledge their pain, and their partner dives so deep into shame or anger that the session has to shift its focus to helping that partner contain and regulate this emotion, it can leave the partner who is needing that acknowledgement feeling alone, misunderstood, and unloved.

These are some of the landmines of couple therapy with childhood trauma survivors, which may explode if therapists do not actively address emotion regulation capacities at the onset of the therapeutic process. It is essential, therefore, that practitioners help survivors build strong and consistent emotion regulation capacities before opening doors that might lead to the emergence of new traumatic memories, painful disclosures, or difficult secrets in the therapy. We would be failing our survivor clients if we did not adequately prepare them for the difficult emotional work of couple therapy.

In the following transcript segment, I was talking to Gary and Geoffrey about their challenges with emotion regulation. Geoffrey was quite aware of how overwhelmed and distressed he gets and could acknowledge that he tends to pursue Gary in a frantic way that appears to trigger Gary. He felt helpless to do anything to change it. Gary, on the other hand, began therapy somewhat less aware of his tendency towards dissociation in response to being triggered and found it very difficult to engage in the conversation in a direct way – also a sign of his challenges with avoidance and dissociation.

THERAPIST: The next area we will be talking about is the issue around emotion and how we experience our emotions. This seems to be a really important area for us to explore given that you have told me that sometimes you [to Geoffrey] feel very overwhelmed with feelings of sadness and anger and you [to Gary] feel shut down when that happens and get very dissociated. As that happens you [to Geoffrey] feel more and more upset until you feel you can't control yourself and around and around you go. Survivors can have a really hard time staying present when there are big emotions happening and that can make it very difficult for you, as a couple, to learn how to talk and resolve difficulties in your relationship. For both of you, big emotions are terrifying for all sorts of reasons. But it sounds as though you are both working hard to stay present in difficult conversations and avoid dissociating.

GARY: There is definitely a part of me saying this is stupid you should just get out of here (dissociate). I have to try to not listen to that voice.

THERAPIST: It sounds like you have been working hard to make a choice not to listen to that voice. Is that the voice that often takes you out of the situation? Like when something is emotionally stressful and difficult that voice might say, "hey, hit the road!"

GARY: Yeah, I think so.

THERAPIST: Okay, so, Gary, when you are feeling distressed, your go-to strategy for managing your emotions is to dissociate or "just get out of here". Geoffrey, it sounds as though your strategy is to try to contain your distress but eventually you just can't do it anymore and you end up in an overwhelming state of despair and devastation. That must be so challenging for you both.

GEOFFREY: Yeah, I don't know what happens to me. Every time I think – keep it together, you'll be fine – if you get upset again, he's just going to disappear again. And then it happens again and I end up a blubbering mess in the corner!

THERAPIST: So, much of what you are both describing is "internal": struggles with finding strategies for tolerating and managing your emotions when they start to feel overwhelming. Things that you try to do by yourself, inside of yourself. It seems as though, when you are both distressed, the things that you need to do, to help yourselves feel emotionally in control, send you further apart from one another. And the thing that feels really difficult is being able to feel as though you can find comfort and calm in your distress with each other.

GEOFFREY: That's all that I want but I know that that makes Gary feel trapped and I don't want to make things worse.

As we discussed their current strategies for emotion regulation, Geoffrey was able to talk about his experience of feeling desperate and his awareness that his attempts to get close to Gary to feel safe and contained led Gary to become overwhelmed and to dissociate. He was able to talk about how abandoned and fearful he becomes when Gary dissociates. Over the course of this discussion, Gary had a hard time staying present and began flickering his eyes and seeming to drift in and out of the discussion. He was able to respond to my efforts to help him with grounding by putting his feet on the floor, focusing on keeping his eyes open and rubbing his hands on his thighs, which was the part of his body he was most comfortable with being engaged with in a tactile sense. When clients struggle with dissociation in sessions, it is the first order of business to help them get grounded and return to engagement with you and their partner. The section on managing and reducing dissociation, will go into detail about various strategies to address dissociation in sessions. In early sessions, however, before these important self-capacities have been developed and are online, the simplest way to reorient the survivor out of a dysregulated state is to shift from open exploration to more structured cognitive activities: shorter sentences, closed-ended questions, and a clearly focused direction of discussion. In the case of Gary and Geoffrey, I turned to the handout and continued to explore the challenges survivors may have with emotion regulation, and how emotions can be used as vital sources of information and guides for making decisions and taking action in one's life. We further discussed how challenges with emotion regulation can impact a couple's capacity to support and connect with one another even in the case of difficulties or conflict. As you might expect, Geoffrey was very interested in this conversation, but Gary was not so keen; his tendency towards avoidance and dissociation was very evident in his tendency to dismiss the value of emotions and emotional life, especially when related to building deeper intimacy with Geoffrey.

When I asked Gary and Geoffrey to think about the most recent time they could remember having struggled with emotion regulation together, and to discuss the strategies they used to deal with these challenges, we were able to talk about a situation where Gary and Geoffrey resorted to using text messaging as a way to stay in contact during a difficult conflict. It seemed that Gary could continue to engage, in spite of his dissociative state, through texting. Geoffrey, in turn, felt a little less frantic when he could at least have some kind of contact with Gary. The two were quite eager to talk about this newfound strategy, using text messages to continue communicating in the face of distress that had become so overwhelming that they simply could not stay in the same room with one another and were certainly unable to talk to one another.

THERAPIST: So you feel that part of the struggle is the pressure you experience to not trigger one another when you are in conflict?

GEOFFREY: I think so, yeah, but it's like we seem to be able to resolve conflict a lot better through text or chat because . . . he doesn't have to see me getting upset, doesn't see me being emotional, which puts more pressure on him. And so we've actually gotten through more conflict just by doing that.

THERAPIST: Gary, how do you understand that it's easier for the two of you to resolve conflicts and to sometimes be closer and more affectionate when you're further apart?

GARY: It's just easier.

THERAPIST: Can you say more about why it's easier?

GARY: Well sometimes because . . . I can articulate things that are not comfortable saying when we are together.

THERAPIST: Okay, so like in a text it might be easier to say something more vulnerable than you might be able to say in person?

GARY: Yeah.

THERAPIST: Okay. Are there other things that come to mind?

GARY: Well, I can separate myself from my problems, I guess.

THERAPIST: Can you say more about that?

GARY: Well, I can sort of separate from my feelings, like they don't exist so I can just talk from one perspective, and I can think more clearly . . . it's like all of the chaos just goes down to one dimension.

THERAPIST: So, when you are in that one-dimensional space in texting with Geoffrey you can also have more space in your mind to think and be close and vulnerable.

GARY: Yeah.

THERAPIST: That's really interesting. Do you understand how you do that?

GARY: I just sort of . . . I guess thoughts come out of my brain through my hand instead of going through my whole body and I can tolerate it.

THERAPIST: So it is less embedded, less embodied. When your mind, when your thoughts are going through your hands, you don't have to feel all of the dimensions of your emotions, it's not as overwhelming, and you're able to comfortably feel that one dimension and, through the texts, to say things that are maybe really important but that may be hard to say when you are so distressed.

GARY: Yes, but, it's good but it's not good, like Geoffrey would say that it's like I'm two different people.

THERAPIST: So, if Geoffrey was sitting in the room with you when he sent you a text and you replied, which "you" would he get?

GARY: Well, I guess it would be the more positive me, more of what he wants, more feelings, I guess.

THERAPIST: So, when you aren't texting, there is something that happens, something about feeling all of your feelings through your whole body, something that pushes you down and holds you back, subdues you?

GARY: Yeah, I guess, it's like I just can't.

THERAPIST: And, Geoffrey, it sounds as though when you experience Gary as being warm and positive, able to share his feelings and be close to you in the texts, and then when he's with you and he's shut down and subdued, you interpret that as meaning something, that maybe he doesn't want you. Is that what happens?

GEOFFREY: Yeah, I mean. . . . We fight about it a lot . . . I do have such a hard time not taking it personally, not thinking that it's about me. I think Gary is really mad that I can't get over that or . . . it was just that I don't get how hard it is for him sometimes. I do think that I really heard that finally.

THERAPIST: And what is it like for you when you have one experience of Gary in a text at a distance and another experience of Gary when you're with him?

GEOFFREY: I mean I think . . . it's very confusing, it's really disappointing because I get very excited when I get a warm loving text from him and I think that . . . he wants to see me so finally I'm waiting, waiting for him to be present and engaged and happy to see me, happy to be with me and he communicates all of this over text and then . . . when I see him it's like the opposite. And I'm like okay I understand that it's . . . when he's not doing well or he's really tired or he's mentally exhausted, that he can't be with me in that way but . . . it's just that I got my hopes up and got really excited to like be with him again and then he's kind of not there.

THERAPIST: So for you, and please correct me I'm just trying to get close to it and understand it as well as I can, for you it feels like the Gary you experience in the text goes away when you're with him in person. That person is no longer available to you. Like you want that person! You're excited about that and then that person is gone and the Gary that you're with is more subdued, less present.

GEOFFREY: Yeah.

THERAPIST: So it feels to you that something's been taken from you, withdrawn.

GEOFFREY: Yeah, like if he hadn't sent me those texts about wanting to be with me, I'd still be disappointed, but I wouldn't be as disappointed.

THERAPIST: So you felt a little bit like you got hyped up about it and then boom.

GEOFFREY: Yeah.

THERAPIST: And the Gary who sends the texts, where is he when the two of you are physically together?

GARY: I don't know, it's not like we really are two different people, I just, feel different.

THERAPIST: What happens to that part of you, the part of you that can connect, that does share his vulnerable feelings, and is able to communicate?

GARY: I don't know . . . I . . . just don't know. I just can't.

THERAPIST: You don't know, that part of you is just shut down when you are together. There's a kind of irony, for many survivors one of the things that they need to be close is distance. For a lot of survivors when there's some distance between them, it's easier for them to express themselves and to be close . . . and the closer the person gets to them physically, emotionally, the harder it is for them to be close. It's almost like they need the space to feel close.

In this segment, struggles with emotion regulation were directly intertwined with the negative cycle in which this couple is caught. As the couple tried to stay connected – ironically, being further apart – this also intersected with shame, as Gary and Geoffrey were bathed in self-doubt and self-loathing over their repeated, failed attempts to find ways to stay safe and close. As the session came to an end, and with it the end of the psychoeducational process, we discussed the next steps in the treatment, moving forward into the skills-building stage.

EMOTION REGULATION

Emotions and childhood trauma

- For survivors of childhood trauma, feelings can sometimes feel dangerous, out of control, or confusing. Often survivors have difficulty naming or understanding their feelings, tolerating feelings that may feel overwhelming and frightening, and then managing those feelings in ways that would allow them to feel strong, capable, and safe.
- However, it is essential that survivors start to really understand that emotions serve an important purpose. Emotions give us information about situations, ourselves, and others, and they help us decide what to do in our lives and our relationships.
- Emotions can be uncomfortable, but they are always "healthy". They do not last forever, and we ARE NOT our emotions. Emotions are simply information messages. We can control our behaviour regardless of the emotions we might be feeling. For instance, you might feel very anxious about asking your partner for a hug when you are feeling insecure. However, that anxiety is just a message from inside of you telling you that this is something you feel some worry about. Maybe, in the past, hugs were dangerous or led to abuse. Maybe, in the past, you were with a partner who rejected or refused you when you were having emotional needs. So your anxiety is just the message from inside of you telling you that something about your desire to ask for a hug is worrisome – new, different, and a little bit hard. That said, you can still ask for that hug! If you ask for that hug, you may still feel a little anxious or worried, yet you might get the hug and that would be information, or you might not get the hug, and that would be information too. No matter what you do in response to a feeling, you learn something, which you can use going forward into new situations.
- Sometimes, we fear that emotions are dangerous or a big problem. BUT what IS the problem are all of the things that we do to avoid or get rid of feelings that seem overwhelming or frightening. Things like pushing feelings away, going numb, dissociating, self-injury, eating behaviours – these things are problematic. Having feelings, understanding them, and learning to know how to use the information they provide is NOT dangerous or bad!
- It is possible to:
  - Be aware of our emotions and what they are trying to tell us
  - Express emotions in positive ways
  - Increase our ability to tolerate unpleasant emotions
  - Cope with stress effectively and in positive ways
  - Behave effectively to match our values and reach our goals in stressful situations.

What do we mean by emotion regulation?

- Affects, feelings, or emotions are three words that mean the same thing: how we feel, emotionally, in response to the world around us and the relationships in which we engage.
- Feelings exist in many ways, and different people might feel very different things in response to the same experience.
- For survivors of childhood trauma, feelings can sometimes feel dangerous, out of control, or confusing. Often survivors have difficulty naming or understanding their feelings, tolerating feelings that may feel overwhelming and frightening, and then managing those feelings in ways that allow them to feel strong, capable, and safe.
- When survivors face these difficulties, couple relationships can feel very difficult. If you find it hard to name, tolerate, and manage your emotions when experiencing conflicts or difficulties with your partner, the emotions that you feel about these conflicts or difficulties may quickly overwhelm you and make it really hard for you to work through the problem in a healthy and constructive way. In fact, the problem becomes the feelings instead of the original conflict. This can leave conflicts and difficulties unresolved and partners feeling angry, hurt, resentful, and even frightened of bringing their concerns to their partner for fear that things will get worse or explode.
- This same problem happens in couple therapy. Often couples come in to therapy to work through difficult conflicts that they have been unable to resolve on their own or they come in to therapy to work on the negative interaction cycles or dyadic traumatic reenactments that we explored in the last section. When they come in to work on these issues and the survivor finds it difficult to name, tolerate, and then manage their feelings, the therapy quickly becomes focused on helping them feel emotionally safe again and the couple does not get the opportunity to really engage in the process of resolving these important conflicts.

How do you see emotion regulation issues impacting in your life and relationship?

- What are your experiences with feeling, naming, and managing emotions?
- How do you deal with feelings that are strong and threaten to overwhelm you?
- How do you, as a couple, work together to support each other in emotion regulation?
- How have you, as a couple, struggled with the impacts of difficulties with emotion regulation on your ability to work together as a couple and support one another?

Recommended readings for the therapist before starting this topic

Cloitre, M., Chase Stovall-McClough, K., Miranda, R., & Chemtob, C.M. (2004). Therapeutic alliance, negative mood regulation, and treatment outcome in child abuse-related posttraumatic stress disorder. *Journal of Consulting and Clinical Psychology*, *72*(3), 411–416. https://doi.org/10.1037/0022-006X.72.3.411

Cloitre, M., Cohen, L.R., & Koenen, K.C. (2006). *Treating survivors of childhood abuse: Psychotherapy for the interrupted life*. New York: Guilford Press.

Cloitre, M., Miranda, R., Stovall-McClough, K., & Han, H. (2005). Beyond PTSD: Emotion regulation and interpersonal problems as predictors of functional impairment in survivors of childhood abuse. *Behavior Therapy*, *36*(2), 119–124. https://doi.org/10.1016/S0005-7894%2805%2980060-7

Fonagy, P., Gergely, G., Jurist, E.L., & Target, M. (2002). *Affect regulation, mentalization and the development of the self*. New York: Routledge.

Schore, A.N. (2003a). *Affect dysregulation and disorders of the self*. New York: W.W. Norton & Co.

Schore, A.N. (2003b). *Affect regulation and the repair of the self*. New York: W.W. Norton & Co.

Chapter 4

Containing conflict

Conflict is part and parcel of the process of couple therapy. In many ways, the role of therapists is as coach and mentor to couples as they learn to manage conflict, work through difficult impasses, and develop new skills to help both partners feel as though their feelings and needs are valued and respected. For childhood trauma survivors, conflict can be particularly terrifying given that, for many, conflict and lack of safety was a defining aspect of their earliest experiences. We also know that childhood trauma survivors are more likely to end up in high-conflict relationships and that survivors are at a higher risk of raising the level of conflict to abusive and violent levels. Throughout the process of Stage One, an emphasis is placed on containment of conflict, setting the stage for a safe and productive therapy process. Until a couple can engage in effective communication without falling into dysregulated conflict, often fuelled by Dyadic Traumatic Reenactments (DTRs), it is difficult to work together effectively.

For our purposes, it is important to differentiate couples along a continuum of conflict. At one end are couples who have had such terrifying childhood experiences that they will avoid conflict at all costs, who struggle with emotion regulation and mentalizing in such a way that the normative conflicts of daily couple life (*Who is going to take the kids to soccer? Who is going to make dinner? Why aren't we having more sex? Why does your mother treat me like that?*) become messy, frightening, and overwhelming for the couple. Their emotion regulation and mentalizing capacities simply go offline in the context of everyday conflicts and they end up not even attempting to solve problems, while tiptoeing around one another. Over time, these accumulated tensions lead to a powder keg of potential conflict. These couples often report that things are just "fine" for a few weeks and then have massive blowouts, often on the weekend when they spend more time together. The conflict erupts over something that completely stumps them (*Why did we lose our minds over who would be taking out the garbage?*) Meanwhile, at the other end of the continuum are couples where emotion regulation and mentalizing capacities become overwhelmed, go offline, and conflict erupts in episodes of interpersonal violence. These couples may have absolutely no role models for what resolving conflict without violence might look like and may be unable to reflect on their own feelings and behaviour in ways that help them contain themselves from saying and doing hurtful and even violent things in their relationship. It is important that the first phase of treatment be used to assess the level of capacity for containing conflict to ensure that interpersonal violence does not erupt as a result of the emotional challenges of therapy, feelings of vulnerability, or fear and retaliation arising out of issues raised in sessions that continue to escalate after the couple leaves your office.

Where do we draw the line: interpersonal violence and DCTCT

Ask any couple therapist about whether they work with couples where there has been a history of any kind of interpersonal violence (IPV) and you will get as many different answers as there are therapists. This has been a highly contentious question in the field and one which continues to be discussed in the literature. IPV is pervasive and destructive. Many couple therapists and treatment guidelines from different theoretical orientations are clear that working with couples dealing with IPV is contraindicated. For others, the decision about working with any particular couple in the context of IPV is based on a careful process of weighing risks and potential benefits.

IPV is frequently equated with physical assault and abuse and sometimes fails to acknowledge the insidious and devastating impacts of psychological and emotional abuse in relationships, especially for survivors of childhood trauma for whom this abuse may be the extension of a lifetime of abuse and violence. IPV ranges from psychological abuse – such as name-calling, yelling, insults, and belittling – all the way to severe physical abuse and homicide. The Centre for Disease Control estimates that 1 out of 6 families experiences some form of IPV and, of these, 1 in 18 families struggles with severe violence.

In the cognitive behavioural tradition, specific models have been developed to address IPV in the couple context. IPV is seen as a learned behaviour that is triggered by negative interaction patterns in couple relationships. These models focus on reducing violence, building up skills such as communication, social skills, anger management, problem solving, and listening skills (Babcock, Green, & Robie, 2004). These models also focus on helping abusers take responsibility for their behaviour, while abused partners learn how to be assertive and set limits with their partners (LaTaillade, Epstein, & Werlinich, 2006). One particular model focuses on increasing the capacity for reflection in the couple through the use of meta-dialogue and a reflecting team. This model assists couples to attend to their perceptions of one another's behaviours, cues, and signals. It is thought that couples experience an increase in reflection and self-awareness through the therapists' use of the reflective dialogue. From the perspective of mentalizing, this might be interpreted as a kind of scaffolding of mentalizing capacities through exposure to the mentalizing of others (Vall, Seikkula, Laitila, & Holma, 2018). Implicit in these approaches is a focus on emotion regulation and mentalizing: helping couples learn to manage their emotional responses to conflict and anger, and how to listen and communicate, all of which require mentalizing capacities.

The originators of Emotionally Focused Therapy (EFT) have suggested that couple therapists not work with couples dealing with severe IPV, which they define as being a situation where one partner feels disempowered, voiceless, and dominated by the other partner (Woolley & Johnson, 2005). There is concern that when partners express strong emotions and high levels of vulnerability, which is a cornerstone of the EFT approach to treatment, violence might be exacerbated and/or escalated. For couples where IPV is less severe, it is suggested that psychoeducation be incorporated into the treatment, but that EFT proceed as normal (Johnson, 2004). Jarry and Paivio (2006), also EFT researchers, suggest that therapists need to create a safe place for the expression of strong emotions without fear of reprisals or angry outbursts, using such techniques as validation and containment.

The traditional approach for treating violence in couples has been to separate the couple and send the perpetrating partner, usually male, to a group for violent men that is focused on psychoeducation, anger management, gender equality, and helping the abuser take full responsibility for their actions. Typically, then, the abused partner, usually a woman, is sent to a support group for survivors of IPV (Oka & Whiting, 2011). The rationale for this approach suggests that, for safety reasons, couples should be separated and that abuser and abused have different issues to work on. However, when abusers are put together in a group there can be undesired consequences, such as abusers empathizing with one another and reinforcing or even creating new strategies for being abusive. Some have suggested that this just morphs the violence into something more insidious as the abuse goes underground, shifting the emphasis from physical violence to belittling, undermining, and other forms of psychological violence (Augusta-Scott & Dankwort, 2002). Additionally, the "divide and conquer" approach does not deal with IPV that is mutual, reflecting an escalating conflict related to couple distress. The "traditional" model is based on assumptions based on heterosexual couples where "perpetrators" are cisgendered men and "victims" are cisgendered women; it therefore does not address issues arising in IPV couples that may be diverse in terms of gender identity, sexual orientation, and other aspects of coupling that do not fit within these assumptions. The traditional approach also does not address the real issues of distress and lack of safety experienced by the many couples who do not want to separate and do want help with reducing the conflict, aggression, and violence in their relationships (Stith, McCollum, Rosen, Locke, & Goldberg, 2005). If couple therapists turn these couples away, they may not seek help elsewhere and are then left in the same situation with no help (Levin, 2007). Also, while only 6% of couples who seek couple therapy disclose IPV as a presenting problem, when asked directly 53% will acknowledge that some form of aggression has been a source of distress in their relationship. Often the treatment process is well underway when therapists become aware that there has been a history of IPV in the relationship (Stith et al., 2005). It is important to ask, right at the beginning of treatment, how conflict is expressed and whether aggression and violence are present, to make decisions about whether and how to work with a couple based on all of the information available, knowing that couples may find it difficult to talk about unsafe conflict for fear that a therapist will refuse to work with them.

A review of the literature on understanding IPV suggests that the phenomenon can be categorized according to different typologies. At the most basic level, violence may be categorized into two primary classes to help therapists make decisions about whether to work with a couple presenting with a history of violence. The first group, characterized as the most severe, involves typically one-sided violence motivated by a desire to control and coerce the partner. This dynamic can involve significant psychological abuse, such as threats, insults, intimidation, ridiculing and berating the partner, and limiting their partner's freedom, including access to finances, friends, and family. This more severe form of abuse also may include such physical aggression as slapping, punching, biting, hitting with objects, choking, and assaulting with weapons, and in the severest of cases, rape and murder (Kelly & Johnson, 2008). In some of the literature, these abusers are called intimate terrorists. It is universally recommended that therapists not work with couples where this kind of abuse is present.

The second class of IPV is not connected to a pattern of subjugation, coercion, and control. This form of violence is more likely to be mutually escalating, involving both partners. This dynamic is still potentially dangerous but is less likely to be severe and result in injury, and is often more closely related to difficulties in emotion regulation than a desire for control, intimidation, and power. Verbal and psychological aggression is often reciprocated and related to levels of distress in the couple (Holtzworth-Munroe, Meehan, Rehman, & Marshall, 2002; Johnson, 2008; Kelly & Johnson, 2008). These couples may be suitable to working in couple therapy.

When we look at the causes of IPV, they are complex and determined by many factors; however, trauma appears to be frequently associated with the development of violence in couples. Those who go on to be in violent relationships are more likely to have grown up in homes where IPV was present, and with parents dealing with addictions. Those who go on to perpetrate violence in their relationships are also characterized by low self-esteem, high levels of jealousy, challenges with assertiveness, and difficulty taking responsibility for their own behaviour (Oka & Whiting, 2011). These could be considered characteristics of those trauma survivors who struggle with emotion regulation and overwhelming shame and attachment anxiety.

Gender differences in IPV are also complex (Archer, 2000; Frieze, 2005). Women typically experience the most severe forms of violence, including physical and sexual assaults and violence with weapons. Men are far more likely to experience milder forms of violence, such as being spat at, bit, hit, or hit with objects, although it is also believed that violence against men is under-reported (LaTaillade et al., 2006). While rates of perpetrating aggression are surprisingly equal between sexes, women tend to use verbal IPV and milder physical forms, while men are more likely to perpetrate more severe forms of IPV including physical and sexual assault (Archer, 2000; Frieze, 2005).

Many couples engage in psychological IPV that is reciprocal and escalating. Partners report that once the violence starts, negative behaviours continue in response to each other's ongoing negativity. As violence escalates, it seems that, for women, abusive behaviour escalates in response to their male partner's physical and psychological abuse, while for men, violence appears to escalate regardless of whether their partner disengages from the conflict. In other words, even if a woman withdraws and attempts to end the exchange, once conflict has begun, men are more likely to continue to escalate conflict towards violence (Jacobson et al., 1994). As couple therapists, we need to be aware of and acknowledge each partner's role in IPV, while being clear that verbal and psychological aggression, committed by either partner, never justifies escalation into physical violence (LaTaillade et al., 2006).

Bearing all of this in mind, how do we, as couple therapists, make informed and responsible decisions about whether to work with couples where there are reports of violence? There are some clear risk factors that should be considered before deciding to go ahead with couple therapy. Factors that warn that couple therapy may be contraindicated include:

- The couple comes to therapy because they were ordered by the courts
- Severe violence with a goal of controlling the partner
- The partner is unwilling/unable to take responsibility for the violence
- An abusive, defensive partner who is hostile in discussions about abuse
- Reports that violence occurs beyond the home
- Untreated substance abuse in one or both partners
- Resources are unavailable for longer-term treatment
- The couple is unwilling or unable to commit to longer-term treatment
- One or both partners reports feeling afraid of retaliation in response to disclosures in therapy.

Factors that suggest that a couple may be appropriate for therapy include:

- Motivation and willingness by both partners to address the violence
- The couple is willing to commit to treatment

- The couple is willing and able to talk about violence openly and without hostility
- Acceptance and acknowledgement of responsibility for violence by any partner who is perpetrating violence
- A non-offending partner is able to talk about the impact and experience without fear of retaliation
- The level of violence is low and there is no history of hospitalization or severe injury
- Resources are available for longer-term treatment.

(Bograd & Mederos, 1999, Holtzworth-Munroe et al., 2002; Johnson, 2008; LaTaillade et al., 2006; Oka & Whiting, 2011)

These are lists of factors that may help a couple therapist decide whether to work with any given couple, but these issues are extremely complex, and each couple must be assessed as a unique unit. Given how many couples do not disclose a history of IPV in their relationship until well into the treatment process, it is important to be assertive, at the beginning, in asking about violence. It is very difficult to terminate an ongoing if a couple discloses IPV well into the process.

If we look to the example couples, you may remember that Chris and Camille reported episodes of IPV when they came in for their intake session. This couple described experiences of violence, both psychological and physical, which occurred after long, escalating conflicts. While this was a concern for me as I considered working with them, the couple had none of the factors that would cause me to lean towards turning them down for treatment. In fact, the couple demonstrated quite a few factors suggesting that working with them could be productive and not dangerous. They were motivated to address the violence, both partners were willing to commit to treatment, the couple could talk about the episodes of violence without becoming unduly dysregulated, both partners accepted responsibility for their own role in the escalation of conflict, the level of violence was very low, and because they were a part of a research study, the cost of the treatment was not a barrier to receiving the longer-term treatment they might require. Based on these factors, I decided to proceed with Chris and Camille, and there were no further episodes of IPV in the couple following the onset of treatment.

At this point, I will step away from these three couples and bring in another example, to discuss how I made a decision, over the course of three assessment sessions, not to provide couple therapy in the context of IPV.[1] In this case, I determined that couple therapy might escalate conflicts and prove destructive or even dangerous for the partners. Lilly and Lyle were a couple in their mid-thirties who had been together for 4 years, living together for 2. Both partners came from homes where physical violence by their fathers was commonplace. Lilly was close to her father who seemed to adore her and, at the same time, would terrorize her when he was drunk. Lilly defended her father to her mother while at the same time tiptoeing around him. Lyle was not close to either of his parents and approached dealing with the violence in his home by becoming quite reclusive, quiet, and withdrawn. The couple were referred by a respected colleague for trauma-focused couple treatment given their extensive childhood trauma histories.

Throughout an extensive assessment process dealing with attachment, emotion regulation, mentalizing, and trauma assessment, neither Lilly nor Lyle mentioned anything about violence in their relationship. Both appeared to be excited about the prospect of a treatment that might help them deal with how the past was repeating itself in their relationship. All couples are told that the first few sessions are to introduce the couple to the treatment and to help the therapist get to know the couple and their particular needs and suitability for the treatment. So when, in the first session after the assessment process, the first words uttered by Lilly referred to violence in their relationship, I immediately shifted into a stance of both engaging in the initial tasks of the treatment – introducing the couple to the model, and assessing their baseline levels of attachment security, emotion regulation, and mentalizing capacities, while also tracking their capacity to engage safely in couple-based treatment. These two segments are taken from the first and third sessions and outline the process of going back and forth in a stance of exploration and assessing suitability. It was clear by the middle of the third session that this was not a couple that would be safe or suitable for treatment, and I shifted into managing safety and dealing with the practical issues of trying to clearly indicate the need to make provisions for safety.

THERAPIST: So. Tell me about this fight. I want to know a little bit more about what life is like in your home, between the two of you.
LYLE: I guess it started in the morning.
LILLY: Mmh. [nods]
THERAPIST: When we say that a fight started in the morning that might suggest that it continued into the afternoon?
LILLY: No, it continued until late in the night.
THERAPIST: Okay, what can you tell me about it? Is this a fight you've had before?
LILLY: Ugh, every weekend!
THERAPIST: Is it THE fight?

Here I was looking to see if the couple can immediately identify a negative cycle or DTR, and also to assess the severity of their emotion regulation challenges.

LILLY: One of them. [rolls her eyes]
THERAPIST: One of them? Okay. So, tell me about this one. What got it started, what kept it going all day?
LYLE: We got up late I think and uh [silence] what's the first thing you told me? You wanted coffee and I reacted by being grumpy.
LILLY: The first thing you told me was "you snored, I couldn't sleep!"
LYLE: Yeah.
LILLY: Wow nice. Good morning to you too. [sighs] Yeah but then, as always, he grabbed his phone and just surfed, just lay around without a plan about what to do in his life and it just gets me furious.

I was starting to notice some mentalizing issues: rigidity, automatic assumptions along with a tendency to blame the other for couple-related distress.

THERAPIST: So, this is Sunday morning? [to Lyle] You woke up, you hadn't slept well.
LILLY: I didn't sleep well either!
THERAPIST: You didn't sleep well either. So, you were both a little cranky, not feeling well rested. . . . Where does coffee come in here?

While at this early stage in the treatment, I did not want to be distracted from the process by the content details of their interactions, I was very interested in how they perceived these details. Staying with content keeps things cognitive, rather than escalating emotions, and it told me a lot about how they view their couple distress, their emotion regulation capacities, and whether they mentalize well in their relationship.

LILLY: I asked him for a cup of coffee.
THERAPIST: You asked for him for coffee and his response was "you kept me awake with your snoring"?
LILLY: Something like that.
THERAPIST: Okay. So when that happened, what was going on inside of you? What were you feeling?
LILLY: I felt like he wasn't grateful because I let him sleep in and all I heard was "yeah you didn't let me sleep!"
THERAPIST: So it made you angry?
LILLY: Yeah!
THERAPIST: Okay, and Lyle, what was going on inside of you?
LYLE: The first thing I remember, I didn't even finish opening my eyes as you asked for coffee. I didn't even see you. I just heard "I want coffee".
THERAPIST: And you were still half asleep?
LYLE: Yeah.
THERAPIST: And you say it with a smile but what was going on inside of you? What were you feeling?
LYLE: I was just . . . thinking . . . what? Go make it yourself.
THERAPIST: So, you were irritated?
LYLE: Yeah. I got up at 7 to make the kitten's food. That's when you started snoring. [she rolls her eyes and shrugs shoulders] You slept through the whole thing.

By this point I had noticed high levels of hostility, belittling, and low levels of self-responsibility, all risk factors for escalating violence. They were able to articulate their thoughts in relation to my questions about their feelings, while remaining immersed in a state of anger, which I articulated in the form of a question. The feelings were so soaked into their experiences of the events that they were not even registering as responses. The couple spent the next few minutes recounting the "facts" about the onset and continuation of the conflict. Both partners were defensive, blaming the other and struggling to prevent the conflict from escalating within the session.

THERAPIST: So, it's Sunday morning. And you said a little while ago "he" didn't have a plan?
LILLY: Yeah.
THERAPIST: Do you usually have plans for Sunday morning?
LILLY: No, but I like my days planned. I like structure.
THERAPIST: And, what is it like for you when other people are not organized?
LILLY: Drives me nuts.
THERAPIST: What is it about it that drives you nuts?
LILLY: Chaos. I can't deal with chaos.
THERAPIST: Say more?
LILLY: It makes me panic.
THERAPIST: You start to get very panicky? What are you afraid might happen?
LILLY: The stuff that I have to do piles up and piles up and I just get unhappier and unhappier. I just have more and more to do and just can't handle it anymore.
THERAPIST: Is this something that has happened to you before? That you've gotten to a state where you couldn't cope?

LILLY: [nods] Yeah.
THERAPIST: And that's a big fear for you?
LILLY: [nods]
THERAPIST: So when Lyle was lying in bed and didn't have a plan, you started to panic that that might happen again, that you might get into that state again. [Lilly nods] What's that like for you? [to Lyle]
LYLE: The planning part?
THERAPIST: Yeah, the organizational. . . [cut off by Lyle]
LYLE: It's very un-flexible. And we end up not doing it anyway, most of the time.
LILLY: Mostly because we fight, we stay in bed too long and nobody gets up!

Both had been in bed and both were unmotivated, but Lilly felt that this was Lyle's fault while Lyle felt fed up and angry at Lilly for wanting him to do and be something that he could not. It was a struggle to refocus the couple from finger-pointing and trying to identify the cycle that was getting activated between them. At this very early point in the process I was straddling a stance of getting to know them to start therapy and assessing the risk that violence could escalate with treatment. Lilly was able to distil something of her own role in the cycle as she expressed her frustration about things not getting done.

THERAPIST: And what is underneath all of this? What is the master motivation?
LILLY: I hate standstill. With him I feel like I'm standing still, nothing is getting done.
THERAPIST: And on your own?
LILLY: I am super accomplished.
THERAPIST: You get lots and lots done?
LILLY: Tons.
THERAPIST: But together?
LILLY: [shakes head] Absolutely nothing.
THERAPIST: How do you understand that?
LILLY: No I mean, when I'm single, I am super accomplished.
THERAPIST: What do you think that means? How have you made sense of that in your mind?
LILLY: He drains my energy because he's completely unmotivated to do anything.
THERAPIST: Okay, so you feel drained?
LILLY: Yes.
THERAPIST: Because you feel like he doesn't have the same. . .
LILLY: Drive.
THERAPIST: Drive, to do. . . ?
LILLY: And I constantly push to get things done.

Lilly was cutting me off here, her speech was pressured, and she seemed determined to make sure that I knew that Lyle was the problem. While both of them had been lying in bed doing nothing, Lilly placed the blame on Lyle and said, "with him I feel like I'm standing still". This statement seemed to be connected more to trauma than to current context, pointing towards a DTR in action. I did not know enough yet, but I tucked this away for future consideration.

THERAPIST: Okay, so you push?
LILLY: And that drains my energy. I constantly have to be pushing for everything.

THERAPIST: So you feel like you're the ox pulling the cart?
LILLY: Yeah while I can't pull myself anymore. Just pulling him. Or the relationship.
THERAPIST: So you're depleted.
LILLY: [nods] Completely.
THERAPIST: For you, not only does not doing things make you panic and fear that you might end up in a place you've been before but also you feel like you're doing it for both of you?
LILLY: Yes.

I was tracking mentalizing in Lilly at this point and trying to ensure that as I reflected her emotional state, I was reflecting just that: her experience, not her "reality". From a mentalizing perspective, Lilly interpreted the external behaviours of Lyle according to a meaning that may or may not correspond with what these behaviours mean for Lyle. Because Lilly has so rigidly constructed this narrative meaning in her own mind, there was very little room for Lyle to engage in the conversation about the meaning of his own feelings and behaviours. I felt a strong need to bring the attention around to Lyle, so that he would have a moment to speak for himself.

THERAPIST: What about you Lyle? What is your feeling about getting stuff done?
LYLE: Well, it feels good, getting stuff done but, I don't know, it's not super . . . urgent, I would say. There's always. . . . Life has to be enjoyed. But it's . . . it's very draining also.
THERAPIST: You find it draining too?
LYLE: Yeah.
THERAPIST: Sounds like you find it draining in a different way. Can you say more about what it is that's draining?
LYLE: The "to-do list" has to be planned in the calendar with the day organized minute by minute. And if something goes wrong or the time goes wrong, and the plan is going wrong – bang, that's it. It's so . . . I mean the things that I get done most is when you're out of the house.
THERAPIST: So you get more things done on your own?
LYLE: [nods]
LILLY: But that's because I wrote down what needs to be done!
THERAPIST: So you're afraid that if it's not written down, nothing would be done?
LILLY: I know that for a fact!

Clearly Lyle was also feeling a lot of pressure, and there might even be aspects of his own trauma embedded in their cycle, in ways it was too early for me to fully understand. At this point, I was not following the model: I was not discussing the model, the couple guidelines or other first-session topics. I was too concerned about the potential of the treatment to lead to escalations in the IPV to dive right in. But while, at the beginning of the session, the couple had been very forthcoming about the IPV, they then avoided discussing the violence directly. I therefore became more direct, to get to the crux of the recent episode of violence with enough time left in the session to wind down and regulate any stray emotions.

THERAPIST: How did this fight escalate throughout the day?
LILLY: He got violent.
THERAPIST: In what way?

LILLY: Shoving me into walls or on the bed, restricting me from moving.
THERAPIST: How often does this happen?
LILLY: Right now, seven or eight times and it's getting more frequent.
THERAPIST: When was the most recent episode?
LILLY: Yesterday.
LYLE: You were throwing water bottles because I didn't listen to you.
LILLY: Yeah because I wanted to get your fucking attention because it's so hard to get your fucking attention!
LYLE: And you were happy as you destroyed things.
LILLY: That's ridiculous!
LYLE: You told me you were happy. Finally, something is destroyed. That's what you said.
THERAPIST: Okay, let's slow it down a bit. It sounds as though you both were getting more and more frustrated. Where did the water bottle come into the story?
LILLY: He didn't listen to me and I wanted to get his attention.
THERAPIST: Okay. . .
LILLY: So I threw a water bottle. I warned him before I did it that if he didn't start listening to me, I would throw it and he refused to listen.
THERAPIST: Okay so you threw it at him?
LILLY: [shakes head] No.
THERAPIST: Where did you throw it?
LILLY: Outside the room. It took three water bottles for him to actually do something!
THERAPIST: And what did he do?
LILLY: The first time he got up, got it, got angry. I tried to make him listen to me because he still didn't want to listen.
THERAPIST: How?
LILLY: By saying something.
THERAPIST: Do you remember what the words might have been?
LILLY: [shakes head]
THERAPIST: No? Okay. And so, what is happening for you? [to Lyle]
LYLE: You told me that I don't take care of you. And I asked you, "what do you need?" and then you said, "if you don't listen to me, I'll throw it" and I kept asking you what you needed. Then you threw the water bottle and said that you haven't had a drink for 2 days so I went and got the water bottle back and gave it back to you. Then you said that you're not drinking it because there was something wrong with it. So then I went to get the smaller one . . . and then you threw that one twice!
LILLY: Because you weren't listening to me. You just weren't paying attention. . .

In trying to bring the attention to details I was attempting to bring the conversation back to a more cognitive focus, to pull them back to their conscious autobiographical memory and away from the dysregulated sensory memory that may be tied to earlier traumas both in their relationship and in their lives in the past. In doing this, I hoped to get a sense of their capacities to mentalize and regulate their emotions when discussing difficult issues. They remained stuck in the space of defending and blaming, so much so that they were unable to track my questions. They seemed determined to answer me with their narrative of blame.

THERAPIST: Okay. Then what happened?
LYLE: I just grabbed her phone.

THERAPIST: You took her phone, and then?
LILLY: She fought back! My phone is my life.
THERAPIST: So, you grabbed her phone, you fought back how?
LILLY: He had it already in his hand. He looked like he would squeeze it to break it. And the next thing I thought he would do if I didn't stop him, was to throw it at the wall.
THERAPIST: Okay, so what did you do next?
LILLY: I grabbed it. I tried to get it out of his hand and then he shoved me.
LYLE: I don't know what happened after that.
LILLY: I don't know . . . At some point I got my phone and I tried to call the police. But he tried to rip it out of my hands again.
THERAPIST: Okay. Did you call the police?

The couple recounted an ongoing struggle for the phone, whether to call the police, and escalating name-calling and blame. This struggle included a very fast fuse of escalating emotion dysregulation leading to impulsive actions.

THERAPIST: So how did this episode end?
LILLY: I went and took a shower and packed my stuff.
THERAPIST: Where were you going to go?
LILLY: A shelter.
THERAPIST: Okay. So, at what point did it escalate again and you called the police?
LYLE: She went outside and drove the car up onto the front yard and practically turned it over.
THERAPIST: What happened?
LILLY: I was angry at him so I drove it on purpose onto the lawn.
THERAPIST: You drove the car on purpose onto the lawn? Were you okay? Was there damage to the car?
LILLY: He didn't even give a shit about it. I was okay. All he did was grab his phone, call the police, he didn't come a step further towards me. He stood there in the front of the house.
LYLE: You got out of the car and started walking right away.

It was clear to me, at this point, that things were not stable enough with this couple to start couple therapy. I was, however, committed to offering them a couple of sessions to help them make some decisions about how to ensure safety, whether to separate and, if so, to provide them with information about resources. The session ended with a discussion about immediate safety and immediate plans for where they would live and how they would communicate.

THERAPIST: So here is the thing. You know that this isn't acceptable. You both know that you shouldn't be throwing things, pushing each other, and all of that. That can't continue. It's not safe for either of you. Physically, emotionally . . . in all ways it's not safe. But it's also not a way to create an environment where we can work to help you heal your relationship. So can I ask you both to, as much as possible, to agree that if you start to feel this way again, to get up and walk away? That I know you feel desperate.
LILLY: Then I will never be at home anymore.
THERAPIST: Well then, we need to talk about that. Because if you're feeling that desperate, then. . .

LILLY: All the time, yeah.

THERAPIST: Then, it might be time to take a break. Because we have to avoid doing more harm to you both as people and to the relationship. Right? When you have been feeling so frustrated, you act in ways that hurt each other and it's really important that we find ways to avoid doing more harm than has already been done. And this is a really great example, in a sad way, of how trauma gets activated in a relationship. In a relationship where there isn't a history of trauma, one person might be feeling unheard and the other person might be feeling frustrated and pull away. When those emotions escalate, they might feel frustrated or angry but the escalating emotions don't feel so overwhelming, so unbearable, so unmanageable that they can't walk away or settle down or even maybe help each other. When you two get frustrated, at this point in the relationship, it feels completely unbearable and intolerable and that's a lot of old trauma piling onto new trauma that you haven't learned how to feel safe with each other, to feel heard by each other, and to be able to turn to each other when you're distressed in a way that helps you. In fact, when you turn to each other, it feels worse by the sound of it. You start to feel worse. So if we are going to be able to work together we have to make sure that you stop any kind of violence between you, and if that means you need to be separated physically for a little while, then that's what that means.

The session ended with a discussion of how to access shelter beds for Lilly and an agreement from Lyle that he would leave the house and go to visit his mother for a few days if things got out of hand again. Both partners expressed a desire to work on their relationship, but I was not certain that this would be wise. In terms of risk factors, neither member of this couple was able to acknowledge their own role in the escalating conflicts; both were engaged in blame and belittling and were extremely hostile towards one another. Both were highly defensive in these discussions, and both seemed quite unable to lift the veil of their rigid mentalizing to allow any other perspectives into their minds. However, if, as is suggested by my experience, conflict in a couple can be moderated by improving emotion regulation capacities and building skills in mentalizing that would allow each partner to more flexibly tolerate and integrate perspectives other than their own, the goal would be to ensure that violence does not continue or escalate while still providing treatment. However, in this case, I was quite doubtful, but agreed to see them for a follow-up session to continue to assess their situation.

In the second session, I was quite prepared to discuss with them the need to refer them to other programming, given their risk of continuing to escalate violence if they engaged in couple therapy. However, the couple came to the session looking happy and positive. They had gone on a holiday and had a lovely time with one another, had been able to avoid any kind of escalating conflict for 3 weeks, and were both feeling more positive about the possibility of taking action to improve their relationship. The couple were open, talkative, and optimistic about the possibility of making change in their relationship. I decided to continue my assessment for one further session and to track any patterns that might emerge over time such as escalating conflict leading to violence, followed by a honeymoon period, and then a repeat of escalating violence: a cycle of violence frequently articulated by IPV researchers. And so when, in the next session, Lilly arrived half an hour late and began the session with another revelation of an episode of violence between them, I felt fairly certain that working with this couple would not be wise, safe, or productive.

THERAPIST: What happened?

LILLY: He attacked me twice yesterday [Lyle shakes his head] and I wanted to pack my stuff and go. I called the police yesterday also and instead of coming here, I was going to pack. Unless he convinces me that staying is the right thing to do. He didn't want to. He didn't want to make any commitments so no I didn't want to come here today.

THERAPIST: So you didn't want to come today?

LILLY: Yes.

THERAPIST: I see. So what changed your mind? Why did you come?

LILLY: I had to ask him three times, and at some point he finally wrote something, and I had to ask him many more times until he finally said something that was okay with me.

THERAPIST: Which was?

LILLY: That he is willing to do everything it takes to repair this relationship.

THERAPIST: Okay.

LILLY: Because he's violent and I'm not accepting this anymore!

THERAPIST: Take me back because I'm just coming in now to a story that started some time ago. So, Lyle, when you got here you thought she was going to be here?

LYLE: I told her to be here because . . . this is the only place we can try to solve something whether it's splitting up or trying to work things out.

THERAPIST: So you felt like coming here might be a way to have a conversation that you've been having a hard time having?

LYLE: Yeah.

THERAPIST: Regardless of what the outcome might be?

LYLE: Yeah.

LILLY: He didn't say that at all. He just told me I should be here.

THERAPIST: Okay. So you changed your mind and decided to come because he said he was willing to do whatever it takes to fix this relationship.

LILLY: No, for him to get better.

THERAPIST: For him to get better?

LILLY: Yes. We only have a chance if he gets better. So if he is not willing to work on himself, then I don't want to be with him anymore. He has to be working with all his energy on it or I'm not willing to do this anymore.

THERAPIST: Okay. So when you say you are not willing to do it, does that mean you're done? You're finished with the relationship?

LILLY: I am currently packing at home.

THERAPIST: Okay. Where do you plan on going?

LILLY: Currently a shelter before I find a place to go.

At this point I felt quite certain that this couple was not going to be safe in couple therapy. In fact, both recent episodes of violence occurred on the day preceding their sessions. Additionally, the level of blame was very high, the level of self-responsibility was very low, and both partners were struggling with even basic mentalizing. While I am very much a proponent of working through trauma together, in this case I came to believe that both partners require more individual therapy prior to making any further attempt at couple work: they would simply be escalating an already escalated situation. The previous day, once again, police had been called after a similar daylong escalation of conflict, and neither partner was able to take any responsibility for their actions. Of course, when there is physical violence, especially by a male aggressor over a female partner, this must be called out as unacceptable and the aggressor must be able to see this as an unbalanced act against a smaller partner. However, in this situation both partners had been actively engaged in the escalation: Lilly's verbal assaults and insults were raw, hostile, and unrelenting. While nothing justifies physical violence, her behaviour must also be labeled as abusive. I spent the remainder of the session trying to deal with the practicalities of helping the couple communicate about where they would live until things are sorted out, how they would communicate with one another, and how to avoid further conflict.

LILLY: He has not respected my boundaries at all. I cannot trust anything he does. I tell him how I feel and he doesn't do anything. I am scared of him. He has no control over himself.

THERAPIST: So at this point you don't trust him. [Lilly shakes head] You want to separate. How are you feeling? Do you agree?

LYLE: I don't trust her.

THERAPIST: You don't trust her. So you both feel very attacked in different ways: [to Lilly] you feel physically attacked and frightened, and [to Lyle] you feel emotionally attacked. You both feel distrustful of each other and you both feel like unless something very significant changes, this is not going to work.

LILLY: Exactly.

THERAPIST: Now I agree that there's a lot of work that you both need to do in terms of your own processing of your lives, your histories, and so forth. But I also agree that if there's no trust and if there's a risk that as you try to work on these things, things become violent, that it isn't a good idea to do that work together because it can be dangerous. And both times that the police have been called, it has been the day before a session with me, which may be related to feelings about coming, feelings about how you feel in terms of trust and willingness to continue to work on things together.

We discussed housing, communication, finding a mediator, and how to help them sort out their financial entanglements and access legal assistance. The couple continued to go around and around with deep ambivalence about any concrete plans for even a temporary separation, while holding with absolute clarity that the relationship had to end.

THERAPIST: I'm going to reiterate how important it will be that you work hard to stop future violence – physical, emotional – and how important it will be for both of you to continue with your individual therapists. The things that have been said and done have been devastating for both of you and you need to find ways to take care of yourselves and to begin to heal.

LILLY: That was my last try. I knew I shouldn't have come.

THERAPIST: I think it was very important that you did come so that we could have the conversation about how to move forward clearly and safely.

The last few moments of the session were focused on providing Lilly with phone numbers for shelters and engaging the couple in a discussion about safe communication, publicly funded mediators, and resources for separation without high conflict. As I reviewed the session, I was very aware of the knot in my stomach, my own countertransference response to partners who don't take responsibility for themselves, my anger that gets aroused when couples are cruel to one another, and my frustration with myself for not being able to help this couple accomplish more than was possible in a shorter time than was realistic. Therapists need to be mindful of the impact of being in the direct line of fire of this kind of hostility, blame, and defensiveness. I tell my students to "never swim alone": you have to have colleagues to turn to, supervisors to consult with, and a life that is balanced enough and free enough from your own traumas to be able to be fully present to couples – in these cases, fully present enough to guide them to safety. In the cases of the couples with whom we decide to work, that means fully present enough to tolerate high levels of emotion dysregulation, low levels of mentalizing, and trauma oozing out all over the place, while moving slowly along the path to greater containment and empathy, and less conflict.

One of my fears in sending this couple back to their individual therapists was that their rigid beliefs and assumptions about their partners and their ongoing inability to accept responsibility for their own roles in the conflict would be solidified. Without partners in the room, individual therapists can only ever see part of the picture, and that part of the picture is seen through the eyes of patients who cannot yet perceive the ways in which their assumptions and interpretations are constrained by their rigid, non-mentalizing stances.

Note

1 Like the others, this is a fictional couple based on my work with many couples over the course of many years. It is a good representation of what I have seen while working with couples where the treatment would likely have been too unsafe for the couple to manage without falling into more escalating violence.

Chapter 5

Stage Two

Building capacity in the attachment relationship context

The goal of this stage of the DCTCT process is to help couples acquire the skills necessary to navigate the process-oriented approach of the third stage of DCTCT and, ultimately, to work through their couple-related difficulties and conflicts on their own in the future. For couples to tolerate, integrate, and benefit from the work in Stage Three, they will need to be able to mentalize effectively – to be curious about, tolerate, and engage with the perspectives and mental states of their partners and therapists; and to regulate their emotional states, ideally in relation to their partners. Without these capacities, the work of Stage Three may be retraumatizing and ineffective.

Mentalizing

It is difficult to gauge how many sessions will be required to build the capacity for mentalization; it will depend heavily on the level of skill already present in the individuals within the couple and how they mentalize together. Do not move on to the next stage until the couple has demonstrated that skills are well-established, as these skills are very vulnerable to collapse under the stress of attachment conflicts that may arise in Stage Three. While the DCTCT model is demarcated into stages, as with other models that incorporate stages and steps these are artificial divisions that may not be reflected in practice. The sole focus on mentalizing in this section is artificial, but I make that attempt to clarify how to work with this specific self-capacity. At the same time, it is impossible to isolate mentalizing from the other concepts, and the work to build capacities in both mentalizing and emotion regulation begins in the first assessment session and continues throughout the treatment. This section will describe specific strategies to use in helping couples develop and strengthen mentalizing capacities so that they are able to continue on to Stage Three, where these skills will be vital to the success of the processing stage of the treatment.

One of the first and most important strategies at this point in the therapy is for you, as therapist, to actively mentalize for each partner: to reflect their feelings, help them make sense of their experience, and help them feel seen and understood. Mentalizing for and with the couple provides a model and a proxy for missed developmental experiences, something that might feel very foreign and new for them. As you work with them at this stage, use your strong clinical skills to help them take turns talking and slow things down so that thoughts, feelings, and behaviours are fully explored and attended to with growing curiosity, interest, complexity, and flexibility. It is important to keep checking with each partner to ensure that you have fully engaged with their perspective, and with the non-speaking partner to ensure that they are hearing, understanding, and tolerating their partner's expressions as well as having the space to try to articulate their own. As you do this, check in and repair misinterpretations also. Through your openness, curiosity, and willingness to correct faulty assumptions and interpretations, you are also demonstrating what a good mentalizer might do in a relational context. You might ask questions like: "What did that feel like?" "How do you think he/she felt/thought/meant when that happened?" "How do you understand what has happened?" "What might have happened for you to feel differently about this?" "What other possibilities might there be to understand that?"

Slow down and even stop the process whenever automatic assumptions are made, explore the origins of these assumptions, work on building shared understanding through growing dialogue between partners, and help the couple open up to the experience of being curious about one another rather than staying stuck in their own rigid, untested assumptions. Whenever one partner finds it difficult to tolerate or acknowledge the other's perspective, take the opportunity to explore what makes this difficult and how they might learn to tolerate and even welcome the situation. The struggles survivor couples experience make sense, given that they may have spent their lives avoiding engaging with the minds of others for their own protection: who wants to imagine what their abuser might be thinking or feeling when they are hurting you? Expanding, opening, and bridging a rigidly protected and certain internal world that was built up around the necessity of blocking out other minds, and opening up to new perspectives and views, can be extremely painful and challenging and may even feel dangerous. Be gentle, compassionate, and persistent. One of the biggest challenges in this process is how this unfolding expansion can trigger difficulties with emotion regulation as you and the couple start to work around old ruts in mentalizing that have become so automatic they are not even noticed. Persistence, patience, and compassion are required to continue to push the boundaries of the isolated minds of traumatized partners without sending them into a dysregulated spiral – go very *slowly*!

As this process moves along, the couple learns how to mentalize their relationship, taking time in each session to piece apart what is happening right here, right now in the session. Include yourself in this dialogue where opportunities arise to further expand the mentalizing narrative and to include relational experiences, exploring the mental states of other important attachment figures.

Another strategy to help the couple build their capacity for mentalizing is to contextualize experience in ways that disrupt rigid assumptions and interpretations. Help the couple put their stories into context – past, present, future – to help them expand their relational narrative beyond rigid definitions they have created for themselves which have limited mentalizing within artificial boundaries erected in their lives lived through trauma.

Take time to explore triggers to emotion dysregulation and collapses in mentalizing, including their causes and impacts, by asking questions that prompt mentalizing about those experiences when they occur. These questions push the partner to expand their mentalizing capacities by being cued to explore beyond the automatic as it is happening. These kinds of questions ask the partner to assume the other's perspective, to explore alternative interpretations, and to consider their own emotional responses as having meaning. Questions might include:

"What happened before you felt so ashamed?"
"When you said that, how did she respond?"
"How did you imagine he felt?"

At every opportunity, help the couple remember the importance of integrating information from all aspects of themselves – thoughts, feelings, and behaviours – remembering that feelings are not enemies to be avoided, but rather they provide important information about ourselves and others. Explore the different ways others might feel in response to the same situation. This is an important opportunity to begin to explore situations that have happened and are happening in the couple's life together, to help them see these in a different way, to heal them, and to expand their ways of mentalizing as individuals and as a couple. Begin with small wounds or stories and work your way up to the more difficult ones.

As with any developmental capacity being encouraged, make sure to validate moments of strong mentalizing when they appear unbidden. Highlight moments of curiosity, openness, flexibility, and self-awareness, as well as acknowledgements of responsibility and demonstrations of the capacity to hold more than one's own mind in mind. You may also notice, where appropriate, moments when it seems as though feelings may be more complex than what has been perceived, when perspectives remain hidden, or when mentalizing begins to fail.

Some questions you might use to help encourage partners to mentalize about one another include:

"How do you think your partner would feel about the situation?"
"What do you imagine was your part in that argument?"
"How do you imagine your partner is feeling right now?"
"When you look back over the past week, what do you think your partner would say has gone well?"
"How do you imagine your partner would know that you were feeling upset?"
"If this happened again, could you imagine trying something different?"
"What might that be?"

You might also try using questions to begin to open up a dialogue about the impact of the trauma on their relationship – when the couple is ready to tolerate this.

"How do you understand your partner's response to this event given what you know about the traumas they have experienced?"
"When you think about your own history with your family, how does that help you make sense of what is happening right now between you?"
"What do you imagine the impact of your traumas might be on how you are feeling about her anxiety in relation to you?"

By way of providing some more concrete examples of this process, I would like to follow Chris and Camille over the course of the treatment and look at how their mentalizing capacities expanded, became more flexible, and strengthened. At the beginning of couple therapy, Chris and Camille struggled with even the most basic of conversations in navigating their couple world. For instance, throughout the history of their relationship, Camille interpreted all of Chris's attachment anxiety and preoccupation as intentional intrusions that failed to respond to her needs in relation to her traumatic triggers. She built up a narrative based on how his behaviours would make sense if she were performing them, about what his behaviours meant – something like, if I did X, then that would mean Y. She focused solely on the external aspects of his behaviour rather than the mental states that might motivate his behaviour, and she has made rigidly held automatic assumptions about the meaning of his behaviours based on her own mental states, or what they would mean if she were performing them. In early phases of the therapy, Camille found it almost impossible to even try to imagine alternative explanations or to tolerate listening to Chris discuss his own mental states that arise as he gets pulled in to pursuing her. One of the key strategies at the early stages of therapy, therefore, was to help both Chris and Camille articulate their own mental states in relation to one another, building a new narrative that included both of their minds and histories of trauma into their relational dance to help them tolerate the diversity of their inner worlds of experience. This was a huge challenge and one that took many months to begin to crack open. Over time, the couple was able to develop some capacity to put their emotional responses into their relational context – past, present, future – and to hold on to their understanding of the other in ways that allowed them to begin to expand their capacity for mentalized affectivity, recognizing how emotions and cognitions are embodied and integrated.

Camille's mentalizing strategies were predominantly focused on self-preservation, managing any interpretation of the mental states of others by using her own mind as the only safe reference place. Her mentalizing was characterized by rigidity, automatic assumptions about the meaning of the behaviour of others, and a tendency towards psychic equivalence – interpreting the meaning of the actions of another based solely on external features. Camille could become quite hostile with Chris over the lack of a shared understanding of her own perspective which, in her mental world, was the only "right" one. The perfect key to Camille's mentalizing lock was Chris's inability to tolerate more than one perspective. In his mental world, only one person can be "right", which means that the other person is "wrong". While Chris frequently agreed with Camille that her perspective was the "right" perspective, he struggled mightily with any kind of dialogue where his needs, ideas, beliefs, or mental states were in opposition to Camille's. He would suppress his frustration about feeling perpetually "wrong" in the hopes that he could please Camille. As a result, the couple struggled to establish any kind of dialogue. For instance, for Chris and Camille, rigid, automatic assumptions served a purpose of regulating their individual emotions, as they focused exclusively on their own mental states as a way to maintain self-cohesion and self-regulation. Early in therapy, a source of pain and conflict in the couple stemmed from their shared feelings of being misunderstood and not accepted. Both were experiencing painful states of mental isolation, filled with hope and longing that the other would understand them and meet their needs; without ever sharing their desire, both were left hanging, lost, and despondent.

In early sessions, the possibility of seeing the other's perspectives, let alone accepting and understanding them, was essentially out of the question. In this session, Camille talked about how Chris does not care about her because he does not notice things that are missing in the fridge and automatically replace them. She equates a behaviour – or in this case, a non-behaviour – as having meaning, a kind of psychic equivalence, and she makes an automatic assumption that she holds rigidly. She is making meaning about his behaviours and feelings about her based on what these behaviours would mean if she were doing them or not doing them, in this case; all the while, all of this interpretive energy is going into an action Chris has no idea he is even not doing. It is impossible for her to imagine that he might not notice something that he does not, himself, consume.

CAMILLE: I run out of milk and suddenly, oops, I can't eat breakfast anymore. He doesn't even notice.

THERAPIST: Do you drink milk?

CHRIS: No.

THERAPIST: Given that Chris doesn't consume milk, why would you imagine he would notice its absence?

CAMILLE: Because he opens the fridge all the time.

THERAPIST: Okay, he opens the fridge but what does it mean, in your mind, that he doesn't notice that something you consume and he doesn't isn't there?

CAMILLE: I notice things if they are missing.

THERAPIST: Right, *you* notice everything.

CAMILLE: I expect him to notice.

THERAPIST: You expect him to notice.

CAMILLE: He just looks through his tunnel, tunnel vision and I don't exist or matter. [makes a tunnel with her hands]

THERAPIST: How do you understand your not replacing the milk?

CHRIS: I had no idea it was even a thing that needed replacing.

In attempting to explore their experiences of mental isolation and their feelings of hurt and longing, I am trying to highlight the irony of deeply longing to be understood, while at the same time expecting the other to read your mind so that it is essentially impossible for your partner to ever know what you really need and respond to it.

THERAPIST: Okay, so, let's try to make sense of this pattern that's happening between you. There is this thing happening that's really got both of you up against a separate wall . . . you have this clear sense of how things should be and you [to Camille] feel like if he really cared about you, he would do things the way you need them because that would keep you from feeling so panicky and upset. And Chris, you feel pushed up against a wall in a different way. You feel as though if she cared about you she would be more affectionate, more loving towards you, that would help you feel safe in the relationship. And so, you both have really strong needs and you both believe that if the other really loved you they would just know what to do and they would willingly do it. Does that fit with what it feels like?

CAMILLE: Well, he should know what I need.

THERAPIST: He should know what you need without you having to tell him, if he really loved you, you wouldn't have to tell him.

CHRIS: I do want to but it doesn't make sense to me, I just can't get it.

As we moved along, we worked towards trying to open up both Chris and Camille to the existence of each other's minds, to the idea that different perspectives might not mean that someone is a threat or danger, to begin to imagine what the other might be thinking and feeling. Learning how to infer the mental states of others was a real challenge, because neither Chris nor Camille was able to think about mental states as flexible, subjective, and changeable. Camille's anger that Chris did not share her perspective, the "right" perspective, continued as Chris struggled to tolerate both his own and Camille's mental states.

THERAPIST: Okay, this looks like a good example of the idea of mentalizing that we've been talking about, so let's explore it a bit more deeply. I have some of the details, some of the facts. So there was a misinterpretation of the word "ready", that the two of you have a different idea about what that word means, and that caused you to feel out of sync with each other. What does that do to you emotionally? What happens inside of you?

CAMILLE: Well, I just feel like – ready means ready. Ready does not mean that I need 5 more minutes, or 10 more minutes, or 20 more minutes. I'm not even the type of girl that says I need 5 minutes to put on makeup. It just pisses me off, he should know! And the fact that I continuously have to remind him of things that are my way of looking at the world pisses me off, because he's supposed to get it. We've already had this argument, this is the way that I see things and no it's not the way you see things, but, can you just take into consideration when you talk to me and when you deal with me on a day-to-day basis, that I am not somebody that has your perspective of the world, and so therefore you should take that into consideration?

THERAPIST: So it makes you angry that Chris doesn't hold your point of view in mind and that he should know what you mean when you say the word "ready"?

CAMILLE: Yes.

THERAPIST: It feels like he's not holding you in mind, keeping you in mind, or your perspective in mind, when he uses language in a way that's different from how you use that language. It makes you feel angry?

Camille was angry both that Chris does not share her perspective and that he does not acquiesce to her perspective, which he would if he cared for her. Although she was beginning to use the language of mentalizing as she began to talk about divergent perspectives, this demonstrated an increased awareness along with an ongoing struggle to tolerate and navigate divergent perspectives. In a way, she was talking about mentalizing while not mentalizing. As we continued, I tried to help the couple explore their differences in terms of their contexts – past, present, and future.

THERAPIST: So for you [to Camille] "ready" means, ready, set, go?

CHRIS: To me, "ready" means like, we're getting ready now to go.

THERAPIST: Getting ready to go. So there's a language difference, a meaning difference, an interpretation difference, but there's also something about what the difference means.

CHRIS: But she's right too, though, because I should have known, I just – I need time. I need 5 minutes to collect myself so I can face people in the morning.

THERAPIST: So there's a difference of interpretation or language. But it takes on meaning. For you [to Camille] it means – correct me if I get this wrong – something like, if he knew me, if he cared about me, if I mattered to him, he'd understand that this is important to me. This is important, because it's something that keeps me calm.

CAMILLE: Yes, that's it!

THERAPIST: And it reminds me of what you have told me about your parents, how you wished that they would have understood what you needed after your trauma, that they would have known and they would have done what you needed. Your feeling that they should have known and they should have responded.

CAMILLE: Well, yes, but, it's not the same, Chris really should know, it's not like we haven't talked about it.

THERAPIST: Okay, so, let's just check over here with Chris. When Camille says, if you really got me, you wouldn't do these things, it sounds like there's a part of you [to Chris] that feels the same way, that if she really got me, if she understood me, she wouldn't expect this of me, or she would give me more space, she would understand what I need and she would accept that.

CHRIS: Yes, she would give me more leeway, because, I just – I don't operate like, oh, I just can't do it her way . . . I need more time.

THERAPIST: That also reminds me of what you have told me about your experiences growing up, that you couldn't express your needs because you never knew what kind of response you would get, that you would shut down your needs to protect yourself from disappointment or someone's anger. When you get shut down and feel overwhelmed by Camille, does that connect with those experiences for you?

CHRIS: I guess so, it's just how I am.

THERAPIST: So, okay, you are having this conflict . . . how do you collaborate around getting a shared understanding of each other's perspective? What does that look like?

CAMILLE: It often doesn't . . . I dunno . . . it's often very messy. I feel like I'm trying to explain my perspective, Chris jumps in trying to explain his perspective, there's a struggle about whose perspective should be said first, then eventually both of our perspectives are said but I don't feel like I'm being listened to, and then he doesn't feel like he's being listened to.

THERAPIST: It does sound messy.

THERAPIST: Chris, how would you add to Camille's description or change it?

CHRIS: No, that sounds right. It usually comes down to whose perspective is *right*, you know? Like, sometimes I just refuse to admit that she's right, and then other times she refuses to admit that I'm right.

THERAPIST: Why would there be a "right", given that perspectives are wholly subjective?

CHRIS: Well, I dunno. I guess maybe that's my problem, then. I need to know who's right.

THERAPIST: What does that mean?

CHRIS: If I don't believe that it's true or right, if I don't believe in the logic behind whatever is being said, then I won't accept it. Just period. Like, I can't – I won't – I'm not allow – like, I can't – I don't allow myself to do that, because it confuses me.

As we moved further into the expansion and building up of mentalizing capacities, Chris and Camille became more comfortable with the language of mentalizing, with the idea of mental states as separate, shareable, and flexible. However, both continued to tend towards rigid and automatic assumptions. Camille experienced ongoing automatic assumptions that were rigidly fixed and developed emotional dysregulation in relation to Chris when he did not know what she needed or act accordingly. Chris, meanwhile, became anxious in relation to Camille: his capacity for mentalization shut down and eventually he fell away into dissociative states when he felt overwhelmed with Camille's disappointment and disapproval of what he perceived to be his failure and the inevitable loss of connection with Camille.

THERAPIST: We are always making those choices. On the one hand, you might *want* to do one thing but you might *need* to do another thing. Every choice involves choosing one thing and not getting something else.

CHRIS: Yeah, my friends were at the bar and I . . . sometimes it's hard to say no to my friends, to hanging out with them.

THERAPIST: But, you did make a choice to be with Camille when she needed you. You made the choice to not go with your friends to be with Camille when she hurt her back, to be with her and take care of her physical needs, but it sounds like you didn't quite get there psychologically, you weren't entirely present anywhere, but you went to be with her.

CHRIS: Yeah, I guess so.

THERAPIST: Change takes a long time. It sounds like this was a very positive change and that you really held Camille in mind and tried to make a decision about something in your life, something where she really *needed and wanted* care from you and you were able to hear her, understand her need, and respond. That's positive change! But you weren't quite at the place where you could do that and also be really emotionally present.

CHRIS: Yeah, I *did* want to be there, but I also *didn't* want to be there. Does that make sense?

THERAPIST: Right! That's the kind of self-reflection that builds a healthy relationship. You were able to hold those two desires in mind, and hold Camille in mind, and make a decision to care for your partner. Sometimes you don't do something you want to do but you *can* tolerate the conflict inside of yourself and not dissociate or shut down. And sometimes we stay home and do the dishes instead of going to a party.

Chris was able to tolerate having more than one thought and feeling at the same time without dissociating, although he struggled to be emotionally present with Camille. He was able to hold his two mental states in mind as well as Camille's mental state, and tolerate the complexity of these divergent states, hold the options in mind, and then make a decision based on doing something to care for his partner rather than "play" with his friends. This is a sign of increased mental flexibility and tolerance of mental complexity. He continued to grow in his capacity to infer the mental states of his partner and take action based on her needs while simultaneously holding his own thoughts and feelings in mind. This was a significant shift from the beginning of the process, when even acknowledging more than one possible perspective would send him into a dissociative state.

As things moved along, I became more able to challenge their major dyadic mentalizing challenge, a challenge common to trauma survivors. "If my partner knows that X triggers me, they wouldn't do it". Or, "my partner should know that X triggers me", even if the partner has no way, beyond the unspoken desire of the partner, to know about X. Perhaps this is the remnant of a child's rigid adherence to the internal fantasy of a just world that cannot be disrupted by exposure to the real world of relationships where people know that you need to be safe and abuse you anyway.

THERAPIST: What do you think it means?

CAMILLE: It means that he didn't listen to me. I don't feel like my opinion matters to him and that sucks.

THERAPIST: So if he doesn't . . . it's water, you can clean it up, but for you it means something, it means that he hasn't listened, that there's something important to you now, and not making a mess is important to you because it triggers anxiety about your childhood and being in trouble.

CAMILLE: Yeah.

THERAPIST: And if it was important to him too he would listen?

CAMILLE: Yeah.

THERAPIST: That it seems as though he doesn't, means to you that your opinion, your feelings, don't matter.

CAMILLE: Yeah.

THERAPIST: Can you imagine that there might be another way of interpreting that? Are there any other possible interpretations than, if he knew it was important to you he wouldn't do it?

CAMILLE: Maybe but it's just – I just don't buy it because, if he listened he would stop doing it.

THERAPIST: That's how it feels, right: it feels as though if you mattered to him he would listen. If your words mattered, he would change his behaviour.

CAMILLE: Yes!

THERAPIST: Has it always been that way?

CAMILLE: It's just automatic. It's like a reaction that I'm trying to prevent something from happening.

THERAPIST: And, if Chris didn't do that thing. . .

CAMILLE: Yeah.

THERAPIST: Then you wouldn't have those feelings.

CAMILLE: Yeah and that sucks.

THERAPIST: Yeah and it could be something else that was a trigger that you might feel the same way about but, in this case, it brings up that feeling, that feeling of being unloved and unimportant.

CAMILLE: Yeah.

Slowly, Camille was stretching her mind to consider the possibility that her traumatic history played a role in her automatic assumptions and feelings in response to Chris's "failure" to respond to her in the way she felt would demonstrate his love. She was tolerating the possibility that his behaviour might not mean that he does not love her, that there might be alternative interpretations. At this point in the therapy, I had a relationship with Chris and Camille, and we had spent a lot of time exploring their triggers and automatic assumptions, so I felt I had some space to push the envelope a bit. Earlier, I would not have challenged Camille to consider alternative interpretations; she would have become angry and belligerent and Chris would have become anxious and dissociative. As they began to stretch their mentalizing capacities and there was now trust between us, it was time to start challenging, stretching, and going deeper into the complexity of possibilities present in strong mentalizing, without triggering emotion dysregulation and dissociation.

As we continued, Chris and Camille began to use mentalizing language but still struggled with rigidity and difficulties with being flexible or maintaining curiosity about each other's mental states. Fear and the resulting rigidity really interfere with emotion regulation: how can you keep your emotions regulated if you are always terrified of making a wrong step? In the next example, we were discussing Camille's changeable responses to sexual contact: sometimes she was triggered and sometimes she was not, but Chris found it close to impossible to be flexible and responsive to her cues. This tied in to both of their trauma histories and would also be a good example of a Dyadic Traumatic Reenactment (DTR) in action – Camille felt she needed someone to respond to her unspoken pain, while Chris needed to be living in an environment where he was not perpetually terrified of making a wrong step and triggering an explosion. The couple was struggling mightily to find a way to even begin these conversations.

THERAPIST: Both of you feel like you're trying really hard and still not getting it. And it all feels connected to your trauma histories. There's that piece of – for you [to Chris], the unpredictability – "I'm going to try really hard, but I'm not going to get it right and something's going to blow up in my face" – and for you [to Camille], this feeling that things are dangerous – mess is dangerous, too much touch or too much closeness can feel overwhelming. There's a way in which the just right, the Goldilocks and the Three Bears kind of just right, you never quite get there. There's always too much or not enough, and you never quite get there. Chris, you're suggesting that you wish you could get it, but you don't know how, and you wish Camille could tolerate your efforts to get as close as you can to helping her feel safe.

CHRIS: It's hard to find the just right. It's hard – it's really hard for me to find the just right for her because it changes, too. It's not like it's always the same.

THERAPIST: Well, part of that is because, in a way, you're approaching this with the logic of a child looking for rules, they look for rules to make the world safe for them. So if the rule is, don't talk to daddy before 10:00 in the morning because he'll be hung over and scream at me, a child doesn't have the nuance to say, if I talk to daddy before 10:00 a.m. am on a morning after he's been drinking, he might cuff me in the ear but if I speak to him at 10:00 a.m. on a morning when he hasn't been drinking, it'll probably be okay – kids just don't have that nuance, that complexity. Kids just get – I shouldn't talk to daddy, that's the rule. So you're trying to make a rule, in a situation where what's required is to pick up on the cues and be responsive, the rules protected you from getting into trouble. And you're [to Camille] looking for a kind of responsiveness, because you don't always feel the same way. Sometimes you're quite triggered by sexual abuse memories, sometimes you're not. So you need Chris to be flexible.

CHRIS: [cuts off] And that frustrates the hell out of me because, like you said, I need that specific rule, otherwise, it's – I feel like – today you want purple, next day you want rainbow. Like, can you pick a colour, so I can bring it to you? [laughs]

THERAPIST: You want to get it right! There isn't, between you, a flexible navigation of how you negotiate these things. You haven't figured out how to stop guessing, expecting, hurting, and just find a way to talk openly about your needs.

CHRIS: I want to give her what she needs but I bring her the wrong damn thing.

THERAPIST: It's hard for you to imagine that Camille's ways of showing her feelings, is something that you can learn to read, and learn to respond to.

CHRIS: I, well, I don't think it's something that I can't do, I just think it's something that I'm not – I'm really not used to, yet. I just need to figure it out, I'm sure I can do it.

THERAPIST: And I just want to be really careful that we're not searching for a new set of rules. That what we're really searching for is a way of communicating and sharing, that you come to learn about each other, how to talk about your needs and feelings, and be able to respond even when something is different from time to time.

CHRIS: Yeah, that is going to be tough for me, because, like, I just do – develop rules for everything.

Chris became somewhat disorganized and dysregulated as he discussed what happens to him when he tries to allow even the possibility that two people might have different perspectives but that these different perspectives can both be "right". For Chris, it seems that the purpose of mental rigidity is to maintain a kind of self-cohesion. If one or the other isn't "right", the rules of my internal world will collapse, and where will that leave me?

Nearing the end of this phase of the treatment, mentalizing became stronger as Chris and Camille were more able to share their minds with one another, in spite of not always being able to explore one another in curiosity. However, their budding capacities for mentalizing were still vulnerable to getting lost in trauma triggers.

THERAPIST: So in that moment, it is so real there could be no other explanation.

CAMILLE: Yeah.

THERAPIST: That is what it is.

CAMILLE: Outside, I can recognize that it's not, but at that moment, it's just unstoppable – it's just basically being hit by a whole ton of rain, and the other person saying, I don't feel any rain.

THERAPIST: So, in that moment, the feeling and the interpretation that makes meaning of it for you is very, very real.

CAMILLE: Yes.

THERAPIST: And it sounds as though it feels inescapable. However, you also seem to be becoming more aware of the difference between how it feels and that there could be more to it.

CAMILLE: Yes.

THERAPIST: And you just need help, or you need it to stop.

CAMILLE: Yes.

THERAPIST: Okay. So this time, when it happened, all of those things happened?

CAMILLE: Yes.

THERAPIST: And then what was different, that you didn't end up in a fight?

CAMILLE: I just felt like Chris was helping me to make it stop rather than saying that it's not raining.

THERAPIST: That's a big difference.

CAMILLE: Yeah, for me – if somebody says it's not raining, it makes me feel even more wet, and more drenched, and even more incomprehensible, it just makes it feel even more real. Like, even though I understand that people – maybe you're underneath like a roof, or something, and you're watching me in this rain, but, like, it doesn't help for somebody to deny that it's raining.

THERAPIST: Okay. So he said, okay, I can see the rain, I'm going to help keep you dry.

CAMILLE: Yeah.

THERAPIST: Well, that's a huge difference.

CAMILLE: Yeah, and for me, that helped me calm down.

THERAPIST: Right. He helped you calm down; he didn't say you shouldn't be upset.

CAMILLE: Exactly. As soon as I feel like somebody says I shouldn't be upset, it just gets worse.

THERAPIST: But it also sounds as though there's a difference in you, in that you let him soothe you, and you didn't blame him. And [to Chris] you didn't have to get into your defensive mode. You were able to get into protector mode.

CHRIS: Well, it was easy this time, because I recognized why – the reason why she was upset.

THERAPIST: Right.

CHRIS: I knew it was no longer tied to the actual action itself, because before, I always thought it was like, really? You're freaking out this much about that? Like, really? That's not even a big deal. And now I know, it's not that, she's just feeling threatened about other things that are bigger than just the thing that is happening, so I could react to that instead.

THERAPIST: So, you understand the trigger, and what it's connected to, historically, so you could understand the gravity of it. It didn't seem so stupid.

CHRIS: Yeah, because to me before, it was, ridiculous, like, who cares? I was inconsiderate, because I thought that, she would think that too.

As these capacities continued to grow, I saw the couple starting to use metaphor, a sign of expansive mental flexibility and comfort with the awareness that the partner experiences the same experience differently, rather than a threat.

THERAPIST: There was a problem, you talked about it, you dealt with it collaboratively, you've come up with a solution, you're going to give it a try. That's amazing, you are learning to understand each other a little better, and starting to be able to see each other's perspective a little more, so that when there's conflict or distress, when things are hard, it's easier for you to turn to each other and to trust that you will be there for each other.

CHRIS: I think that's happening, there are some things that I get, now. I still don't feel like I've got everything.

THERAPIST: Can you be more specific?

CHRIS: I generally know what physically upsets her now. And, like, I guess just things I do that antagonize her, or stress her out, or put her in anxious mode. I understand those things, but there are still times where I have a very specific way that I like to do things and I don't understand when she doesn't get that the way that I did it was meant to be good, and it wasn't meant to be a slight.

THERAPIST: Okay. And when those things happen, are you more able to try to understand her perspective, than you might have been before?

CHRIS: Definitely.

THERAPIST: So, it's getting better; you're finding yourself more able to understand her, more able to get her perspective about certain situations, but sometimes you fall into the trap of coming up with a solution that might be the best one for you, that might not be the best one for her, and it takes you a while to catch up to it.

CHRIS: Or, I just do it, and she gets mad at me because I didn't include her in the decision-making process.

THERAPIST: Right. And it takes you a while to kind of find her mind. To find what would work for her, and to start to collaborate around a solution.

CHRIS: Well, just collaborating in general, I don't do very well.

CAMILLE: Like, I get why – for example, if we disagree on something, I get why my perspective is different than his. But I don't get how to explain my perspective in a way that he'll understand it.

THERAPIST: Okay. And what do you think gets in the way?

CAMILLE: It's like I don't know what – it's like I have a lock inside of me, and I've got no clue which key I'm supposed to use

THERAPIST: Right; and you might have a keychain full of keys, but you don't know which one to use.

CAMILLE: Exactly. And there's just – there's only so many keys and then I start getting upset, and I start finding it really difficult, and I don't know what I'm supposed to do, because I don't know how to get – it's like I don't know how to get through to him, sometimes.

At this point in the therapy Chris and Camille were working hard to understand one another. They continued to struggle with falling into mentalizing holes that sucked them back into a place of losing sight of one another and into an isolated, traumatized state.

However, this happened less and less and as the couple moved along through the remainder of the therapeutic process, Chris and Camille grew stronger and more flexible, resilient, curious, and open in their mentalizing processes. By the end of treatment, Chris and Camille had developed a shared narrative about their couple difficulties, the role of history in these challenges, and new skills and strategies to deal with conflicts that arose old non-mentalizing instincts.

Emotion regulation

Building emotion regulation skills is facilitated both through exercises and activities to help the couple work together to build these vital skills, as well as through the therapeutic process. It is difficult to gauge how many sessions will be required for this stage of the treatment: it will be heavily dependent on the level of capacity present in the couple and the individuals within the couple. For many couples, working within the sessions on the issues with which they present, and helping them to explore, tolerate, manage, and express their emotional responses and experiences, will be sufficient to build up emotion regulation capacities.

Incorporating emotion regulation techniques into sessions, such as slowing down the process and helping couples breathe together or coach each other in regulating their distress, will help the couple prepare for the emotionally challenging work of Stage Three. For couples who have some capacity to regulate their emotions, you may not engage in all of the structured exercises. For example, Anush and Amira used avoidance as their primary emotion regulation strategy and were both capable of some strong mentalizing already at the beginning of therapy. Based on this, I did not spend many sessions on exercises but rather focused on identifying and reducing avoidance in sessions and suggesting strategies for the time between sessions that would increase engagement. Through this approach, I was trying to increase opportunities to practice feeling feelings in the couple without resorting to avoidance. Each of the exercises will need to be practiced and applied many times by each couple, both in sessions and at home. Couples like Gary and Geoffrey require slow and intentional practice and review of the exercises during the sessions, along with clear and specific homework for between sessions and reminders to return to their practiced emotion regulation strategies later in therapy when the emotional going gets tough. Do not move on to Stage Three until you feel that these skills are fairly well-established, as these are self-capacities that are vulnerable to collapse under the stress of the exploration inherent in therapy, especially couple therapy where attachment conflicts may trigger deep and painful traumatic emotional states. For couples dealing with impacts of trauma, talking about their sexual relationship or their attachment vulnerabilities, and sharing undisclosed trauma stories with their partners, will call upon both mentalizing and emotion regulation skills, which must be strong and resilient to withstand the challenge. Without strong emotion regulation capacities in Stage Three, there is a possibility of retraumatization and even of survivors feeling betrayed and hurt in the couple and therapeutic relationships. Couples are taking huge risks to enter these murky waters; they are counting on practitioners to keep them safe.

Some couples report that they feel that I am holding them back, in insisting on these exercises while life's challenges are raining down upon them. While this is true in a sense, it is also true that couples who are really struggling with emotion regulation will benefit from these exercises in all aspects of their daily lives. Remind them that while these exercises may not be directly about trauma and the conflicts they are experiencing with their partners, they are about how they deal with their trauma. They can bring these daily life stressors to bear on the exercises as they work on them at home with their partner helping the couple grow together. For couples who feel impatient and in a hurry to get to the more process-focused trauma work, remind them of the importance of safety and containment for the therapeutic process to work; going into the processing work too quickly may be harmful for the couple and will limit the effectiveness of the therapy. If the couple is not regulated, they will not benefit from the work they are doing – they may simply become overwhelmed and unable to be present as they end up flooded or dissociated. Remember, it may be easier for therapists to tolerate that the couple is not ready to tolerate the tough work of Stage Three than it is for the couple to acknowledge and tolerate that they are not yet ready. It is a delicate balance between affirming that the couple are experts in their own lives and experience while also holding gently an informed understanding of the challenges that lie ahead.

In addition to the exercises themselves, therapists continually work in sessions, to help couples develop emotion regulation capacities. This will be a challenge for you, as therapist, to really focus in on the small, moment-by-moment emotional interactions that are happening in the room. For instance, Gary might say that he is feeling overwhelmed and shut down, and the goal would be to rewind the process, go back to the first moment he remembers feeling triggered, and follow that moment in freeze-frame slowness until arriving at the moment of dissociation and shutdown. The more we can take this apart thought by thought, feeling by feeling, sensation by sensation, the more we are modelling a non-dissociative way of exploring triggers and strong feeling states. Helping Gary learn how to be present with his own emotional experience rather than dissociate will also help him understand himself, his relationship, and his needs in ways that he simply cannot while fluctuating in and out of a dissociative state. As I help Gary, I am also helping Geoffrey to see that Gary's dissociation is rooted in a trigger and a response that can be understood and to see that there are ways of being with Gary that can help him become able to stay with those triggers and feelings and, eventually, with him.

Titration of emotional arousal is essential for this work to be safe and successful. I find that the analogy of driving a car works for me and my students. Imagine that you are learning how to drive a car, and you are trying to figure out how to keep the speed of the car steady at 60 km/h. Over time, you learn how to titrate your pressure on the gas and the brakes to keep yourself at a steady speed. In the beginning, however, it is jolts and jogs and fits and starts. Emotion regulation work is the same: you learn how much gas you can apply before the survivor gets triggered over the line of regulation and how strong an application of the brakes will send the survivor under the regulation line, becoming numb and disconnected. A key role for practitioners is to help titrate the level of emotional arousal in sessions, and also to model tolerance of strong emotions and the capacity to maintain mentalizing capacities in the face of dysregulation. For partners who have felt overwhelmed or even frightened by their partner's emotions, your capacity to be present, to continue to mentalize with them and to help the partner engage with some tentative mutual regulation with you, is a wonderful model for them that there are possibilities for helping their partner and supporting one another in emotion regulation.

Exercises

This section will focus on building specific skills within and outside of sessions. Take one exercise, work on it in the session with the couple, and then take the opportunity to explore how this exercise might provide insights into individual and couple issues. These active exercises include Naming Feelings, Exploring Learned Emotional Relationships, Dyadic Breathing Relaxation Exercises, and Dyadic Emotional Coping.[1] For each exercise, explain the rationale, what you hope the couple will learn, how they can work together to help each other, and how they can apply the exercise in their daily life together.

During this process of skills acquisition, it will be important for couples to complete weekly logs in areas of particular challenge, to discuss these with one another, and to bring these back to sessions to continue to process and strengthen insights and new skills. It will be important to help the couple to understand that completing these exercises is an important precursor to the more active couple-focused work that is to come. Help the couple to work on these exercises together. They can start by taking turns and then, as they improve in these skills, they can try to do them together in tandem, thus working on the important capacity of mutual emotion regulation. As they learn to regulate their own emotional states, they gradually become more able to tolerate and help regulate the emotional state of their partner. While you do not need to complete all of the handouts, be careful not to misinterpret over-control, numbing, or excessive intellectualizing as the equivalent of vibrant and strong emotion regulation!

Throughout the remainder of the treatment, should one or both partners appear to be struggling with their emotion regulation, ask them to name one of the strategies that works best for them. If they appear to have difficulty naming one of the exercises, you can suggest two that they have rehearsed and ask them which one they would like to try, right now, in the session. If they have chosen a breathing exercise, for example, have both partners perform that breathing exercise in the session with you. If the exercise requires someone to take the lead, ask the partner who is not having difficulties with emotion regulation to take the lead. If both are finding this to be difficult, you may take the lead as therapist and then ask them to do the exercise independently. Over the course of the therapy, it should be possible to provide shorter and less frequent prompts for emotion regulation strategies and skills in the sessions, with fewer moments of needing to fall back to more basic skills and exercises in periods of distress. The couple builds new relational habits as they learn to help one another and coach each other in mutual regulation.

As sad and surprising as it may seem, many survivors simply have no words for their feelings. All of their feelings have turned into one toxic, unwelcome mush of overwhelming danger. Also, for many survivors, all emotional responses quickly turn into one predominant emotional state. As discussed in the psychoeducation section, many survivors do not have the capacity to stay attuned to the primary emotions at the core of their experience, such as sadness, hurt, and anger. Even joy and happiness can feel dangerous. All primary emotions are quickly smothered by old trauma-induced strategies into secondary emotional responses which, for survivors, are often simply one emotion. For many survivors that one emotional response is shame. For another, smaller fraction, that emotional response is anger, which can serve as both a primary or a secondary emotion, depending on the context. The first task is to explore the multi-faceted and broad range of emotional responses to help survivors begin to identify and label their emotions. Using the *Words for Expressing Feelings* worksheet, discuss the survivors' experiences with identifying and tolerating feelings. Many trauma survivors have never had the developmental experiences required to help them identify feelings within themselves. They may also be unable to tolerate these feelings without needing to suppress them, dissociate, or engage in problematic strategies to push the feelings away, such as addictions, self-harm, or compulsive sexual behaviours. For survivors, emotions are often dangerous harbingers of bad things. Exploring the value of emotions as providing essential information about situations, people, and events, as well as reminding them that when you screen out the "bad" feelings, the "good" ones are also eradicated, will be important as you lead up to beginning to explore their relationship with their emotions.

Use the following questions to guide the discussion:

Can you identify three or four feelings that you have experienced now as we have discussed your feelings?
Which of these feelings do you feel comfortable with?
Which of these feelings feel foreign or even dangerous to you, and why?
How do you usually experience your feelings?

At the end of this session, provide the couple with the *Words for Expressing Feelings* handout and ask them to keep a daily log. Suggest that they set a timer in their phone or watch for every 3 hours and that, each day, they stop what they are doing, tune in to themselves, identify the feelings they are currently experiencing, and write a short note about this in a notebook that they will then bring back to the next session. If the couple is not engaged in a lot of conflict, ask them to share their notebook entries with each other at the end of each day and discuss what they have learned about themselves and their emotions. If there is a lot of ongoing conflict within the couple at this point, it would be better to ask the couple to bring their notebooks to the next session for sharing and discussion.

In the next session, you might work on the exercise *Exploring Learned Emotional Relationships*. This handout explores how the survivor learned about emotions in their families, community, and culture and through their traumatic experiences. For instance, it was clear to Anush, a first-generation Canadian Muslim whose family had escaped atrocities in their country of origin, that very few emotions were acceptable. As the firstborn son, his role was to shepherd younger family members; to support his parents, aunts, uncles, and grandparents; and to be calm and supportive at all times. There was little room for fear, anger, or hurt. Shame dominated Anush's inner experience of emotion, while no emotions were acceptable to him for outer expression. Adding the impacts of sexual abuse to the weight of the expectations he held for himself as the eldest son was emotionally crippling. As therapy moved along, it seemed that these messages were his own deeply internalized beliefs about what was expected of him. As he disclosed to family members and shared his struggles, he learned that his family did not share his ideas about what was expected of him: in fact, they were deeply supportive and experienced myriad complex emotional responses that Anush had believed to be anathema to his family.

It is fascinating to see what the couple learns about one another by working through this worksheet. For many, it is the first time they hear how their partner's family dealt with emotions. For many, it is the first time they learn how their partner experienced their trauma, in relation to others – family, community, culture; up to now, trauma has been a hidden, unspoken spectre in their relationship. As they discuss their individual experiences of learning about the "rules" of emotions, bring the discussion back to the couple and explore how these rules and expectations have been played out in their relationship.

Moving from more cognitive explorations of what emotions are all about and how the couple has learned about the rules of emotions, a good place to start with couples struggling with emotion regulation is breathing exercises. Breathing exercises are a staple strategy to help people reduce anxiety and emotional arousal and to tolerate and regulate their emotions. One of the best things about breathing exercises is that they do not require any tools or costs; everything you require is with you at all times and in all places. You can start by explaining to the couple how deep and regular breathing will help a person maintain calm, reduce tension in the body, and maintain focused attention. Bringing a couple's attention to their breathing is a first step to help the couple notice some of the bodily cues of stress and dysregulation. For many survivors, emotions are already well out of regulation before the survivor even notices them. Trying these exercises while the couple is not in a state of distress helps the couple instil these skills so that they are well-practiced before they are needed.

Start with the couple practicing noticing the rhythm and sensations of their breathing, where do they feel the breath in their body, do they breathe through their nose or mouth, do they breathe deeply or shallowly? Once the couple is comfortable with just noticing their breath, ask them to try to change the rhythm of their breathing, by putting their hand on their abdomen and slowly breathing into their hand and then exhaling, slowing the rhythm and noticing the abdomen moving in and out. If the couple has trouble doing this organically, suggest that they breathe in to increasingly longer counts. This would lead into the next breathing exercise: the square breathing exercise. This exercise involves:

Breathing in to a count of four,
Holding to a count of four,
Breathing out to a count of four, and
Holding to a count of four.

This is repeated until a state of calm has been achieved. I have found that this exercise works really well for couples to do together. One counts and the other does the exercise, and then they switch. Another adaptation involves the couple drawing a square on their partner's hand while they engage in the breathing exercise. The couple can also take this exercise home with them. Ask the couple to set aside 10 minutes each evening to practice. Ask them to take turns doing the exercise while the other partner counts for them and then ask them to try doing it in tandem, one partner beating out the rhythm of the count on the other partner's hand. Asking them to begin engaging in these activities as a pair, I also see how well they are able to adapt to the idea that they are not alone with their emotions, and that their partner can be there as a resource to help them.

Following the introduction of breathing exercises that are focused on the individual in relationship, we move to a breathing exercise that is dyadically focused. The *Dyadic Breathing Relaxation Exercise* is designed to help the couple begin to develop new strategies for dyadic or mutual emotion regulation and to help them learn how to respond to one another when in distress. This exercise brings the partner in to the process of using breathing for relaxation, as each partner is asked to bear witness to each other's attempt to deepen and expand their breath, slowing the pace and growing calmness in breathing. Once this is established, the couple is asked to breathe together and to expand the breathing exercise into sharing the rhythm through putting one hand on their own chest and the other on their partner's abdomen. Of course, this may be quite triggering for some survivors, so feel free to adapt the exercise as fits the tolerance and triggers of your couple. The goal is to begin to help the couple "use" one another for support and mutual regulation rather than turning away from one another when they are in distress.

The last exercise in this section is one that you will continue to come back to over the course of couple therapy. The *Dyadic Emotional Coping Exercise* is an adaptation of an exercise from the Skills Training in Affective and Interpersonal Relations treatment model (Cloitre, Koenen, Cohen, & Han, 2002), which helps the couple come to understand the patterns and triggers that lead to specific emotional responses. The exercise involves invoking a situation that is fresh, identifying feelings, thoughts, and responses, and expanding these to exploring possible alternative responses. I also use this to explore the relationship between current responses and any ongoing negative patterns and as an opportunity to closely examine DTRs that the couple is working on. At first, I ask the couple to fill these out forms separately, but over time I will ask them to work on this together as a way of learning how to turn to one another, talk about difficult experiences and emotions, work together to solve conflicts, and practice taking responsibility for themselves in the relationship as a matter of course rather than getting stuck in shame or anger. Couples are asked to identify an interaction that occurred between sessions that led to emotional distress and/or conflict and to fill out this form. After trying this in sessions, partners are asked to work on these forms on their own, and eventually with their partners, and to return with their completed forms for exploration. Over time, the couples learn that feelings are not as terrifying, shameful, and dangerous as they once believed, and to be aware of, tolerate, attempt to understand, share, and explore their emotional lives with each other.

This exercise is one where problematic ways that survivors deal with emotional distress may be exposed. Depending on your experience working with childhood trauma survivors, it will be more or less distressing for you to hear about self-injury, suicidality, drug and alcohol misuse, the use of food as an emotion regulation strategy, and all the other creative ways that survivors find to manage the overwhelming distress in their lives that may cause them to feel deep shame. It may also be the first time that their partner is hearing about these strategies. The take home message then is: tread lightly. Shame is a powerful force that can stop the therapeutic process and leave people feeling isolated and incompetent. If survivors are in individual therapy, when they discuss emotion regulation strategies that have the potential to hurt themselves, this is an opportunity to ask how those issues are being addressed in the individual therapy. However, if survivors are not in individual therapy, it is important to find a balance between exploring strategies and alternatives to self-harm while maintaining the focus on the couple relationship as the primary "unit" of the therapy. This is challenging: therapists cannot ignore self-harm, but also need to be ever mindful of supporting individual therapy while not diverting the couple therapy process. Where discussions of emotion regulation strategies that involve self-harm arise, you might use these as a vehicle to move back into discussions about the couple relationship. The following questions may facilitate an exploration of the relational impact of self-harm and of shameful emotion regulation strategies that may draw each partner into secrecy and isolation.

To survivors who use strategies of emotion regulation that they find shameful or that must be hidden or take up a lot of time away from their partner:

How does this strategy hold you away from your partner?

How might your partner help you when you are feeling like you want to cut yourself (drink, binge, etc.)?

What is the impact of your weight (cuts and scars, hangover, debt from buying drugs illegally, etc.) on your relationship?

To partners who are just learning about these strategies:

> What is it like to hear that your partner has been struggling in secret in these ways?
> Are there strategies that you might use when you are distressed that help you understand your partner's cutting (binging, drinking, etc.)?

More often than not, both partners have emotion regulation strategies that have been turned inward, away from the relationship, that can be used as examples to mirror the struggles that both are having and the isolation they experience trying to tackle these on their own. For some survivors, the ways they struggle to deal with overwhelming emotional states are too shameful, and they simply will not share the details. However, it cannot be underscored enough how significantly these kinds of secrets impact the relationship. Any kind of secret about which the survivor feels deeply ashamed builds a barrier between partners and makes it very difficult for them to develop the capacity for mutual regulation.

Managing and reducing dissociation

Dissociation lies at the extreme end of emotion regulation strategies that lead to isolation, alienation, and pain. For many survivors, especially those whose trauma was early, chronic, and severe, dissociation was really the only strategy that could protect them from the ravages of their experiences. Dissociation is extremely creative, resourceful, and functional when it is needed: never doubt that those who have learned to dissociate in response to trauma did so because it was the best – and perhaps the only – strategy for psychic survival. The problem with dissociation, as with so many responses developed by resourceful and resilient people to survive atrocities, is that it becomes the go-to strategy for dealing with emotions and attachment stress rather than the response of last resort. In effect, emotional responses to life in the present are built upon life in the past; they are geared to responding to all emotional triggers as though the horrible thing that has already happened is about to happen again, regardless of the external context of current life and relationships.

The process of building emotion regulation skills will definitely be helpful for survivors who use dissociation as their primary strategy for regulating their emotions. As they engage with the exercises they may, for the first time, allow themselves some awareness that their bodily sensations can carry emotional messages; they may now begin to track the relationship between triggers, emotions, and responses as they engage with the exercises. They may start to become aware of the importance of sensing and acknowledging their own emotional lives to be able to live a full and rich life with their partner. However, for some survivors, working in sessions as dissociation arises will also be very important. For instance, Gary and Geoffrey really struggled to find ways to regulate their emotions, where one partner would use distance, avoidance, and dissociation as his main emotion regulation strategy while the other was desperate to get close to him in any way possible. This couple engaged readily with the emotion regulation exercises and as therapy continued, I also took an active role in sessions to help Gary stay present, oriented, and attentive to the process. This became less and less of a challenge as therapy moved along. In early sessions, it was an unceasing struggle to attend to Gary's slipping away into dissociation while continuing to move couple therapy along and ensure that Geoffrey felt that his emotional needs were also being considered, acknowledged, and responded to.

I will share some transcript segments to demonstrate some of the moment-by-moment work with Gary and Geoffrey, as Gary's tendency towards dissociation played itself out in sessions.

As a starting point, simply noticing and acknowledging that dissociation is a part of this couple's relational dance shifted them out of a paralyzing level of conflict and pain. As we worked through the psychoeducational material on emotion regulation, Gary was able to relate to some of the content around dissociation.

GARY: Some of this speaks to me a little bit in my life, yeah.

THERAPIST: Can you say a little bit about how?

GARY: Well, . . . I often lose "who am I", or feel like I have lost myself. I don't remember a lot of my life, like people say, "where have you lived?" and I have to go like hmmm, and I don't remember when or where. And that kind of happens a lot with Geoffrey, he will say to me that we have discussed one thing or another and I have no memory of it at all.

GEOFFREY: That definitely is a thing that happens. There's definitely been times where we got into arguments that, to me, are like just arguments or heated fights, but to him I can see now that he is no longer in control. He often doesn't remember what he said or what happened.

THERAPIST: [to Gary] How much do you remember of those experiences?

GARY: I often remember some parts of them but I mostly don't remember what was so upsetting.

THERAPIST: You don't remember what you were fighting about?

BOTH: Yeah.

THERAPIST: So you remember being angry and triggered?

GARY: I guess. . .

THERAPIST: It seems like at some point you get very overwhelmed, like you couldn't think straight anymore . . . can you help me understand what it is like?

GEOFFREY: I guess when we argue I just feel like I have nowhere to go, I start to feel trapped.

THERAPIST: Nowhere to go. . .

GARY: Yeah.

THERAPIST: And feeling secure about having a place to go, being able to feel safe and free is big for you?

GARY: Yeah.

THERAPIST: So those kinds of situations make you really panic and then you take off, emotionally, you disappear inside of yourself and no longer remember what is happening and even what you are doing?

GARY: I guess so, that sounds right.

GEOFFREY: I mean I've learned now that actually because of trauma that kind of arguing really like . . . any kind of heating conflict, I find, has always ended really, really, badly. I'm someone who is okay with arguing and I can get very upset but it's not traumatic to me like I mean it's like really hard, but like I'm okay.

THERAPIST: You can keep thinking and pushing through.

GEOFFREY: Yeah, I can still communicate my feelings, I'm in control of my body . . . I know what's going on, I remember, I can process information, but for Gary, I see his eyes glaze over.

GARY: I get really dissociated.

As we dove deeper into the impact of dissociation in further sessions, the challenge was to help Geoffrey discuss the impact on him when Gary disappears into himself while holding Gary and helping him not to descend into shame and the dissociation he uses to deal with feelings of any kind.

GARY: I still suffer from childhood trauma every day. I go through feelings, triggers all the time. Like last night I was just talking to somebody about HIV stories, and I just couldn't hear anything he was saying anymore because I just had a huge flashback about being abused. I had to wait until that subject was over. I didn't like being dissociative. I have to struggle with my closest friends even, to be like "actually I didn't hear you you'll have to repeat that" . . . you know?

THERAPIST: You have to struggle to hear, to listen?

GARY: Yeah.

THERAPIST: So it sounds as though you get really triggered and then you dissociate and can't follow what is happening, you really take off inside of yourself. What is it like when that happens between the two of you?

GARY: Sometimes I'm a bit self-absorbed and I have to struggle to realize that I do care about what he's talking about 'cause I'm just so . . . wrapped up in my head that I don't have room to care in that moment.

THERAPIST: And you need to remind yourself to go back and to be present.

GARY: Yeah.

THERAPIST: And you're nodding. [to Geoffrey] That's something you feel?

GEOFFREY: Yeah, sometimes we end up in a fight, I'm like "why don't you pay attention to me, or care?"

THERAPIST: What it is like for you when you notice or feel that?

GEOFFREY: Well I just notice that . . . my feelings and my thoughts and my emotions – I'll notice if I'm talking about something that's going on in my life or something that I'm upset about, he doesn't seem to really care, he'll just like change the subject.

THERAPIST: What is that like for you?

GEOFFREY: I mean it doesn't feel good . . . I try to not get to upset about it. I try to either bring it up or understand that what's going on for Gary. Sometimes he's not doing that well or he's stressed and so he's not there, not available to me to be emotionally supportive about some things, but I try to remember that on a regular day, he would be . . . like he does really love me. Then I try to think of ways that he is really supportive. I try to get out of a negative thought.

THERAPIST: So you remind yourself that he does care and you try to do that for yourself. What is the feeling state that you're trying to soothe through telling yourself these things and thinking these things?

GEOFFREY: Well that . . . Gary doesn't know or doesn't care to be emotionally supportive or doesn't care about my life.

THERAPIST: So a feeling that he doesn't care about you?

GEOFFREY: Yeah, I know he does cares about me.

THERAPIST: The head knows. Gary, what are you thinking as Geoffrey is talking about this transition and how shifting from a focus on how difficult things can be for you to a focus on where both of your needs are being considered?

GARY: I kind of checked out a couple of minutes of what you were saying just now.

THERAPIST: Can you describe what happened when you checked out?

GARY: I just started feeling tired and thinking about my own thoughts and. . .

THERAPIST: And what were your thoughts?

GARY: I actually don't even remember right now.

THERAPIST: Can you think what the trigger was for you to go away?

GARY: Just that . . . maybe I just hadn't heard my own voice in a while. . .

THERAPIST: And what is that like for you?

GARY: Well I don't know, it's probably the abuse, I just wasn't communicating for a long time in my life and I didn't really have much of a voice so sometimes maybe I get triggered back to this place where I'm not existent, not actually in the conversation, even though he was talking about me. . .

THERAPIST: So something happened at some point, I could see you moving your body back and your arms seemed heavy.

GEOFFREY: Was it because I was saying something not positive about us or about you that made it harder for you to listen?

GARY: Maybe?

THERAPIST: And that's something you notice, that sometimes there's a point where you just slip away.

GARY: Yeah, I definitely had an easier time staying focused at the beginning.

THERAPIST: And do you notice when you start to drift away?

GARY: I did this time, yeah.

THERAPIST: And is there a way that you could signal to us that you're starting to drift away?

GARY: Hmm . . . maybe I'll just say "I'm just asserting my voice to stay in the conversation".

THERAPIST: Okay, so that is something that we can work on together, how we can be aware of when you get triggered and start to slip away, and for you to find ways to signal to us that you are finding it hard keeping your voice in the conversation. And, for the two of you to start to learn to be focused on each other in a way that doesn't feel too stressful or difficult.

At this early stage in the process, we are just noticing, attending, and looking at small strategies like developing signals to help the couple maintain connection during moments where dissociation is drawing a partner away. I had noticed that Gary was sinking back in the chair, moving his body in ways that suggested that he was uncomfortable, and he did not appear to be attending or tracking the conversation as I was talking with Geoffrey about his experience in the relationships. It is important to not abandon a partner mid-exploration at the first sign of dissociation in the other partner, both to assess regulatory capacities but also to clarify that the focus of the therapy is on the couple and to model capacity to attend to the partner's distress without collapsing into dysregulation or dissociation. However, I was interested in finding out more about that process and how he experienced it, rather than stopping it. As the therapy moved along, as I became more cognizant of Gary's triggers, I was more on top of it, more focused on helping him manage the triggers and to stay present in the session. After this session I became very aware of the need to manage Gary's exposure to anything that could be experienced as shaming or critical. While it is essential for partners to become able to tolerate their partner's expressions of distress or dissatisfaction, for someone like Gary who is so smothered by the annihilation of shame, finding ways to help him tolerate, hear, stay present for, and eventually engage with areas where he is not meeting his partner's needs is a real challenge. I say manage, not avoid, because it is essential not to become sensitized to a survivor's dissociation and entirely avoid things that might trigger them but to learn what these are in order to scaffold, coach, and contain them as they learn to ride the wave of the emotional response to their triggers. Eventually, with enough exposure and coaching to tolerate and manage, the triggers lose their power. In the next small segment, you will see me working more actively with Gary to help him stay present in a session where Geoffrey is talking about his emotional dysregulation and how this impacts Gary and their relationship.

GEOFFREY: I feel like that was also the state where I would be freaking out or I'd be like crying or I would be upset and Gary just couldn't handle it and then he would just go . . . like just disappear, I guess, into a dissociative state.

THERAPIST: So it feels dissociated to you?

GEOFFREY: Yeah.

THERAPIST: Do you have a sense of losing touch with different parts of yourself in those moments?

GARY: Um . . . what's the question?

THERAPIST: When those times happen, when you feel really triggered and it sounds as though maybe you're saying or doing things you later regret and don't entirely remember, when those times happen, what is going on inside of you? Do you feel like you're losing some part of yourself or disconnecting from some part of yourself?

GARY: Yeah I think so. It is really draining and . . . I lose myself and it makes me really tired . . . I do try to come back.

THERAPIST: Okay, so part of it is that this experience makes you tired, and you seem to be getting tired now, as we talk about this experience.

GARY: Mmmh.

THERAPIST: So what's going on inside you now as we talk about this?

GARY: Umh, I'm just looking for a place where I can feel okay and things are good . . . I can't help it. I'm thinking about something that makes me feel like I'm not the best person in the world.

THERAPIST: So something about us talking about this experience is triggering some feelings of not being a good person?

GARY: Or not being as healed as I thought I was.

THERAPIST: And that has the effect of pulling you away?

GARY: Mmh . . . yeah, I mean I could probably try to work on it and talk about it more but . . . it's the first time I've ever talked about with somebody else.

THERAPIST: What is that like for you, to talk with me about these things that make you feel like maybe you aren't as healed as you thought you were?

GARY: Very hard.

THERAPIST: It feels very vulnerable to have someone learning these things about how you cope with these strong feelings and about the way the two of you interact?

GARY: I just feel like I'm . . . yes . . . it's a not a good feeling.

At this point, Gary was barely holding on to the conversation. He was talking but very slowly, in a monotone, his eyes were half closed, and while he was clearly trying very hard to stay with the conversation, he was also slipping away. I wanted to take a break, to help Gary and Geoffrey work on these strong emotions together and to help Gary find a way out of the dissociation that was threatening to envelop him.

THERAPIST: Okay, let's slow things down a bit and see if we can find a way to help with those very strong, not very good feelings. Would that be okay? [both nod] I'm going to suggest that we try out one of the emotion regulation exercises that we have been working on, right here in the session, to see if we can find a way to bring the feelings into a tolerable zone so that we can all be present together. [both nod – Gary appears to be coming in and out but is still with me] Let's try one of the breathing exercises together. Let's put both feet on the ground, sit forward in our chairs so that we are sitting up straight, relax our shoulders and abdomen and put one hand on our chest and one hand on our abdomen. [both do this but very slowly] Now, remember that the goal is to breathe in very deeply, hold the breath, and then exhale very slowly. Sometimes people like to close their eyes when they are doing this exercise as it helps them focus on their heart rate and breathing and helps them calm down. I'm going to suggest that we don't do that because that might make it easier to get sucked into our inside selves and not stay present in the room together. Does that sound okay? [both nod] Good. So, I'm going to count for us, we'll breathe in for four, hold the breath for four and then exhale for four.

We went through the exercise about five times. The first three times, we had to stop and help Gary calm down – even doing the deep breathing was overwhelming. Therapists need to remember that for many survivors there is a paradoxical response to any kind of relaxation exercises. There are various reasons for this but one which is important to remember is that children are often taken unawares from a restful sleep, reading a book, or simply walking idly down the street, and thrust into a violent abusive situation. So, hypervigilance is a really good thing and relaxation becomes a really bad thing. Shifting through that paradoxical response may take many attempts.

THERAPIST: Gary, stay with me. I want you to open your eyes and look at something in the room. Can you do that? [Gary opens his eyes and flutters them off and on for a few minutes until he can reliably keep them open. I am simply waiting, calmly, but clear in my goal.] Okay, good, can you look at Geoffrey? [This is less of a challenge and he is able to look at Geoffrey fairly quickly.] Good, would it be okay for Geoffrey to put his hand on your hand? [Physical touch can be very grounding if it is safe and with a partner in the room; again, where safe, you can have the benefit of physical touch without you, the therapist, violating any boundaries. Gary signals that this would be okay, and Geoffrey puts his hand on top of Gary's in a gentle and loving way.] Okay, Gary, can you tell me what's going on, what's triggering you?

GARY: [speaking very slowly] I don't know, it's okay when I breathe in but when I hold the breath I get freaked out and panic.

THERAPIST: Hmmm, I wonder what that might be about. Do you have any theories?

GARY: Um, well, I. . . [seems to be slipping away again]

THERAPIST: Stay with me Gary, I think this is really important and understanding more about this trigger may help us understand more about other triggers and your struggles with dissociation.

GARY: [starting to cry] I just can't hold my breath like that! It's like when I couldn't breathe with . . . I couldn't breathe. . . [crying and pulling away from Geoffrey]

THERAPIST: It's like when you couldn't breathe. What happened when you couldn't breathe, Gary?

GARY: He, he . . . I couldn't breathe . . . he made me. . .

THERAPIST: You couldn't breathe, he was hurting you, he was hurting you in a way that you couldn't breathe?

It is clear, at this point, that, for Gary, some aspect of his abuse is triggered by holding his breath in the breathing exercise. Both Gary and Geoffrey tried this exercise in an earlier session without appearing to trigger anything, but at that point in therapy it was introduced into a session where emotions were not already in a dysregulated state. In this case, he did not appear so much to be having a flashback in the session as having a hard time telling us about what happened in his abuse. The difference can often be discerned by whether the person's eyes are open, whether they are speaking in the present or past tense, and whether they are talking to you or seem to be inside of themselves talking about the trauma. Gary appeared to be talking to me about something from the past, so I was thinking that he was trying to tell me something difficult and very triggering.

GARY: Yes! [coming to the present in full force] He put his fucking dick in my mouth and he slammed my head against the floor and I couldn't breathe and it lasted forever and then he came in my mouth and I couldn't breathe and I couldn't swallow and I thought I was going to choke and I was suffocating and I was sure I was going to die and he just laughed at me!

When Gary made this clear, present, direct statement of his abuse, I was of course filled with compassion for him, but I was also very pleased to see that he could recount this story in a clear narrative with a beginning, middle, and end, with emotion and emphasis and mental clarity. It was a real sign of progress for Gary that he could be so clear and have feelings without dissociating. A traumatic event becomes a memory rather than a reliving when it is told as an autobiographical event with a beginning, middle and end, with words and feelings firmly rooted in the past. This disclosure was helpful for Geoffrey who, all of a sudden, could see so much of Gary's behaviour around emotions and sex in a new light. Geoffrey reached for Gary and took his hand in a loving and soothing way, and Gary was able to accept this gesture of caring.

THERAPIST: Oh, Gary, I am so sorry that happened to you. It sounds unspeakably terrifying and, of course, a breathing exercise where you have to hold your breath could really trigger all of that terror. I'm so sorry.

GARY: [crying but not dissociated] He said that he loved me. . .

THERAPIST: That is NOT love, that is abuse and I am so sorry that happened to you.

GEOFFREY: Baby, why didn't you ever tell me about this? I feel like an ass because I, well, you know.

It seemed that Geoffrey was starting to make associations between this traumatic event and their sex life. At this point, I wanted to stay focused on emotion regulation and understanding triggers so I steered the conversation back to the exercise. I also did not want to end the session without wrap-up, so I went back to the exercise, discussed adapting it for Gary's particular triggers, and wrapped up the session.

THERAPIST: Geoffrey, it sounds as though you are starting to make some connections between Gary's trauma and your relationship, maybe even your sexual relationship. That is important; that is a big reason why we do this work together. However, I am aware that this has been a really challenging session, and I want to make sure that we go back to the exercise and see if we can find a way to help you both use this exercise together in a way that is helpful and not triggering so that you have that as a resource to use between sessions. Gary, what would you think about trying the exercise again but removing the part where you hold your breath?

GARY: Okay, we could try.

The session ended with Gary and Geoffrey trying the adapted exercise and finding that it worked well for them at that point. Both were well-oriented, calm, and connected to one another at the end of the session. In case they are not in this state at the end of the session time, I always provide a small area where couples can regroup before going out into the world. I do not go overtime with sessions, even when couples are feeling dysregulated. My goal is to always keep at least 10 minutes for grounding and debriefing at the end of a session; however, it is not uncommon for a survivor to bring up emotionally laden material at the end of a session and I am aware that the nature of trauma means that emotions will not be easily packed up and tied with a bow at the end of all sessions. At the same time, the overall message is clear: we are working on developing these emotion regulation skills, I am here to help you during the session, and at the end of the session I trust that you will use the skills we are working on to regroup and get ready to go back to your life. It would send the wrong message if I were to become dysregulated and could not keep the boundaries around session times, suggesting that the couple's emotions were not safe, containable, and tolerable or even that my own emotional states are not regulated. While not encouraging avoidance, we also do not want to flood or retraumatize clients. In this case, I removed the part of the exercise that was particularly triggering; in future, I could revisit this to consider adding that element back into the exercise. This really depends on my assessment of the value of pushing through the avoidance trigger. Sometimes it is necessary to push through something that someone is avoiding because it is a trigger, and sometimes it is not worth the effort and potential for retraumatization. For example, a client who avoids bathrooms because their abuse happened in a bathroom may develop health problems such as chronic constipation, inflammatory digestive issues, or chronic urinary tract infections because they avoid listening to the cues in their body that tell them it is time to go to the bathroom. For them, the feeling of discomfort of holding everything in is better than the terror of going into the bathroom. In such a case, pushing through the avoidance of the trigger is important. However, in the case of avoiding holding one's breath, I would need to consider how often it would be important for Gary to be able to hold his breath in a real-world situation. If Gary had a lifelong dream of being a scuba diver, for example, I might have to sort that out with the couple.

As we moved forward, Gary was more able to talk about the origins of his disconnection and how when he feels responsible for Geoffrey or when he feels that Geoffrey really needs him, his dissociation and disconnection is triggered. This is a clear statement of past impacting present, with a narrative that allows for expansion and exploration, where previously we just experienced Gary as disappearing any time their couple interactions were discussed.

GARY: Part of me is like, well, it's good that he talks to me about this, but the other part of me is like, "I've done too much work in my lifetime, I don't need to do this", you know. . .

THERAPIST: What kind of work?

GARY: Like . . . caring for everyone else. My mother was so mentally unstable that whenever I did spend time with her, it was all about her. My abuser, well, he just pretended to care about me and then he used me for his needs, and other people in my life, people we haven't talked much about, people who really took advantage of me over and over again and I just let them.

THERAPIST: So there's a way in which you're protecting yourself from repeating history, a history where you got really taken advantage of, hurt and abused. That's become the template for your relationships, especially when someone seems to have needs that might trigger that pattern emerging in the relationship.

GARY: Yes, I know that Geoffrey is different but, well, what if he isn't, what if he is just sticking around until. . . ?

THERAPIST: It sounds as though, in protecting yourself from something that has already happened, and isn't currently happening, you're losing something very important. And it sounds as if you're so in that protective space that you may not even feel what is really happening in the present. Geoffrey, what comes up for you when you hear Gary say that he is afraid that this could happen again with you?

GEOFFREY: Well, I guess it makes sense, most of his life people have taken advantage of him. I guess it also kind of hurts because I don't think I've ever done that and I don't think I ever would, that's just not me.

THERAPIST: It seems as though, in fact, you have a tendency to put your needs aside and try to suppress them so that Gary doesn't experience this trigger.

GEOFFREY: Yes, that's true.

GARY: Yeah. I know, but, well I guess because I'm dissociated a lot and like, it just feels like someone may be like hey, forget about that good stuff, now I'm going to turn into a needy jerk. And it's hard to not get stuck in that place. Dissociation is just where I live, you know.

THERAPIST: Yeah, I think you've helped us see more about how dissociation is really embedded in how you experience the world of other people and the world inside yourself. I think habitual dissociation is like surfing, you're just on the wave, you're just doing your thing and someone comes around and puts their foot in front of your board and over you go!

GARY: Yeah! [laughs] Like most people I can get by like, "yeah okay, sure", you know, like . . . pretending I'm paying attention.

THERAPIST: And it sounds like you are very good at that and you even maintain relationships that way with some friends. . . . But, you know, you can't do that in a love relationship, it has an expiry date, your partner is going to come to you and need you to be there with him and, after a while, he's going to know. . .

GARY: Yeah, I know.

THERAPIST: You need to come out from behind there every now and again. Coasting . . . dissociation is a very powerful protective mechanism, it protects us from lots of things. But it also keeps us away from people. Dissociation keeps us from deep connections with others. You've been able to coast in this relationship because the two of you love each other very much and you can stay in that sort of dissociation and Geoffrey has been really trying to be okay with the level of engagement up to now but now he's saying, if we're gonna stay together, I need it to be more balanced, I need to feel more connected.

GEOFFREY: I haven't really thought about dissociation that way. It's interesting. I have a really hard time thinking of it as anything other than him being self-involved or not wanting me, but, I guess, it could, it could be trauma-related, it could be . . . like he's experienced enough trauma, enough hardship . . . that it makes sense but it's just, well, it's hard.

THERAPIST: Well I suspect there's somewhere in between where you could find balance, find a way to be present with one another and your needs without being overwhelmed and triggered back into all of those old relationships. There might be somewhere in between these opposites of being either completely subsumed by the needs of another person or completely gone to the wall of protecting yourself. There's a probably a way that we can find what's in the middle where you can ebb and flow a bit. That's probably going take a lot of work. And that work involves being less dissociated and at some level, that takes energy and self-care.

GARY: Yeah.

THERAPIST: And at another level, it's also a decision. Like, "okay this is something I want to do in my relationship with Geoffrey". It's really hard to come out of that kind of dissociation, it's nice and quiet in there.

Over time, Gary became more able to be present in sessions and with Geoffrey in their lives. It was a slow and challenging process for both of them. As will be examined in the section on getting stuck, Geoffrey moved more quickly to a place of feeling that he was worthy of having his needs met than Gary moved in the direction of being able to be present and meet those needs. It was a slow but steady process with one step forward, two steps back.

THERAPIST: It's a struggle for you two when you get into that particular dance of you [to Geoffrey] feeling like Gary doesn't care about you and your needs while, for you, Gary, it sounds like sometimes you can feel confused about how Geoffrey goes from 0 to 60 when he gets distressed and then you start to shut down and it escalates from there.

GEOFFREY: Yeah, now he's more like pissed off when it happens. He used to be just shut down, now it seems that it's happened so many times that now he's just angry.

THERAPIST: Would you agree with that?

GARY: I don't know; I just panic when things are out of control.

THERAPIST: You're afraid of losing control?

GARY: Yeah, it feels out of control when Geoffrey gets so emotional.

THERAPIST: Okay, so if Geoffrey's really upset, you start to feel things and you start being upset as well?

GARY: Yeah.

THERAPIST: Even if you might feel angry, fear would come up for you also?

GARY: Yeah.

THERAPIST: You know, as uncomfortable as it is, I have to say that feeling angry is much more real than shutting down. There's something really positive about that, to actually be feeling a feeling rather than trying to shut them all down.

GARY: I guess.

THERAPIST: That strikes me as progress, as hard as it is when it happens.

GEOFFREY: [laughs] Yeah I definitely noticed some change. You get angry more quickly than shut down. It's not just me escalating the conflict also. I really just said, "can you just show a little bit of concern?" and then Gary was like "What! I can't do this anymore!" I can't remember everything that he said, but we broke up for those 20 minutes.

THERAPIST: Is that your go-to when you have conflict? It seems that that has happened a few times, that when things escalate and you are both present in the conflict, instead of dissociating, you bring the conflict to an end by breaking up for a while.

GEOFFREY: I think it has started to be a little bit of a pattern. This is exhausting, me always being angry at him or disappointed or whatever.

THERAPIST: It sounds like there's something that we don't yet understand. Something that I'd like for us to understand more, that I don't think we've dug deep into yet because we've been trying to clear the underbrush. I do think we're starting to get a closer, clearer picture of what's happening in the conflict when you both get triggered, the relational dance where you [to Geoffrey] feel like Gary doesn't care about you and, in that upset state, as you move towards Gary, you [to Gary] feel overwhelmed with those feelings of need. You end up straight back in your childhood of people using you in ways that were really harmful for you. That pattern is living in the moment, but it is deeply tied to the past, your experiences earlier in your life with people who should have cared for you both but who used you for their own needs or didn't care for you in the ways you needed.

So, as we continued, I began to see the direct links between the strategies that this couple used to manage emotion dysregulation, their trauma, and their negative cycle, all wrapped up into one big DTR. The couple could not imagine that there were any alternatives to how they had been dealing with their conflicts: Geoffrey getting upset, Gary dissociating or – their new strategy – Geoffrey getting upset, Gary getting upset, the couple exploding and breaking up for a while. It was difficult for them to tolerate this new pattern even if it represented progress. A little psychoeducation about the fact that it is normal for couples to fight was called for at this stage. When survivors come from families where there was a lot of conflict that led to violence, or where nothing was ever talked about but really bad things were happening, it is challenging for them to understand or even tolerate the idea that there is such a thing as healthy, normal conflict. Learning how to have conflict, to fight even, and to trust that you will come out the other end emotionally and relationally intact, is something that takes a long time to learn; Gary and Geoffrey needed to learn that every conflict did not spell doom for their relationship.

THERAPIST: Every couple fights, it's inevitable if you are going to be a part of a couple. How we fight, what the outcome is, and the things that are said, that's what we hope to change. There's nothing wrong with fighting; fighting is how you resolve conflict. It's when couples never get to the end of the fight or never resolve one, or when conflict leads to violence, that's when we have a problem.

GEOFFREY: Does this way feel better for you?

THERAPIST: The intensity feels pretty overwhelming to you when the fight starts to feel too big or really difficult?

GARY: Yeah it makes me really tired and I have a hard time not taking off.

THERAPIST: One of the things I'm noticing though is that as Geoffrey talks, you're really listening to him in a way that I think sometimes is difficult for you but it seems like you're really interested in what he's saying as it relates to how the two of you interact together. That's a really nice change to see in you.

GARY: I guess. It's good to know that you see it as progress. I just have to think about it to feel it.

GEOFFREY: I don't quite understand it but obviously not getting into fights where Gary then checks out for a few weeks is good but, this feels really hard. I guess if I hadn't brought up the issue we wouldn't ever actually address anything fully, but I don't like the conflict, it's really yucky. And, I know you said that it isn't the goal, to avoid situations entirely but. . .

THERAPIST: We'll just keep exploring this as we go along. And the more we can talk about these situations as they happen, the more we can talk about what feels good for you, what works for you as a couple and as individuals and. . . . We'll keep working on this. You've come from a place where every conflict led to you [to Geoffrey] being completely flooded and overwhelmed and you [to Gary] getting triggered and dissociating. Now, there is less dissociation and less feelings of being overwhelmed and more instances of actually communicating with one another. We have a way to go before you both are feeling confident that you can tolerate, regulate, and eventually resolve conflicts between you. This all takes time and neither of you has had any good role models for how this should be, so try to trust me that this is good progress and you are doing really well.

The case of Geoffrey and Gary is a good example of a couple where dissociation is the primary strategy for dealing with any emotional arousal and trauma triggers. Gary's dissociation was quite severe and impeded our capacity to dive into any material in sessions until some new strategies for emotion regulation were in place. However, Gary's dissociation was a strategy, not a structure. What I mean by that is that Gary used dissociation as a strategy to deal with overwhelming emotions and trauma triggers, but his dissociation was not structural; it did not impact the overall structure of his personality or psychic life. For those where dissociation is structural, you may be working with individuals whose personality drastically changes depending on the emotional challenge they face in the sessions. This includes those who have been diagnosed with such dissociative disorders as Dissociative Identity Disorder (DID). A whole book could be written about working with couples dealing with dissociative disorders, and I cannot even begin to do the topic justice in one chapter. Most of the work you would need to do in the case of a couple where one or both partners has been diagnosed with DID would be exactly as discussed so far, only with a broader lens to ensure that all of the parts of your clients are in the room, listening and learning. If you do find you are working with a couple where one or both partners experience their inner worlds as having more than one state that feels like "me" – referred to as "self-states" for the present purpose – it is important that all of the self-states are included in the therapy and the therapeutic relationship. Challenges can arise if certain self-states are not engaged in conversations about the couple relationship, even if those parts of the self live on the back burner within the relationship. For instance, a common issue is that of sexual consent, where the adult self-state consciously consents to sex while other self-states are triggered or traumatized by sexual activity that does not feel consensual. Strategies for this situation include finding ways for self-states that have been sexually traumatized or those that experience their psychic world at earlier developmental stages to be "put to bed" so they are not exposed to sexual activity that would feel traumatizing. This is just one example of an issue that can arise when working with couples dealing with dissociative disorders, and unfortunately, there has been very little written directly on this topic so far. A couple of articles on the topic that you can refer to if you find yourself needing more resources include:

MacIntosh, H.B. (2013). Dissociative identity disorder and the process of couple therapy. *Journal of Trauma and Dissociation*, *14*(1), 84–96.

Panos, P.T., Panos, A., & Alred, H. (1990). The need for marriage therapy in the treatment of multiple personality disorder. *Dissociation*, *III*(I), 10–14.

Exploring learned emotional relationships

The goal of this exercise is to begin to understand our habitual patterns in our couple relationship by exploring how we learned to respond emotionally.

1. Fill in the following table on your own.
2. Consider the role of your traumatic experiences, the example of important people in your life and community, and the lessons of your culture about feelings.
3. Compare your responses with those of your partner.
4. Consider how similarities and differences between your responses influence the challenges you experience in your relationship.

	Family	*Community/Culture*	*Traumatic Experiences*
Which emotions are acceptable?			
How do you cope with difficult emotions?			
How do you express emotions?			
What are the benefits of following these rules?			
What are negatives of following these rules?			

Source: Adapted, with permission, from exercises in the STAIR 12-week treatment programme. Cloitre, M., Koenen, K.C., Cohen, L.R., & Han, H. (2002). Skills Training in Affective and Interpersonal Regulation followed by Exposure: A phase-based treatment for PTSD related to childhood abuse. *Journal of Consulting and Clinical Psychology*, *70*, 1067–1074.

DYADIC BREATHING RELAXATION EXERCISE

- One important approach to help you deal with distressing emotions is to calm your body down using breathing strategies.
- Often couples where one or both members have experienced trauma in childhood find it difficult to calm themselves down when they are distressed about something happening in their lives or relationship, or by reminders of their traumas.
- Often couples find it difficult to turn to each other for support and help when they are feeling distressed, because turning to other people when they were little was not helpful, at best, or was even dangerous and frightening.
- The goal of this exercise, then, is to help you work together as a couple to learn how to use a simple breathing exercise together, to reduce feelings of anxiety, and to help you get grounded.

Getting started

- Sit together facing one another. Find a position in which you feel comfortable. Take turns with one of you placing one hand on your chest and one hand on your stomach. If you feel comfortable, let your partner place their hands over yours. Take slow deep breaths and try to focus on isolating your breathing so that only the hand on the stomach moves up and down.
- Once one partner feels that they have been able to master this first step, switch places.
- The role of the observing partner is to provide support and grounding containment and to help their partner calm down should they find the exercise triggering.
- Once you feel comfortable with this first step, take one hand and put it on your chest and put your other hand on your partner's abdomen while your partner does the same. Then, work together to breathe in deeply, hold the breath for a few seconds and then breathe out slowly, together, being aware of each other's body and twinning your breathing with theirs.

Slow down your rate of breathing

- The next step in this exercise is to slow down your breathing. For this step, continue to sit facing one another and both partners will put one hand on their stomach.
- Watching one another, and following the lead of one partner, take in a long slow breath, hold this breath for a moment, and then let it out slowly. Pause briefly after exhaling and before inhaling.
- After four or five breaths, switch the partner who is taking the lead. Practice this exercise until you find it relatively easy to slow your breathing and to follow one another. Alternate breathing through your nose and your mouth until you find which strategy allows you the most control over your breathing.
- Practice this exercise daily for at least 10 minutes.

DYADIC EMOTIONAL COPING EXERCISE

The purpose of this exercise is to explore repetitive emotional responses or patterns that lead to conflict and emotional distress in your relationship.

1 Using a situation that has occurred recently and led to conflict between you and your partner, fill in this log.
2 Identify how this situation relates to ongoing and repetitive patterns of distress in your relationship.
3 Share your log with your partner and discuss the similarities and differences between your responses.
4 Discuss possible alternatives to current ways of responding.
5 The next time you and your partner find yourselves in this repetitive pattern again, try out the alternatives you have thought up in Step 4.

Situation	*Feelings*	*Thoughts*	*Relationship to repetitive pattern in relationship*	*Response*	*Alternative*

Source: Adapted, with permission, from exercises in the STAIR 12-week treatment programme. Cloitre, M., Koenen, K.C., Cohen, L.R., & Han, H. (2002). Skills Training in Affective and Interpersonal Regulation followed by Exposure: A phase-based treatment for PTSD related to childhood abuse. *Journal of Consulting and Clinical Psychology*, *70*, 1067–1074.

Words for expressing feelings

Affectionate
Afraid
Amused
Angry
Annoyed
Anxious
Apathetic
Apprehensive
Ashamed
Bitter
Bored
Calm
Capable
Cheerful
Comfortable
Competent
Concerned
Confident
Confused
Contemptuous
Controlled
Curious
Defeated
Dejected
Delighted
Depressed
Desirable
Despairing
Desperate
Determined
Devastated
Disappointed
Discouraged
Disgusted
Disillusioned
Distrustful
Embarrassed
Enraged
Excited
Frantic
Frightened
Frustrated
Fulfilled
Furious
Generous
Glad
Gloomy
Grateful
Great
Guilty
Happy
Hateful
Helpless
Hopeless
Horrified
Hostile
Impatient
Inadequate
Inhibited
Irritated
Isolated
Jealous
Joyful
Lonely
Loved
Loving
Loyal
Manipulated
Manipulative
Melancholy
Miserable
Misunderstood
Muddled
Needy
Nervous
Numb
Out of control
Outraged
Overwhelmed
Panicky
Passionate
Peaceful
Pessimistic
Pleased
Powerful
Prejudiced
Pressured
Proud
Provoked
Put down
Relaxed
Relieved
Resentful
Resigned
Sad
Safe
Satisfied
Secure
Sexy
Shy
Silly
Strong
Stubborn
Stuck
Supportive
Sympathetic
Tearful
Tender
Terrified
Threatened
Thrilled
Touchy
Trapped
Troubled
Unappreciated
Uncertain
Understood
Uneasy
Unfulfilled
Unimportant
Unloved
Upset
Uptight
Used
Useless
Victimized
Violated
Vulnerable
Withdrawn
Wonderful
Worn out
Worried
Worthwhile
Wronged
Yearning

Note

1 Exploring Learned Emotional Relationships and Dyadic Emotional Coping Exercise are adapted from exercises in the Skills Training in Affect and Interpersonal Regulation therapy model for childhood trauma survivors: M. Cloitre, K.C. Koenen, L.R. Cohen, & H. Han. (2002). Skills training in affective and interpersonal regulation followed by exposure: A phase-based treatment for PTSD related to childhood abuse. *Journal of Consulting and Clinical Psychology*, *70*, 1067–1074.

Chapter 6

Stage Three

Attachment-focused dyadic processing

Introduction

Moving into Stage Three, the focus of DCTCT becomes less psychoeducational and skills based and more process focused. The sessions come to rely less on handouts and containment through cognitive exploration, and place more emphasis on exploring the what is occurring in the session and what has occurred in the couple relationship in the past and in the present. Here we begin to rely on, and continue to build up, the self-capacities developed in Stage Two. While up to this point the psychoeducation and skills-building exercises have been oriented to the dyad, the intervention has primarily been directed towards each individual partner's learning and growing process in relation to their trauma history, as well as beginning to learn and grow with their partner. The primary goal has been, within each couple, that both individuals will have built stronger and more resilient self-capacities, with the hope that the couple would begin to learn that turning towards, rather than away from, one another during times of duress, they could rely on their partner for support in emotion regulation and exploration in mentalizing. At this point in the process, the therapist turns the couple towards each other, to share experiences from their pasts more deeply, establishing connections they will then carry with them into their couple relationship. From this point on, the therapy becomes less directive and focused on the agenda of the therapist and more experiential. The sections within this stage are ordered by how they have most frequently unfolded in couples that I have worked with in my research and practice. However, as you follow a couple's lead, it will become clear where best to focus your interventions. This section of the book is divided into five sections: (1) attachment histories living in the present, (2) working through the Dyadic Traumatic Reenactment, (3) disclosure, (4) trauma processing in a dyadic context, and (5) sex and sexuality.

As with all other stages in this therapy, emotion regulation and mentalizing must be supported throughout. This means that if a partner begins to struggle with emotion regulation – or their mentalizing capacities begin to collapse – slow down, reorient, regroup, and help them regain their capacities in the context of the session. As therapy moves along, you may need occasionally to scaffold the couple by coaching the partners to help one another with emotion regulation – to be able to breathe together, to orient and ground themselves together, and to share the triggers and stressors that might be underlying their moments of loss of capacity, so that they can take that learning into their relationship in the future.

Things to keep in mind as you move through Stage Three

Shame

Before we dive into process-focused work, I want to discuss shame. We talked about shame with our couples in Stage One, exploring various relevant topics to help couples understand the impact of trauma on their lives and relationships. We looked at how shame pervades the emotional lives of survivors and how this shame can ingratiate itself into the bond between the couple, especially as they try to tackle the tough stuff: their needs, grief, pain, and longing for one another. I want to reiterate how important shame is when working with survivors. Shame may infiltrate every nook and cranny of the survivor's emotional world, making the way forward very challenging. Even when approaching the process-oriented work with newfound strong and resilient emotion regulation and mentalizing capacities, shame can rear its ugly head and stop the process flat. Be on the alert for the various ways in which shame may hinder these nascent emotion-regulation and mentalizing skills and how this then impacts the process of therapy. As you get to know the couples, you will identify their vulnerable spots and become more prepared to slow them down and coach them through these shame-filled waters while closely monitoring the survivor's well-being.

Taking care of ourselves – monitoring countertransference

As the emphasis shifts from the work of education and skills building, the therapy moves into the blood, guts, and gore of trauma. Up to now, discussions about the actual details and impacts of the trauma have been held within the realm of thinking and knowing, through deliberate therapeutic containment. The next phase moves into the realm of feeling and sensing. I do not need to tell you how much research there is on the topic of vicarious traumatization; it is voluminous. Providers of mental health care services to survivors of heinous traumas – especially those who were betrayed and violated as vulnerable children – are very vulnerable to trauma symptoms of our own in relation to the stories we see, feel, and hear in our offices every day (Pistorius, Feinauer, Harper, Stahmann, & Miller, 2008; Regehr, Leslie, Howe, & Chau, 2005). In fact, in light of the overwhelming evidence of the impact of work related exposure to trauma, the *Diagnostic and Statistical Manual of Mental Disorders* (DSM) included in its fifth edition the expansion of the diagnostic criteria for PTSD to include exposure to the aversive details of the traumatic event (American Psychiatric Association, 2013).

Every practitioner may have specific vulnerabilities and particular kinds of stories that touch us more deeply than others. These might relate to our own trauma histories or those of our families, prior exposure, or any number of factors that impact our way of experiencing the stories we hear. For instance, I am not a particularly visual person. I am a musician before anything else and process information primarily through my auditory sense. The stories my clients tell me come through my ears, and I do not tend to conjure up graphic pictures of the traumatic details I hear. In some ways this protects me: I do not see images of the bloodied, naked children that I hear about. However, probably because I am so auditory and word oriented, I am particularly vulnerable to stories that are told with strong, sensory language. Those stories penetrate me and have a deep impact. I remember, vividly and at an embodied sensory level, stories that involve graphic descriptions of sensations, bodily fluids, and violence and have a sensory quality; phrases like "the blood was sticky", "the smell was putrid", or "the urine trickled" will paint a picture in my mind that penetrates to my bones and stays with me for a while. Those stories are sticky for me, and I have a hard time leaving them at the end of the day. When I hear stories like that, I have learned that I need to do something to unglue them from my psyche. Ever mindful of confidentiality and the importance of holding these trauma stories with deep respect, I am able to turn to trusted colleagues or supervisors and share the impact and lingering echoes of what I have taken in. It is important that you understand yourself and your vulnerabilities and know when you are falling into a hole. As I tell my students, "never swim alone". If you are doing work with childhood trauma survivors, you absolutely must have a support network of people who get it, people who have been in the trenches, people you trust implicitly, and people who understand you well enough to know your vulnerabilities. Not all workplaces are safe places for you and your vulnerabilities. That does not mean you cannot engage in your own private supervision, keeping the specific details of the stories you hear confidential – and of course, your own psychotherapy is invaluable in protecting you from vicarious traumatization.

Keeping an eye on countertransference is also a way of keeping an eye on vicarious trauma. If you start feeling angry, resentful, or irritated by your couples, it is likely time for a supervision or psychotherapy session. It is hard to work with couples who are in such distress and who carry such hideous stories. These couples become more dysregulated and more distressed; they progress more slowly and more get stuck more frequently; and they are more likely to fall apart or terminate therapy prematurely. When attachment histories are so weak and attachment distress so strong, we feel the anxiety, we see the avoidance, and we may feel unprepared to take on the role of modelling healthy attachment with the couple. When I see myself mirrored in a couple – my own attachment traumas or avoidant habits in my own relationship – I can be triggered into pulling myself away from the couple to protect myself, stepping back behind the veil and hiding my own vulnerability. The problem with this is that childhood trauma survivors can "smell" you pulling back to protect yourself, from a mile away. Staying present is emotionally draining and yet absolutely necessary to gain trust and build safety with a couple that has experienced traumas at the hands of those who should have protected them above their own needs, desires, and self-protection.

Many of us do this work because we genuinely want to have an impact, to offer calm waters in a churning sea for couples who have had so few positive experiences with caregivers. Many of us feel that the work we do is part of our identity, who we are, and it can be hard for us when our best efforts appear to be thwarted by events that occurred decades previously. Frankly, this work is not as overtly rewarding as working with couples who come from reasonably healthy families and have reasonable attachment security between them; these couples progress slowly but surely and usually leave couple therapy more satisfied and connected than they were at the beginning. This is not typically the case with childhood trauma couples. For months and months, the process may appear to make no headway, to achieve no progress. And yet, one day, something breaks open and – wow – there you are, seeing a mind mentalizing their partner in a way that is rich and complex and nuanced, for the first time, or witnessing a survivor turn to their partner to share a deeply shameful secret and experience love, tenderness, and compassion in a gentle embracing response. We need to keep the markers of progress small – each tiny step is progress – and remind ourselves that regardless of how stuck we are and regardless of the outcome of the therapy, this process is providing them with resources they would not have otherwise had access to, as well as new understanding, new skills, and new ways of engaging with others. While this work may not be as overtly and quickly rewarding as work with non-survivors, it can be deeply rewarding if we can keep the long game in view. Helping a couple that has come from the depths of distress with unbearable histories is a long, slow slog with a couple that previously could not imagine feeling safe, loved, close, and content in their relationship. The reward for this work cannot be measured. As a practitioner, you have helped a couple that many or most therapists would shy away from working with. You may have helped their children and their children's children. Just make sure to hold on to yourself, take care of yourself, and know your limits and vulnerabilities.[1] Two books that I have found extremely helpful in my work with couples and in my teaching are:

Dalenberg, C.J. (2000). *Countertransference and the treatment of trauma*. Washington, DC: American Psychological Association.

Pearlman, L.A., & Saakvitne, K.W. (1995). *Trauma and the therapist: Countertransference and vicarious traumatization in psychotherapy with incest survivors*. New York: W.W. Norton & Co.

Attachment histories living in the present

The objective of the psychoeducational section was to help couples develop a cognitive, conscious understanding of the impact of childhood trauma on attachment security. During that process, the therapist usually has the opportunity to learn about the attachment history of the couple and to begin the dialogue about how this history is living in the present. Moving into the processing stage of the treatment, the couple should be encouraged to begin the hard work of trying to shift from insecure to secure ways of being attached to one another. Attachment is not something that changes overnight; it is stable and resistant to change, operating primarily outside of our awareness. At this stage, we are planting some seeds with the hope that, over time, the couple can build up greater security as the partners engage with one another in new attachment-enhancing ways. Before going deeper into trauma-focused work, attachment is crucial, because the couple needs to learn how to turn towards one another, and to comfort and be soothed by one another, before entering into the territory of trauma where they will face significant emotional challenges.

Working models of attachment are both conscious and unconscious. These mental representations guide our expectations in attachment relationships and arise out of early experiences with our caregivers. Over time, we form an understanding of ourselves, of whether we are loveable, and of whether others will be present for us and how we expect them to respond to us (Sandberg, Bradford, & Brown, 2017). For survivors, the idea that we might be loveable, and that others might be there for us when we need them, is often unimaginable. While adult romantic attachment relationships prime similar conscious and unconscious schemas and perform similar relational functions as those of the infant-caregiver attachment system, they are different in at least one important way: they are bi-directional and reciprocal. At any time, either partner may be providing or receiving care and support: being the safe base or using the safe base (Novak, Sandberg, & Busby, 2018).

One of the ways these working models of attachment remain quite stable over one's lifetime is that, as we go out into the world and encounter other humans, we attend to information selectively in ways that confirm our inner working models; in fact, we even engage with others in ways that elicit the responses that fit our expectations about ourselves and others (Pietromonaco & Feldman Barrett, 2000). However, more and more research demonstrates that attachment styles can and do change as a result of interpersonal experiences that disconfirm our pre-existing expectations, including experiences facilitated through therapy (Crowell & Treboux, 1995, Chris Fraley, 2002).

The psychoeducational module about attachment discussed the origins and characteristics of attachment styles, the ways we most typically relate to others (Mikulincer & Shaver, 2007). Moving into the work of shifting couple attachment insecurity towards security, the sessions at this stage will delve deeper into couple's understanding of their attachment styles and how trauma impacts the potential development of secure attachment. They will scrutinize the historical experiences that fuel their attachment representations and expectations of each other. Getting a more detailed understanding of each partner's attachment history is a good place to start, asking questions that explore closeness, safety, trust, and intimacy in childhood. These questions are slanted towards the possibility that the survivor might have experienced some positive attachment-enhancing relationships. The powerful impact on a child when even one person – a teacher, babysitter, coach, or other interested adult – spends time and does not violate the child's vulnerability, cannot be overestimated. In my case, it was my grandmother who accepted me unconditionally, thought I was smart and funny, and simply enjoyed spending time with me. Some questions that you might start with include:

Who were the people you felt close to, as a child?
Who were your role models growing up, and why?
When you were upset as a child, who did you go to?
When you were upset as a child, what did you do?
What is your earliest memory of being taken care of or comforted?
Who were the people you felt comfortable being held or hugged by?
What was it like to be sick in your family?
What can you tell us about your family, the relationships with siblings or your parents, grandparents, aunts, and uncles, growing up?
Do you remember being separated from your parents/caregiver as a child? If so, for how long and why?
Do you remember how you felt when that happened?

The impact of trauma caused by trusted adults cannot be ignored, but the possibility that the survivor might have experienced some positive, security-enhancing relationships or aspects should also be explored. The differences for survivors whose traumas occurred within the family and those whose traumas occurred outside of it will be significant, and this is an important place to begin this conversation. Survivors may find these questions distressing, if they cannot recollect any positive experiences, and become overwhelmed with shame and hopelessness. Normalizing and soothing the survivor in the face of these stark realities is slim consolation, but the therapist can be present in the undissociated process of grieving. Many survivors, especially those oriented towards avoidance, will have avoided facing these realities head-on and have resisted being fully immersed in their grief (Stark, 2002). This resistance makes it even harder to be close to anyone now in the present. Helping the survivor reframe their history in terms of resiliency and the miraculous capacities they have developed that allow them now to be in a romantic relationship, regardless of the couple's struggles, orients the survivor into the present. Some questions to ask, to tap into the traumatic aspects of the couple's early attachment experiences (and to be adapted based on your understanding of the trauma history of the couple), include the following:

> You've told me that the person who abused you was (X – father, mother, etc.). Were there times when you felt cared for or comforted by them in spite of the abuse?
>
> If yes:
> What was this like for you? Were there times when this was confusing for you?
> If no:
> Was there anyone you could turn to for comfort even when you were being abused?
>
> You've told me that your (father, mother, uncle) was your primary abuser. Did your (other parent or family member) know about the abuse?
>
> If yes:
> How did they respond? Did they provide you with any support? Did you have any therapy or help at that time?
> If no:
> Were you able to get any support from them even with them not knowing about the abuse? Did you ever think about telling them? What stopped you?

These questions are directed at learning more about how the abuse impacted the survivor's feelings about closeness and security in relationships. Use your knowledge of the family of origin, experiences of the survivor, and your understanding of attachment theory to tailor your questions to the particular context of each couple.

At this point, the therapeutic process must take into account the two dimensions underlying how we experience attachment: avoidance, the tendency to deny attachment needs and suppress attachment-related thoughts and feelings, and anxiety, the tendency to fear abandonment and assume unavailability by the attachment figure. These questions are oriented in the present and relate to the current adult attachment relationship. The goal is to assess the survivor's level of comfort with closeness (avoidance) and confidence in the availability of their partner-attachment figure to be there for them (anxiety). Some useful questions might include:

> When you are distressed, how confident are you that your partner will be there for you?
> Can you describe a time when your partner really supported you?
> Can you describe a time when your partner really did not support you when you needed them?
> When you are distressed, how comfortable are you talking about your feelings with your partner?
> Do you easily share your thoughts and feelings with your partner?
> On a scale of 1 to 10, where 1 is not at all afraid and 10 is completely terrified, how afraid are you that your partner might leave you?
> How comfortable are you when your partner needs you?
> How easy is it for you to provide comfort and support to your partner when they are having a hard time?

Of course, these kinds of questions can be extremely loaded for survivors and could open up a can of worms. This is a first test of the braking system: does the couple have emotion regulation and mentalizing capacities on line as the discussion deepens about potentially triggering emotional and relational experiences? If they do, off you go. If they do not: slow things down, go back around the block, and start again as many times as required. This is not a test of speed, it is a test of endurance: slow but steady wins the race.

As therapists, we talk about attachment styles and working clinically to help shift couples from insecurity towards security, but what does that really mean and how do we go about doing it? When so much of attachment is unconscious and reinforced by an invisible process of directing attention towards interpersonal evidence that confirms attachment expectations and away from disconfirming evidence, how can therapists intervene? Most of the research in the area of adult attachment has focused on attachment styles – the feelings, beliefs, and expectations about the partner, often operating outside of awareness – and how these play out within a couple. Very little attention has been paid to the behaviours that reflect attachment and that might promote security or insecurity (Alexandrov, Cowan, & Cowan, 2005; Feeney, 2008; Wampler, Riggs, & Kimball, 2004). It seems that attachment styles and attachment behaviours are correlated but different, and both are important for therapists to keep in mind, especially as they work with couples with histories of attachment trauma (Knapp, Sandberg, Novak, & Larson, 2015; Sandberg et al., 2017).

What this means for therapists is that while attachment styles operate mostly outside of individual awareness, we can help couples learn how to respond to one another to enhance security through attachment behaviours. Trying new behaviours associated with secure attachment may help the couple gradually shift from insecurity towards security in their attachment-orienting behaviours with one another. This will deal with the conscious, behavioural aspect of attachment, helping couples *do* something differently in relation to their partner, demonstrating their interest in being accessible and reliable. How, then, do we address the significant contribution of unconscious factors that are not behavioural: deep feelings and unconscious priming of responses and expectations, selective attention to confirming interpersonal experiences, and suppression of awareness of disconfirming evidence? These aspects of attachment can take years of slow but steady work in therapy and in life, with close, reliable, and available others, to come to the surface and gradually change. The reality is that, in most contexts, that kind of long-term therapy is not possible due to financial limitations, agency policies, or other external restrictions on the length of work. One of the ways to nudge the survivor, gently, to dislodge unconscious aspects of attachment is to work from the top down, from the cognitive and behavioural aspects to those that lie outside conscious awareness. Through being coached into engaging in new behaviours with their partners, survivors will confront those unconscious forces – their anxiety about closeness, their urge to avoid an emotionally challenging situation, or the pull away from attending to the new behaviours in their partner. Essentially, a clinical laboratory is established for new attachment experiences during the sessions, holding and containing the couple as they come up against their internal working models, learn to tolerate novel, disconfirming evidence, and try new attachment-related behaviours with their partner. Through trying a new behaviour – through doing – the unconscious underbelly of historical attachment traumas can be awakened, while containing the potential for emotional dysregulation and the collapse of mentalizing as the survivor pushes through to something new.

However, that description makes the process sound much easier than it actually is. Just help couples to do something different, and their attachment towards one another will become more secure – the reality is much harder than it sounds. Therapists are asking survivors to *do* something that they learned *not to do* because it was dangerous for their psychic survival, to try a new behaviour that they have rejected over and over again because it was terrifying even on an unconscious level. Survivors will need help every step of the way. Those internal obstacles to new security-enhancing behaviours generally operate outside of conscious awareness. The incomplete homework and untried new behaviours, the inability to tolerate deeply desired support when it is offered, all of these obstacles cannot be explained cognitively because the "real" explanation defies awareness. It may be tempting to label these stuck spots as "resistance", or to say that the couple is not ready for therapy. However, such an approach will help no one: by those definitions of readiness, survivor couples will most likely never be ready. Like ironing a beautiful pair of linen pants that never seem to be wrinkle free, we need to patiently go back, over and over again, until the thing that makes change seem impossible softens or moves aside and the impossible becomes possible. I often have no idea exactly why this happens, when it will happen or how, but this does not really matter. Some things will never be consciously "known", but the degree of awareness that allows for change is enough. Go slowly, scaffold those emotion regulation and mentalizing capacities, and model the secure attachment figure they need as they come out of insecurity. Let them rely on you as a safe haven and secure base, while they try these new and terrifying behaviours that are associated with promoting attachment security.

The relationship between attachment security and attachment-enhancing behaviours is reciprocal: when people feel more secure, they behave in ways that promote attachment security in their partners (Mikulincer & Shaver, 2007). To maintain attachment security, partners need to be good both at giving and receiving, at being both seekers and providers of comfort and support (Feeney & Collins, 2004). However, a reciprocal relationship between insecurity and behaviours can also get in the way of security. Failed support seeking contributes to failed support giving, and these behaviours become the norm against which the expectations for the couple become solidified. As one might expect, avoidant partners seek support less, but they also provide less support and respond negatively to the support-seeking behaviours of their partners. Avoidantly attached partners are also likely to avoid conflict due to the need to maintain emotional distance, which leaves problems unresolved and results in increased, rather than decreased, levels of conflict in the long run (Mikulincer & Shaver, 2007). The overall strategy of avoidance aims to hold their partner at a safe emotional distance, but this results in a double isolation as both partner's needs remain unmet. Over time, these behaviours escalate, as a vicious cycle increases avoidance in both partners in response to less support seeking, and the resulting decrease in support receiving (Collins & Feeney, 2000; Fraley & Shaver, 1998). Anxiously attached partners also provide less support, tend to be less responsive, and see their partners as needing more support, and their caregiving is often out of synch with the needs of their partners. It seems that, regardless of the partner's level of need, anxious partners provide the same amount of care, as though the care provision relates to their own anxiety rather than their partner's needs (Kunce & Shaver, 1994). Partners of anxiously attached persons may try to increase their level of support to respond to the high level of need, and may themselves become anxious in response to the anxiety of their anxious partner: around and around it goes.

Introduce the idea that the couple can bring about change by gradually, thoughtfully, and intentionally engaging with one another in new and different ways. Secure base processes, or behaviours that promote attachment security, are behaviours that can be learned, practiced, and normalized (Davila & Kashy, 2009). These behaviours are characterized by emotional accessibility, responsiveness, and engagement (Novak et al., 2018). Couples that are stuck in a perpetual cycle of disengagement and unresponsiveness need to learn a few new steps to their attachment dance. The first of these involves distressed partners making a clearly expressed statement of need. The dance continues as the supporting partner demonstrates concern and interest in the distressed partner's expression of need, receives the message, and responds with support. The final step in the dance involves the distressed partner feeling supported and comforted, and thus reducing their stress (Crowell et al., 1998).

For survivor couples, trying these new ways of engaging with one another may feel like a huge risk. Learning how to ask for help, how to provide support, and how to turn to one another to regulate distress: these are risks necessary for the couple to shift into more secure attachment, and may also feel quite terrifying. Overcoming this will take modelling and role playing within the sessions. Many survivors will also believe that they are already doing these things: asking for help, offering support, giving, and receiving. Often, upon deeper exploration, we find that the messages of need are unclear and cloaked in faulty mentalization: he should have known I was in distress – I was crying in the bathroom – when the partner was out of earshot cutting the hedge with a loud chainsaw in the backyard. On close examination, we also often discover that support behaviours are quickly withdrawn in response to any obstacles to open and easy receipt. Details are required here – do not take the couple's word for it – the therapist must take these interactions apart piece by piece, step by step. Simply talking about what behaviours might facilitate attachment security is not enough: the couple must practice new ways of engaging with one another to break through the unconscious barriers that pull them back to their habitual ways of being with one another. We need to find ways to bring avoidant partners in closer, to help them buy into the importance of learning new behaviours. Moving towards their partner to seek and to give support will feel very foreign. Within the confines of a safe therapeutic relationship, your support will be crucial to help the couple explore possible new patterns. It will take many tries before an avoidant partner will not feel daunted when moving towards their partner rather than away. It will take many tries before an anxious partner will be regulated enough to receive support fully and feel confident in and comforted by their partner. Help the couple attend to such new experiences as a way of disconfirming old working models of attachment and beginning to build a new, secure attachment with the partner. Help them notice when their partner is reaching for them; help them find the language and the confidence to respond with support. In the following session segments, you will see an early session that pulls apart the sticky grip of history on current interactions, as well as sessions later in the process where I am coaching the couple to try something new and supporting them as they try and try again.

In this segment, Chris and Camille are struggling with the interplay between Chris's anxiety and Camille's avoidance. You can see vividly the interweaving of mentalizing challenges, attachment expectations, and struggles with emotion regulation into the need to dramatically pursue or frighteningly withdraw. As Chris discusses the origins of his anxiety in his relationship with his father, he is able to make the connection to his anxiety about his attachment with Camille. However, he struggles with the task of mentalizing in relation to Camille as her needs for support do not coincide with Chris's assumptions and beliefs about what it should look like to provide and to receive comfort. Here the importance of both support-seeking and support-providing roles becomes clear. Providing support is important to instil confidence and security in both the relationship provider and the receiver. The capacity to use an attachment relationship for mutual regulation is hindered when both partners, even the support provider, do not feel that their needs are being met.

CHRIS: Well, I can't understand how she can't want to be touched, you know? And, I just forget – well it's not like I forget, I just can't deal with not being physically in contact with her. She tells me she is upset and that she is feeling really triggered and then she just shuts me out and doesn't let me get anywhere near her. I feel like I'm completely being shut out and I'm alone in the universe and nobody cares about me and, and that if she doesn't want me to touch her, then I'm some kind of monster that is ruining her life.

THERAPIST: So, for you, when she doesn't want to be touched and you know she's in distress, it feels as though (a) you're not doing your job, because to do your job would be to be in physical contact, because that's what you would like if you were that distressed, and (b) you feel set adrift, you feel like she's rejecting you. You're all alone. And then what happens?

CHRIS: Well, I usually touch her, and then she freaks out, and then I try to stop, and then I can't, and I do it again, and then she freaks out even more, and then I just keep pushing her to the point where she's completely, shut down and then – we don't have any communication – I just end up getting mad or annoyed, or hurt, or sad, or whatever, and then she's the same way. So, it just doesn't work.

THERAPIST: So you know at the head level. . .

CHRIS: Yeah. I know. But I just can't stop it, it's just, like, I have to.

THERAPIST: So the brain is saying, "don't do it, Chris" and there's something happening at another level that's saying: I have to, I have to, I have to, and what – what can you tell me about that feeling? The strength, quality?

Chris's difficulty with mentalizing was evident, as he tried to adapt his support-provision strategy to fit with Camille's specific triggers and her needs for contact in the context of her sexual trauma. Chris's struggles with emotion regulation were also revealed, as he described how dysregulated he becomes when Camille does not accept his gestures of support. Support provision is an essential aspect of one's feelings of confidence and competence in a relationship. In this case the anxious partner, Chris, was not responding in synch with his partner's needs; as a result, the support provider ended up becoming distressed. This began as an example of Camille being distressed and yet the discussion shifted to how upset Chris became in trying to respond to her distress. As the session continued, I coached Chris to regulate his distress, to facilitate his capacity to better read Camille's cues. As Chris became more regulated, I turned to Camille in the hopes that she would also become more aware of her avoidance and learn how to more clearly signal her distress and her specific needs for support.

THERAPIST: Chris, what is the cue that you get that Camille is starting to be overwhelmed by your attempts to support her with touch?

CHRIS: I don't really know.

THERAPIST: Okay.

CHRIS: I just, kind of, I get it after a while.

THERAPIST: So it isn't something specific, but you start to pick up on it?

CHRIS: Yeah.

THERAPIST: And what are the cues that you get from Camille, when you start to pick up on her distress? Is there something she says, something that happens in her body, in her non-verbal cues?

CHRIS: Well, she'll either tell me that it's too much or she'll start getting colder, which is hard for me, because the more she gets cold, the more I want to touch her because I feel – why do you not like this? It doesn't make any sense to me that you don't like this. I feel like she hates me and I try harder and it's just. . .

THERAPIST: Around and around and around?

CHRIS: Yeah, it's constant.

THERAPIST: So, in your mind, you're picking up on cues that tell you that your touch and approach is too much for her. You're also thinking, "this doesn't make any sense to me; people who love each other touch, and hug, and connect, and if she loved me, she would want to do this; this is what normal people do" . . .

CHRIS: Yes, and for me I need physical contact with someone. I just don't feel like I'm getting any kind of love if she doesn't let me touch her, you know?

THERAPIST: Let you touch her. . . . So it feels like she's. . .

CHRIS: It feels like she's running away from me.

THERAPIST: And if she loved you, she would let you, because she should know, that this is how you feel better, grounded, contained, settled?

CHRIS: Yeah, but it's not easy, because I also know that I'm, like, a lot.

THERAPIST: Okay. So, you [to Camille] know this about Chris; this is not news?

CAMILLE: Yup.

THERAPIST: Can you tell me more about how you communicate the cue that it's too much for you, that you are feeling overwhelmed?

CAMILLE: I'll often say stuff like, "Chris, it's a bit too much right now; can you just tone it down", or, "I'm feeling anxious right now", or, "I had a long day, and I don't feel comfortable doing this". I can feel myself stiffening up.

THERAPIST: So, you start with words and then your body starts to stiffen up.

CAMILLE: I say these things so that Chris knows. At the same time, I just physically don't feel comfortable with it.

THERAPIST: So your head says, Chris needs a lot of physical contact to feel soothed and comforted. Your own body reaction, emotional reaction, is to start to feel tense and uncomfortable – when you feel squished.

CAMILLE: Yeah.

THERAPIST: So you have these messages going on inside of you, and then, ultimately, what happens?

CAMILLE: Well, I don't actually see them as working against each other. I feel like – okay, if this is the level of affection that Chris wants to give me at this amount of time because I'm upset, okay? [lifts hands to mark a high level] I probably only need about this. [lowers hands to mark a low level] I'm willing to meet half way. [lifts hands up to mark a middle level]

THERAPIST: You feel like there could be some space for negotiation so that both of you could find a comfortable middle ground?

CAMILLE: Well, I mean, it's just – I can't stand this, this [high hands] level. That level would be me, if someone died or something. If I'm upset about something I want to hug him, but it's just – I can't go all the way to there. [hands high again]

THERAPIST: So what you're saying, then – and correct me, if I'm getting it wrong – what you're saying is, everybody needs something different; I understand that Chris needs something different than me but I can't quite tolerate what Chris needs when I'm upset. You're willing to meet him half way when he's upset, but you wish he could understand that what you need – is different.

Camille found it easy to express her awareness of the difference in needs for comforting contact between them but demonstrated little awareness of the impact of her own avoidance of closeness on Chris's attachment anxiety. She did, however, express an interest in finding a solution to the disparity between their needs for proximity by finding a middle ground. Remembering that this conversation had begun with a discussion of how Chris attempts to provide support to Camille after she expresses her distress: we have ended up turning attention to Chris's distress when Camille does not accept his provision of care, and this then shifted to an exploration of Chris's anxiety in relation to his needs for contact after feeling rejected. The reciprocity of anxiety and avoidance could be seen here as Chris's anxiety about his attachment to Camille being picked up in Camille's dysregulation around his pursuit of contact with her, and avoidance is reinforced. It was hard for Camille to see that, paradoxically, reducing her avoidance and moving closer to Chris would likely lead to decreases in Chris's anxiety over time, allowing him to back up a bit and eventually, cultivating this middle ground she seeks.

THERAPIST: I think there's something there, Chris, when you feel that need for contact, for reunion after conflict, even when that conflict is about how you learn to read Camille's cues about what she needs from you as support when she is distressed. There's a need to reattach, as though there's a risk you aren't attached, that when you see her you have to reattach.

CHRIS: Yeah.

THERAPIST: It's bigger than just "hey, how are you?". It's "hey, do you still love me; are you still there; do you still want me?" It's bigger than coming back together and feeling secure; it's – are you still there, are you still mine, will you still respond to me?

CHRIS: Yeah.

THERAPIST: So that security, trusting that she'll come back, it just isn't there. And when you can't get close to her in the way that you feel you would like if you were distressed you need to, all of your anxieties bubble up.

CHRIS: I feel like a puppy dog that hasn't seen their owner in 6 hours. You know how ridiculous they are. They chase their own tail; they jump all over – that's how I feel.

THERAPIST: Do you have a theory about why that is that you struggle so much with feeling soothed?

CHRIS: Yeah, because my dad used to not talk to me for weeks and all of a sudden, he'd come back and he'd say whatever, you know? And I was like, okay, I guess we're allowed to be humans together.

THERAPIST: Can you give me an example of a time that happened?

CHRIS: All the time. That was my entire life with my dad. I would make a small little mistake, and then that was the end of the world for him, so then he would not speak to me for the entire day, or the entire next two or three days.

THERAPIST: Can you give me an example? Do you remember a specific time when that happened?

CHRIS: No, I'm not joking. It was all the time.

THERAPIST: I'd really like to get a specific example so that I can really get the feel of it with you.

CHRIS: [sighs] I don't know. I don't really have any specific examples that I can think of. It could be for anything. It could be something as stupid as leaving a bowl on the computer desk. He'd come over and say, "I need you to clean that up". And then I'd forget to do it, you know? I'd get involved in what I was doing and forget to do it and then 2 hours later he'd come in say "I told you to do this, ahahaha, you're so useless and messy blah blah blah blah", and he wouldn't talk to me for hours, and hours, and hours, and I'd have to chase him around the house and make sure we were still okay and he could still be my dad. I would go clean it up and that was it. Basically, it would just feel like, he's my dad, he's my dad, he's my dad, I did something wrong so now he's just this person that lives with me and I need to chase after him to make him my dad again. And then he's my dad again, he's my dad, he's my dad, I did something wrong. I was constantly chasing after him. It never felt like he was always my father, you know?

Chris could not come up with specific examples, which may reflect the way these experiences of unpredictable rejection had become one big, amorphous blob of what attachment is all about. It could also mean that he was using an avoidance strategy to manage his distress about overwhelming experiences of attachment rejection, while his latent anxiety was popping up all over the place with Camille. These experiences were no longer discrete entities but, rather, one big fuzzy, overarching expectation that would overwrite any other or newer attachment experiences, limiting Chris's ability to reflect on his own attachment experiences, new and old. Specific examples can help bridge the connection between unconscious, the accumulation of disavowed memories of rejection bundled up into a working model of self and others, and current behaviours that have not been recognized as having their origins in the past. Persistently trying to find those specific memories can be one way to uproot the dormant, unquestioned expectations and bring them into awareness. With exposure to the memories that have been avoided and that led to current attachment strategies, avoidance of the underworld can be lessened, making room for new thoughts, feelings, and behaviours. As we moved towards the end of the session, I wanted to make sure that Chris had connected the dots from his current behaviour and feelings back to the historical experiences with his father and again back to the present.

THERAPIST: It's not the cognitive level we're interested in: you are good at the thinking part of things. We're interested in your way of being attached to people. There's a deep anxiety in your attachments that can come from these experiences of being rejected and then having to struggle for reunion.

CHRIS: Yeah, but I guess I never really thought about it being about my dad. I always thought it was just, like, me.

THERAPIST: Again, it's not about something wrong with your thinking, it's about what goes on inside of you. So I would love it if over the next week you would sit down, with a journal, and try to bring to mind some specific examples. Right now it's this formless void of a generalized attachment expectation, which is: I'm going to have to fight to continue to be attached to you, because I made some small error which is really inconsequential and you shunned me. What would be helpful to us is to have some specific examples that we can start to dig into, to help us understand more deeply, from the inside out.

CHRIS: I get the same thing from Camille. It's like – the one time that I make a mess, it's just a mess, it's not the end of the world, but we just lost our attachment because of that. Because now I have to chase after you and make sure that our relationship is okay just because I made a mess. That's what it feels like to me. It feels like. . .

THERAPIST: It's broken. . .

CHRIS: We've lost – we were 100% in love and now we're only 40% in love, because I made a mess, a stupid mess.

THERAPIST: For you, the consequence of a small error is to lose attachment. And it's very hard for you to imagine – I think impossible at this point – that Camille could still love you, want to be with you, and also not want to be touched by you when she is distressed. It's like, those two things don't go together.

CHRIS: No, they don't, because dad wouldn't.

THERAPIST: Right.

This process dealt with signal and response: Camille's ability to provide a clear signal of distress and Chris's capacity to receive this signal and to regulate himself well enough to respond in a way that would be empathic to her needs rather than focused around his own attachment anxiety. In the next example, I was working with Anush and Amira to increase attachment security and was actively helping the couple learn to engage more clearly and intentionally in secure base behaviours more clearly. By exploring Anush's unconscious urge to pull away from Amira as she moved closer to him, and the lack of clarity in Amira's signals for support, I was trying to create an opportunity to practice a secure base process and deal with the ensuing feelings. Here, both partners used avoidance as a primary strategy to manage attachment-related feelings – Anush by avoiding Amira's desire to respond to his trauma and Amira avoiding clear signals of her need for communication and sexual connection due to her internalized expectation that her needs would not be met.

AMIRA: I think, in a way, we've just accepted it. There's only so many times you can be rejected before you give up.

THERAPIST: Well, you didn't accept the lack of sexual closeness.

AMIRA: No. Even last week I tried again to talk to him about it and he just shut me out.

THERAPIST: How did you approach him to talk about that?

AMIRA: I guess I just asked him.

THERAPIST: Can you take it apart for me, step by step?

AMIRA: Well, he was in the basement watching hockey, again. I put our daughter to bed and went down and sat with him and asked him what he was thinking about. He said "hockey" and laughed and that was it.

THERAPIST: Hmmm, tell me about the part where you tried to talk to him about sex.

AMIRA: Well, that was it.

THERAPIST: Okay, but what I heard was a conversation about hockey. It sounds as though you were trying to find a way to talk to Anush about sex, but your signal wasn't clear and you didn't persevere after your first attempt.

ANUSH: I had no idea.

AMIRA: I suppose that's true, I just give up.

THERAPIST: It seems like you did give up in some ways and you have both come to accept that you would both be thinking about your emotional connection separately, that there wouldn't be a back and forth about how you talk about your relationship. Like when you're [to Anush] having that feeling of pulling back, you don't say to her, "You know, I don't know what's going on for me – because I think it's great that you're being playful with me – but I'm feeling like pulling back, and I don't know what that means".

AMIRA: Yeah, we don't have that discussion.

THERAPIST: You don't have that. When you are able to have that conversation, you have context and you can know that he's not pulling away because of some negative reaction. It's something going on inside of him that you can then talk about, "Well, I wonder what that might be". It's like all of the feeling and thinking about your closeness and your relationship happens inside your own heads, but not between the two of you. And when there isn't trauma, couples don't necessarily have to have those conversations. Someone gets sick, or something happens, and they are able to turn to one another for support and comfort and talk about what's going on and how they feel. But for you guys, your reactions to things are based on what has happened in the past – instead of what's happening now. You're both reacting to now based on something that's from another time. When that happens in a couple, it's really important to start to learn how to talk about it.

AMIRA: Yeah. I don't know that you're feeling like you need to pull away, how could I know if you don't tell me? You just seem to disappear.

THERAPIST: How would you know?

AMIRA: Well, he just pulls back.

THERAPIST: In the moment, how aware are you [to Anush] of that pulling away and shutting down?

ANUSH: Well, when we're here talking about it, it's easier to think about it than when it's happening. In the moment it's happening, I'm probably not thinking about it to myself, it just happens.

THERAPIST: It's just happening.

ANUSH: It's just happening.

THERAPIST: Right.

ANUSH: Right. And then I'll be just kind of like. . . [makes a gesture indicating turning away]

THERAPIST: At what point do you become aware of the urge to turn away?

ANUSH: After it's happened. When I stop and I'm not busy with something.

THERAPIST: When you have space.

ANUSH: Which would probably be when I'm going to bed. When I'm trying to fall asleep everything comes into my mind.

Anush was not aware of anything that happened inside of himself as he turned away from Amira. Trying to help him tap into any internal signals led to a small window of potential awareness that he was suppressing thoughts and feelings that might allow him to understand himself and of the space he needs to breathe and try something different. In the previous exchange we saw that Amira's signals to Anush for closeness were neither clear nor sustained, while Anush's response was simply to avoid and turn away. I was trying to provide language to make hidden experiences known and to help the couple imagine that there might be other ways to engage with one another. Avoidance that is outside of consciousness cannot be tackled directly, but consistently and persistently challenging avoidance can bring the supports for avoidance to the surface to be explored, understood, and revised.

THERAPIST: I wonder if that might be the time to share those thoughts and feelings, when they start to come up?

ANUSH: Not really, when I'm working around the house – or when we're playing with our daughter.

THERAPIST: It's when you stop. And you don't stop that often.

ANUSH: No. But I mean . . . I've noticed sometimes that when I'm thinking or feeling those things, I will hold on to her.

THERAPIST: Physically?

ANUSH: Yeah.

THERAPIST: Okay. So, you're communicating in one way.

ANUSH: Yeah. I may not say something, but I'll hold her.

THERAPIST: What would stop you from saying something? Letting her know that you want to be close to her?

ANUSH: I'm thinking maybe I'm showing her like that. But I don't . . . I don't know how.

Anush was trying to signal to Amira that he loves her and that he wants to be closer to her, but his message lacked clarity and specificity. He could not tell her with words or respond directly to her statements of need, but in a way he was saying, "this is the best I can do". As I started to unpack this interaction in the session, it became clearer that Anush's avoidance masked major anxiety about his attachment to Amira. However, he was neither able to signal his anxiety clearly to Amira nor could he engage Amira in a way that either of them would find soothing. The sad irony for so many couples, especially trauma survivor couples, is that the very thing they need is something they simply cannot get.

THERAPIST: [to Amira] What do you think?

AMIRA: I think holding on to me . . . well, I don't think that that's expressing that you're feeling like you need to pull back. Or did I misunderstand.

ANUSH: It's just kind of . . . I don't know . . . it's just reassurance.

AMIRA: Okay.

ANUSH: Like when I'm feeling those things, it seems like my response is to hold on to you. And that kind of. . .

AMIRA: That helps you get over the pulling back?

ANUSH: It's that . . . I guess I'm trying to show myself I'm not pulling back.

THERAPIST: You pull back and you busy yourself – busy busy busy busy busy – and you go to bed and you stop moving, and then the feelings and the thoughts start to emerge about what it means to be close, your fears, your discomfort – whatever it is – and you reach for her. You hold her. And that soothes you. So, without Amira ever knowing what she's soothing you for, you feel better.

ANUSH: Yeah.

THERAPIST: What do you think about it?

AMIRA: I think that's okay, if it helps him to feel better.

THERAPIST: How would you feel if he talked to you about those feelings?

AMIRA: I think it would help both of us, because it'll help us get an understanding of where it's coming from. . .

THERAPIST: So you would welcome that?

AMIRA: Yeah.

ANUSH: That'll be hard for me to figure out a way how to say it, describe it, besides just physically showing it.

THERAPIST: Could you even say something like, "I'm feeling that feeling again".

ANUSH: Yeah, I guess I could try.

THERAPIST: It could be a good conversation opener.

AMIRA: But then I would probably annoy you, because I'd want to know, "What does it feel like?" [both laugh]

THERAPIST: You'd be interested in him and his feelings.

AMIRA: Yes, I want to understand him.

THERAPIST: Well, let's see if we can try to have that conversation here. Okay?

ANUSH: Um, I guess so.

THERAPIST: Well, it seems that things get turned upside down when the two of you are trying to find ways to get closer to one another. Let's see if I can summarize the pattern the two of you are stuck in. Amira, you want Anush to come towards you, but you've given up on asking and are waiting for him to come to you without sending him any signal that you need him. Anush, you find yourself pulling back when you feel Amira coming close to you and then you feel anxious and fearful and hold her, trying to show her that you want and need her, but she doesn't get that message. Does that sound about right?

AMIRA: Yeah, that sounds about right.

ANUSH: Yeah.

THERAPIST: Let's start by taking it apart in terms of what we talked about attachment. For a couple to feel secure and close with one another, part of what needs to happen is that they figure out how to signal their distress to their partner and respond to each other. If we look at the scenario you were telling me about, Amira, you were wanting to get close to Anush to talk about your sexual relationship but when you tried to talk to him you were vague and then you gave up before you even began. Amira, if you were to ask Anush to talk, to put words to what you really wanted to say, all of the words, what would they be? All of the thoughts and the feelings in there.

AMIRA: Well, I guess I wanted to say that I was feeling lonely and I was angry at him for pulling away again and again and again. And yes, I wanted to talk about sex, but I guess it was mostly that I was feeling sad about how much we've grown apart over the years.

THERAPIST: That was much clearer. I wonder how Anush would have responded had he heard that. Amira, can you try again? Can you try to start that conversation with Anush and really let him know what it is you need?

AMIRA: Oof, I don't know. I don't know.

THERAPIST: What would make that hard for you?

AMIRA: Like I said, I've given up.

THERAPIST: So might that have had something to do with how hard it was for you to send a clear signal to Anush about your feelings and your desire to have a conversation about your closeness and sexual relationship?

AMIRA: I suppose, yes; I hadn't thought that, but it makes sense.

THERAPIST: Let's try again. I know it will be hard, but let's try.

AMIRA: Okay. . . [long pause] . . . [to Anush] I just wanted to talk about us, really, about why we never have sex, why we . . . I don't know . . . just I'm lonely.

THERAPIST: Good, that was clear and specific. How did that feel?

AMIRA: Okay, I guess. Weird . . . uncomfortable.

THERAPIST: Anush, tell me what you heard Amira say.

ANUSH: Um, that she's unhappy, I guess.

THERAPIST: So, you heard, unhappy?

ANUSH: Yeah.

THERAPIST: Amira, were you asking Anush to talk because you were feeling unhappy?

AMIRA: No, how did he get that from what I said? This is why I feel so hopeless. It doesn't matter what I do or say, he just gets the wrong idea.

THERAPIST: Let's just slow down and back up and try again. Anush, let's look at how you got to hearing "unhappy" from what Amira said. When Amira said that she was feeling lonely and wanting to talk about your sexual relationship, you heard "unhappy".

ANUSH: Well, that's what it means.

THERAPIST: How do you know that's what it means?

ANUSH: It does, doesn't it?

AMIRA: No, it doesn't. I wish you would listen to me. I just want to talk to you, but you don't want to be anywhere near me!

THERAPIST: So you both kind of jumped there – Anush, you jumped from lonely to unhappy and Amira, you jumped from Anush making a jump about what you are feeling to him not wanting to be with you at all. What do you think just happened there?

ANUSH: What happens every time we try to figure this stuff out! [everyone laughs]

THERAPIST: Anush, you're laughing but I think you're right, every time the two of you try to talk about your relationship and your desire to be closer it seems you both end up hearing what you expect to hear rather than what your partner is actually saying – Amira, you hear that Anush doesn't want you and, Anush, you hear that Amira is unhappy with you. Let's try this again, we'll just go as slowly as we need to get to the point that you are actually hearing and taking in what each are saying. Amira, you were feeling lonely and wanting to talk to Anush about your sexual relationship, let's try telling him that again.

AMIRA: That's all, I'm lonely, I wish we could have sex, I wish we could be closer. That's it. I'm not unhappy, well, not all the time, I just want to be closer to you.

ANUSH: Okay, so, why aren't you unhappy if I can't give you want you need?

THERAPIST: Anush, let's back up the truck, Amira is telling you that she wants to be closer to you and it's really hard for you to hear that, to stay with her desire to be closer, you go straight into unhappy again, only this time it's with a question mark. I know that that is what you expect, but let's see if you can focus on what Amira *is* saying and not what she *isn't* saying.

ANUSH: I guess so, but, I don't know what to do.

THERAPIST: Well, Amira has expressed a need, so it seems to me that the thing to do is to listen and respond. What is she asking for?

ANUSH: To talk?

AMIRA: That's all.

THERAPIST: Good, so, Amira wants to talk. Anush, how do you feel about that?

ANUSH: Okay, I guess . . . I'm not so good at that.

THERAPIST: Well, let's start by just listening, maybe that would be a good start.

From there, the couple was able to make a try at a conversation about their current levels of closeness. Coaching the couple to engage in secure base behaviour was challenging. At every turn, their expectations trumped their perceptions, as each "heard" what they expected to hear rather than what their partners actually said. Additionally, it was very difficult for Anush to tolerate remaining present for Amira's expression of need and to respond. After a few tries, he was able to do it in spite of his distress. Using a full session, we were able to enact one complete secure base process. Amira was able to fully, clearly, and specifically express her need – her desire to talk with Anush about their closeness and sexual relationship. She was also able to persist in her signalling, with support from me, until Anush could hear her. After a few tries, which included misinterpretations on both sides, Anush was able to listen and, eventually, engage with her, in spite of his anxiety about not getting it right or even making things worse. Amira was able to receive Anush's efforts to support her by engaging with her and being present in the much-needed conversation about their attachment. In the end, she felt comforted and soothed, and Anush felt more confident and competent. Unconscious aspects of both of their attachment insecurities reared their heads as we attempted to try new attachment-enhancing behaviours. We simply slowed down, clarified the difference between the expected/confirmatory/historical and the unexpected/disconfirming/present, contained the emotional responses to these new experiences, and tried again.

Couples need to be able to turn to one another and engage in mutual emotion regulation as they move into the trauma-focused stages of treatment, so it will be important to work through this process a number of times. Starting with minor, daily events and escalating towards issues and concerns that have more significance to the couple, therapists can slowly help the couple shift towards greater security in their attachment by helping them to establish strong secure base behaviours and to find ways to acknowledge and navigate through all of the unconscious thoughts, feelings, memories, and road blocks that come along with trying new ways of being together as a couple.

Working with Dyadic Traumatic Reenactment

Couples making important strides in their relationships, working hard to shift their attachments with one another, may come up against obstacles that feel insurmountable as they move along on this challenging journey. Therapy often pushes up against invisible boundaries trying to make the unconscious conscious and help the couple find new ways of being together, changing stuck interaction patterns and promoting attempts to try new, attachment-enhancing behaviours. The last section, working with attachment, aimed to help couples try new, secure base attachment behaviours and patiently iron out stuck spots through slow, steady persistence. Many couples will come up against obstacles that do not yield to the slow, gentle, repetition of new behaviours, as unconscious forces fail to relax and refuse to let go in spite of repeated attempts to smooth them over. These couples simply keep on going around and around in their repetitive cycle of pain and distress, diving deep into their Dyadic Traumatic Reenactments (DTRs) in spite of their best efforts to try new ways of being with one another.

This section will look more closely at how to work with couples that are struggling with unyielding DTRs. These kinds of struggles, where insight does not lead to change and attempts at implementing new attachment behaviours are hijacked by old scripts, cannot be transformed overnight. Given that most of our couples do not have the resources to attend therapy for years, we need to find ways to work with DTRs so that the hard packed-layer of old trauma reenacted in the present cycle is opened up, and the couple acquires some armament for their future work together as they continue to learn and grow after treatment. So many of these challenges are easier to learn by watching, listening, and feeling the process as it unfolds, so I do my best to expose couples to ways of engaging with those unsymbolized, dissociated cycles of the past living in the present.

The concept of the DTR was introduced in the psychoeducational section, and couples had the opportunity to consider together how this concept might help them understand more about the ways their traumatic life experiences have become embedded in their distressing relationship patterns. Over the course of therapy up to this point, these ideas have been revisited and fleshed out with the layering of each new concept and the building of self-capacities that allow survivors to hold more in themselves, tolerate greater internal conflict, and regulate themselves in relation to the growing capacity for greater internal complexity. At this point in the treatment, the couple has had the opportunity to develop a more refined and nuanced image of how their past is living in their relational present. Understanding their negative patterns and cycles, and how they are triggered into traumatic re-experiencing, is often not enough to break through the forces that keep them stuck (MacIntosh & Johnson, 2008; MacIntosh, 2017a). The need for more work becomes apparent when working on other issues, especially attachment-related issues, as gentle, persistent perseverance may not lead to an opening up of new secure base behaviours and feelings of safety and security. When these efforts become stuck, we may need to spend some more intentional and specific time working on the DTRs.

As discussed in the psychoeducation section, this work can be broken down into three distinct levels of process. The first two map on to the approaches used by most models of couple therapy, while the third is unique to our work with those who were severely traumatized at key developmental periods. The first level is knowledge: how does the couple understand their negative cycle, what are the factors that trigger and influence it, can they identify it when it is happening, and can they begin to talk about what they are experiencing when it is in full swing? The second level is insight: can the couple understand what fuels the fire of their "stuckness", do they get the unmet attachment needs and longings that burrow under these interactions, and can they acknowledge and see the role of their past trauma in the concrete embeddedness of history? This concrete embeddedness can be conscious and understood because it is living on the surface: my father yelled, my husband yelled; my uncle raped me in the dark, I freak out and run away from you when you initiate sex in the dark. These insights, while painful and sometimes shameful, can be achieved because they relate something knowable to something else that is thinkable. I know about the context and content of my trauma, and I know about the context and content of my couple relationship and our cycle, and I can think my way into connecting those two things. However, by trying to articulate this clearly, I do not in any way mean to suggest that it is easy or simple. It can be immensely painful to realize that the man you thought was so different from your father, on many levels, is so much like your father. However, working with the couple weaves in and out of these levels, piecing apart the many factors that influence their negative cycle and supporting them to understand more about how the past is concretely embedded within their relationship. For many survivors, especially those who have engaged in psychotherapy previously, these two levels will come naturally – they will already have the skills to tackle the tasks of figuring these out. Where the rubber hits the road, however, is at the third level, that which is outside of the couple's awareness and is reenacted moment by moment in ways that cannot be known in words or felt in ways that distinguish the present as separate from the past – a live stream of trauma superimposed onto the present of the couple. This third level is where things get tough. Survivors and their partners typically feel frustrated and helpless as they try to implement change based on knowledge and insight, without success. The thoughts and feelings, sensations and shadows do not allow the past to be pried out from the present; the couple has trouble even identifying how the past is being relived in waking life because it feels indistinguishable from now . . . it feels like an immense, painful, horrible now, still felt as present in the present.

What does all of this mean? How can therapy help couples liberate themselves from the vice-like grip of the past? As discussed in the section on shifting attachment, aspects of this dynamic are conscious and knowable, while others remain outside of awareness and are, therefore, not knowable in a conscious, cognitive way. To help couples, their DTRs must be brought alive in sessions, in the present, so that they can be stripped down and examined in their emotional reality. The therapist helps the couple to smell, taste, feel, and see the past and to disentangle that which has been held outside of awareness as it is brought into painful relief. Focusing on words and what is overt in the couple's current cycle may actually make the unconscious enactment even more stuck and rigid. While working at the first and second levels of the cycle is important, eventually the cycle must be reflected back in the immediate moment, to expose what is being enacted here and now, and to make space to explore the way this DTR is alive for the couple, and for you as therapist, in the session in real time. As a third person in the attachment of the therapeutic relational system, therapists may often be pulled into the DTR: this is both a risk and an opportunity. The risk is that you may be sucked into a dissociative relational enactment and come to represent someone or something within the traumatic cycle. The opportunity is the same: as you are pulled into the enacted DTR you have the opportunity to try to keep one foot on dry land, to help the couple from the inside out, as you feel both the pull of the enacted realm and hold steadily to the outside in the present, you may be able to participate as a new someone or something, a new experience and relationship. In our practice, we need to look at the ways that deep relational unconscious expectations continue to be enacted. When they are enacted in sessions, the therapist has the opportunity to both *be* different from caregivers in the past and, at the same time, to direct the survivor's attention to that difference – to hold their gaze steady in spite of the desire to pull away and not see something disconfirming and new. As these dissociated emotions, sensations, thoughts, and relational expectancies come up in the sessions, your capacity for empathic attunement and containment will help the couple regulate their emotional arousal, tolerate the new information about themselves and their traumas, and acknowledge and process the impact of any new memories that may emerge in their DTR. These experiences of emergence help the couple wrest free of the hold of the past superimposed on the present negative cycle, as its power dissipates away from the dark realm of the unconscious. Over time, with enough runs through the process, the unsymbolized can be symbolized and the past's pull on the negative interaction cycle begin to loosen. Change happens slowly as consciousness dawns over strong feelings and deep-seated trauma memories, which allows partners the psychic space to respond to one another in the present without being drawn into cycles of the past. Through these new experiences, new relational expectancies will gradually emerge, allowing for the more fluid expression of new security promoting attachment behaviours that had been held back by the "stuckness" of the DTR.

To illustrate this, clinically, the next section returns to Camille and Chris. As discussed in the psychoeducational module, at the first level of knowledge, Chris and Camille easily established a cognitive understanding of their negative cycle. Chris was relentlessly and anxiously pursuing Camille who would withdraw at the first sign of pressure, reinforcing Chris's anxiety and pursuit. Over time, in therapy, the couple developed an understanding at the second level, the deeper level of insight. Chris understood that he became fearful of rejection because of the difficult cycles of rejection and abandonment he experienced in his family of origin, which were tightly embodied as an automatic assumption in times of need. Camille continued to experience feelings of hypervigilance and emotional dysregulation, as a present-day echo of her trauma and Chris's intrusive pursuit triggered her into states of dysregulation and withdrawal. Chris and Camille could identify this cycle and could understand it in relation to the longer term-impacts of trauma. As we moved into this stage of the treatment, neither Camille nor Chris could tolerate the idea that the past was still living in the present, or that their cycle was deeply influenced by the emotional responses, sensations, thoughts, and actions associated with living as though the trauma was still happening. Chris was still struggling with reenacting this historical cycle as "real", expecting abandonment at every and needing to be vigilant now, not then. Camille was reenacting the horribly painful experience of never having her needs for care met by those who should have protected and supported her. Her parents' inability to tolerate her distress and support her following her sexual assault was living in her expectation of being failed, but she had no conscious awareness of the origins of these expectations: they were simply there in real time. This aspect of the negative pattern was not conscious for either partner. If asked about his pursuit, Chris stayed within his understanding of what was happening in the present and could not tolerate the possibility that an underlying, unconscious expectation was fuelling his experience of and response to, all of these interactions. Camille was the same, except that Chris could acknowledge the role of history to give insight into their problem but could not pull apart the inner workings of his feelings and urges as they were reliving the past. Meanwhile, Camille could accomplish neither step. In her experience, Chris (and really everyone else) was incompetent in caring for her; history had nothing to do with it. She described herself as vulnerable due to her trauma symptoms and felt that her caregivers should be more tolerant, understanding and responsive. The following segments will demonstrate the rigid embeddedness of expectation in Camille's narrative of an incident with Chris and how, in spite of a lengthy exploration of history, Chris *really was* providing her with incompetent care in the present. The incident in question involved giving her a particular snack food that had a preservative in it that she believed had caused an allergic reaction. For her, Chris *really did* provide her with incompetent care – there was no room in her narrative for human error, or the fact that Chris did not remember that this food additive could cause allergies.

THERAPIST: If we think about how your traumas fit together, lock and key, we can start to understand more about how this negative cycle becomes so terrifying, painful, and frustrating. Neither of you are able to feel cared about, loved and even competent as partners. Chris, you describe becoming so anxious about Camille that you can't leave her alone even when she is completely overwhelmed and shut down and, Camille, you describe finding yourself withdrawing from Chris and feeling like he doesn't understand or care for you and that he can't possibly help you with your distress. These expectations are all about how you were failed as small children who needed your caregivers to be there, to help you feel safe and to take care of you when bad things happened. Chris, you expect to be blamed and left, and Camille, you expected that the people who were there for you would not be able to help you, just like your experiences with your parents following your disclosure. You expect that people are going to be incompetent and so, like a lock and a key, your traumas fit together into a cycle of going around and around only being able to see the ways in which your partner is meeting that unconscious expectation, and nothing else.

CAMILLE: Look, I get that, but I'm just a bit frustrated because honestly I hate to say this but I didn't just randomly have an allergic reaction, you gave me something that I was allergic to.

CHRIS: How could I have known you were allergic to that obscure and bizarre thing?

CAMILLE: I have told you that before, and you should know.

CHRIS: I guess I forgot. I gave her Benadryl and I tried to help.

THERAPIST: So when we go into this discussion around trying to understand what happens between the two of you, again your response is, but it *really was his fault, he really did do something bad*, he really did not care for me, he really did let me down when I needed him. It's hard for you to look at both pieces – the part that is happening now where Chris forgot that he needed to be careful about that preservative and the part that is related to the past living in this moment between you, the part where your parents didn't provide you with the care you needed after your assault. There's a way in which you really need me to hear, "no, no, something bad really did happen and it is his fault!" Can you tell me what that feeling is inside you when you feel a strong need to tell me the truth of what happened in the present?

CAMILLE: Nobody listens to me, I knew stuff (voice raises and changes, like a small child), I knew what happened, I knew I didn't want to go back there, if only my mom would just listen to me.

THERAPIST: You did know, and you did try to tell her, and she didn't do what you needed her to do. It was devastating for you and you suffered for years without getting the help you needed to heal. I'm so sorry that happened to you and that your parents weren't there to be with you and support you in the way you needed them to.

CAMILLE: They would tell you that they did help me. And it's always been like that, and I've known stuff, and it's so bad. Things happen and nobody listens and I'm always the one stuck with it – like I just don't understand what's hard for people to make more of an effort to listen to me, like I'm not stupid!

THERAPIST: You know things, you have things to say, and no one listens. Chris and I are both listening very closely, right here, right now. Your parents couldn't or wouldn't care for you in the way you needed after your horrible trauma and, even now, if I were to ask them, they would tell me that they did help you, they did protect you, they did care for you. And you need me to really understand that that is not true and there is a part of you, a small scared part of you that is still living in that reality, the reality that you are all alone when horrible things happen.

CAMILLE: Yes. [crying openly]

CHRIS: But, I'm here. I'm listening, I make mistakes, but I'm not going to do that to you.

THERAPIST: Can you hear what Chris is saying? Can you look at him? What do you see?

In that moment of feeling, Camille was able to express the past in the present and bring it into our room to start to delineate the old caregivers from the new caregivers. Camille did look up at Chris, like a wounded animal checking to see if the hunter is right around the corner ready to pounce. The look on Chris's face, of love and warmth and protection, was something to behold, and Camille was able to take it in. For Chris, something in the clarity of the past morphing into our immediate moment brought him into the present and helped him see something that he *can* do to care for Camille, a way that he can be there for her. The past intruded in a very vivid way into the session, as Camille's traumatized child self emerged from beneath her angry protestations of the reality of Chris's failing her: like a flashback of a memory, when an enacted relational expectation comes alive, all of the feelings, sensations, and thoughts are alive in all of their developmental purity and are absolutely "true". However, while this was deeply painful for Camille, it did thrust the superimposed image of her trauma into the present in a way that she herself could more clearly recognize, which allowed the couple to start to pry apart the embeddedness of past and present and respond to one another based on what was happening in this moment, understanding the role the past has played in how they experience their relationship.

This was an important moment of change for this couple. Camille had an experience of the past superimposing on the moment in a way that she could really feel it as the past thrusting its way into the present. In this experience, she was able to find a way to see the two – past and present – as separate and to see Chris as the man he is: a loving but flawed human being who will do all he can to support and care for her. Chris was, initially, sucked into his fear, defensiveness, and certainty that he would be abandoned. As his past rejections came alive in the session, they were supplanted by a developmentally strong adult self who saw a way to actually help Camille – right here, right now, in that very moment – and he was able to pull himself out of his enacted experience and to be there for her as the caregiver who *did* notice and provide a needed response. Camille, in return, was able to recognize this "new" Chris who was showing up for her in a new way. The act of looking, the non-verbal relatedness, pulled them both into the now as new people in a new time, to attend to disconfirming evidence that suggested that the past might be able to stay in the past.

However, while this represented progress, the therapeutic process had not emerged from the woods quite yet. This same DTR came alive in a future session, as I became the target of the expectation that no one could or would provide care for Camille in the way she needed. In this later session, Camille became triggered by a conversation about the couple's sexual relationship. As they discussed specific aspects of their sex life in some detail, Camille became dysregulated. The usual strategies for grounding and containment failed, and Camille became silent, withdrawn, and visibly distressed, rocking back and forth and covering her ears. Chris was a gentle, quiet presence, trying to help Camille come back to us. I used traditional grounding techniques, asking Camille if she could put her feet on the ground, look up, and open her eyes, and notice the room around her, and I asked her to do some of the breathing exercises from the emotional regulation skills-building module. Eventually, Camille put her headphones on and retreated even further. Throughout these attempts, I was asking Camille whether she could hear me and other questions that could be answered non-verbally. However, unbeknownst to me, the hand gesture that Camille was using was meant to communicate "stop talking; you're making it worse" when I was interpreting it to mean, "yes, I hear you" or "okay". Needless to say, this activated Camille's deeply held belief that no one – especially me – could possibly care for her in the way she needed, especially when she was in distress. The session ended with Chris ushering Camille away. The couple skipped the session the following week and only returned because Chris convinced Camille that therapy had been helpful to them, and they owed it to me to come for one final session before quitting. Over the course of our sessions I had been filled in on the history of all of the other therapies and therapists that had failed Camille and the number of therapies that she had quit, so I was waiting to be fired but hoping that we could wrestle with that damned DTR a bit before giving in to the deep force of the past trauma.

THERAPIST: So, I didn't see you last week – and then, I heard from Chris that you weren't coming, but I didn't hear from you. I was wondering how you were doing and how things were for you after that difficult session?

CAMILLE: I was fine. I just needed to leave.

THERAPIST: How long did it take you to be fine?

CAMILLE: I don't really want to talk about it.

THERAPIST: Okay. Can you tell me why you don't want to talk about it?

CAMILLE: Because I just don't.

THERAPIST: Hmmm, how about we try talking about not wanting to talk about it? [tries to smile in Camille's direction]

CAMILLE: I don't want to talk about it.

THERAPIST: Here's the thing: when we don't talk about it, we strengthen the belief that getting away from things makes them better. We were here in the session and you felt like you desperately had to get away, so you put your headphones on and you left. You felt like, "I have to get out of here". But, if we don't come back to that, then that becomes real – and then the world just keeps getting smaller. Like, if I have a panic attack in this grocery store, I never want to go back to that grocery store. And then, I go to a different grocery store and have a panic attack there. Next thing, I can't go to any grocery stores and then contagion sets in and, over time, I avoid every place that I feel anxious and the world keeps getting smaller.

CAMILLE: [angrily] I'm back here, aren't I?

THERAPIST: You're here.

CAMILLE: So, I think that should count for something. And. . .

THERAPIST: It absolutely counts for something. I'm really impressed and pleased that you've come back. I'm sure it would have felt easier to not come.

CAMILLE: I don't think that talking about it is going to help, so I don't want to talk about it.

THERAPIST: Okay, you don't want to. I *do* think it will help.

CAMILLE: Well, I disagree.

THERAPIST: Okay. You can disagree. And I would like to explain why I think it'll help. Because I can imagine that it feels like I'm not listening to you if I continue to suggest that we should do something that you are really clear that you don't want to do. So, I'd like to explain why I feel that talking about what happened in the session is important and then, if you still don't want to talk about it, we'll let it drop.

CAMILLE: Well, your first explanation is not relevant. I don't feel it's relevant, so. . .

THERAPIST: Tell me more.

CAMILLE: It doesn't feel true. You thinking that it would help me to talk about it is not my opinion about it.

THERAPIST: No, I totally get that. But that's why we're here, right? We're sharing our opinions. We have a different opinion. And I think this is actually a really good example of something we've talked about that happens between you and Chris – where you have a different opinion, and then you have trouble finding a place to rest when the differences don't shift.

CAMILLE: This is different.

THERAPIST: How does it feel different?

CAMILLE: It just is.

THERAPIST: So, you feel like talking about it doesn't help. I feel like it does help. So, those are different perspectives, right?

CAMILLE: Sure.

THERAPIST: So, my perspective – and I'm happy to explain why I feel that way – is that we should talk about it, and you have a different perspective. And you've described that something similar happens between you and Chris.

CAMILLE: But it's not similar.

THERAPIST: Okay. Help me understand why it's not similar.

CAMILLE: 'Cause it's not.

THERAPIST: It's really important to me that you help me understand. The challenge is that if I don't understand your perspective, it gets really hard for me to provide you with the care that you need in the way that you need it. And, I say need because I think need is often different than want, especially for children.

Camille was sitting in the session still wearing her heavy winter coat, with her mittens and hat clutched tightly in her lap. She made herself as small as she possibly could and was speaking in short, curt utterances with a tone that sounded very childlike: higher pitched, and less sophisticated than her usual voice. I was aware that we were on a precipice. I could feel her desire to bolt. I am also very aware that if I dropped it and did not talk about it, we would have missed the opportunity to challenge the DTR and we would, in fact, validate the reality of her rigid belief that caregivers are neglectful and incompetent. I was also very aware of my own feelings of irritation, frustration, and incompetence. In this instance, I stood in for all the other caregivers who had let her down. As the DTR became alive between the three of us, I was pulled into feeling inadequate, anxious, and defensive, familiar feelings for me when I am aware that a patient is unsatisfied with me as a therapist or I feel that I am not doing good work. The weight of all of the other caregivers' "failures" to shift this very destructive narrative weighed on my shoulders, and I was quite anxious about being the next in the long line of therapists who had failed Camille. Using my own emotion regulation strategies – going slowly, breathing deeply, talking myself down from getting defensive and overwhelmed with shame – and talking to myself about how important this moment was for the future of our therapy, in relation to dismantling the past living in the present, I continued on. I was determined to shine a little light around the closed door that was Camille's expectation that I would be just one more incompetent caregiver.

CAMILLE: Okay, but I don't want to talk about it. Talking about how it's not similar brings back a point of comparison – which means I would have to talk about it. Which means I don't want to talk about it. Which means . . . there's no point.

THERAPIST: I can see that, and I imagine you feel like I'm just playing with language to get back to forcing you to talk about something you don't want to talk about. I do want to explore talking about perspectives, which isn't the same as talking about what happened.

CAMILLE: Well, the fact is, when I disagree with Chris about something, it's different than when I disagree about something with somebody else.

THERAPIST: Help me understand, how is it different? How does it feel different? What is it like?

CAMILLE: It's just a different relationship, different context, different reasons, different everything. So there's no. . . . It's just different.

THERAPIST: Okay. [pause] What do you think? [to Chris] How does it feel different for you?

CHRIS: Well, it's not really that different. It's just that I feel like Camille feels very threatened right now by being here. And . . . I don't know, like, if we're going to have much progress – like she feels attacked, and she feels like she's not going to be able to open up. And her whole body right now is closed off, so. . .

THERAPIST: You say "threatened". Can you explain that? Can you tell me more about what you mean by that?

CHRIS: Well, she was really freaked out in the last session. And all she needed was time and silence. But the issue is, I have to agree with you too: it has to be talked about. But the thing is, I don't know . . . I have not been able to figure out a way to talk with her or communicate about things that happen between us without her feeling threatened. Because she feels like, if she remembers it and then it scares her or she doesn't want to talk about it – if she talks about it, then she is reminded that it existed, and so then, it's like impossible to get any kind of conversation about it. And I don't want to be a source of pain for her. But, at the same time, we have to figure out a way to communicate about it. I don't know, every time I've been blunt, it hasn't helped.

THERAPIST: Okay. So, Camille, would you agree with the word, "threatened" as a way to describe how you feel right now?

CAMILLE: No.

THERAPIST: No. What word would you use?

CAMILLE: Not interested.

THERAPIST: Can you tell me more about what that means?

CAMILLE: It means I don't want to talk about it, because it's pointless to talk about it.

I can imagine that some of you are becoming rather uncomfortable at this point – why doesn't that damned therapist leave the poor girl alone? I get that reaction; I was pretty uncomfortable as well. I think it is very difficult to "read" the emotional tone and feeling of a session, through the resulting transcript. Imagine that you are trying to get into your house. You stepped outside and the door slammed behind you, locked itself, you do not have any keys, and there is a toddler in the house wandering around with a pair of scissors. That is not a good feeling, and so you run around to all of the doors and windows looking for something to be opened or unlocked, and you find nothing. I was trying all of the doors and all of the windows hoping to find one that was open, even a crack. Only by accessing the feelings, sensations, memories, and thoughts of the unconscious reenactment can the trauma survivor shift out of "stuckness": we have to help the person stop paying attention to the evidence that confirms their beliefs and help them pay attention to the new, disconfirming evidence that is right in front of them, before anything will change. Of course, it goes without saying that I have to *be* the disconfirming evidence. I cannot just say that I am a different caregiver, I have to *be* a different caregiver, and Camille has to be able to feel that deep inside the old, wounded places of her self. This is no different: if we cannot help Camille out of her enactment of the past, which feels very real in the present for her, we will only further solidify her belief that the world must get smaller and she must protect herself because no one can or will help her. So, yes, I was being persistent beyond what felt comfortable to anyone but, at the same time, I knew that she had more than one foot out the door, so I did not have much to lose: she already had her coat on and her hat and mittens in hand.

THERAPIST: When you say pointless, do you mean that you feel like talking about it with me is not going to change anything?

CAMILLE: [sighs]

THERAPIST: The more I understand your experience, the more helpful I can be to you as we try to sort this out.

CAMILLE: [starts to laugh]

THERAPIST: Tell me about what's funny. . . ?
CAMILLE: It's very funny to me.
THERAPIST: Okay, tell me more about that.
CAMILLE: I don't want to.
THERAPIST: It's absurd to you that anybody could be helpful?
CAMILLE: No, it's not.
THERAPIST: Say more.

Even though Camille was laughing in my general direction, this was still a kind of engagement; her disdain represented an affective shift in the direction of being with me, if even angrily, so I actually felt a tiny bit more hopeful.

CAMILLE: No. I don't want any more presumptions.
THERAPIST: It's hard for me not to presume, if you won't tell me how you're feeling. I'm trying hard to find my way to understanding your experience.
CAMILLE: We could talk about something else.
THERAPIST: What would you like to talk about?
CAMILLE: I don't care.
THERAPIST: See, therapists are funny creatures – where other people run from fires, therapists run into them. And part of what we do is go places that people are uncomfortable going. So, we start out from a different vantage point, right. Like, therapists run into the burning building; normal people run away. Your instinct is: "Run away!" Don't think about it; don't talk about it, and it'll be over. And even, "It's pointless". There's no point in talking about what happened here – but also what happened afterwards, in terms of how you felt and . . . I'd be really interested in how did you get back here? What was your internal process that helped you come back? I know you were pretty freaked out in the last session but you got back here, and I'm really interested in the process you went through to bring yourself back.
CHRIS: The thing is, like, I had to almost convince her to come back a little bit. Because I felt like we're not finished here. It's not resolved here yet. That last session didn't really help much, because I feel like it's really upset her and made her not, like . . . without putting words in her mouth, I feel like she feels like you can't help her any more. And so, like, the thing is, I want to be on her side – because I care about her a lot but, at the same time, I see the value in what you're saying. So, it's scary for me to be here right now, because I feel like I'm really stuck in the middle here – which is also a terrifying place for me, because that was my entire trauma.
THERAPIST: Absolutely, you were the go between your Mom and Dad. That must be scary for you, and yet you are so clear-minded and articulate about your thoughts and feelings and in your reflecting on what Camille might be thinking and feeling. That's really impressive progress from where you were in the beginning.
CHRIS: Yeah, that's why I thought we needed to come back.
THERAPIST: So, Camille, is there anything about what Chris said that you would like to say more about?
CAMILLE: No, not really.
THERAPIST: Would you say that the feelings you were having in the last session were scary for you somehow and those feelings got associated with me. I was the person who took you into the woods and now you're connecting me with getting lost in the woods and feeling really scared?

CAMILLE: It's not that they got connected.

THERAPIST: No? Can you help me understand then?

CAMILLE: I don't want to talk about it.

THERAPIST: [earnestly but compassionately] I do get that you don't want to talk about it. I totally get what you're saying – but I also feel like there's a bit of a self-fulfilling prophecy here: If I don't understand, I can't help. And, if I can't help, then I fulfill the prophecy that people can't help.

CAMILLE: No.

THERAPIST: No, okay. Say more.

CAMILLE: [giggles]

THERAPIST: It's a trap, right? "I can't explain to you why you can't help me. But I know that you can't!" And then . . . I feel I can't help you or I guess and I do something not helpful because I don't understand well enough. I can guess. But guessing isn't fair for either of us, I think. I do want to help you. Both of you.

CAMILLE: Fine then. Your reaction to me being upset was not helpful.

THERAPIST: Tell me more. What was it about my reaction that wasn't helpful?

CAMILLE: More sound, when the sound is overwhelming, is not helpful.

THERAPIST: So, my talking?

CAMILLE: Yes.

THERAPIST: And was there anything about what I was saying that was making it worse?

CAMILLE: No. It's just the fact that you were. . . . Well, questions don't help.

THERAPIST: Okay.

CAMILLE: Because it's not. . . . It's just not helpful. It doesn't help to ask questions.

THERAPIST: So, what would have been helpful? How could I have been more helpful?

CAMILLE: Just silence – for a bit?

THERAPIST: And how would I have known that? What might I have noticed about what was happening in you that would have helped me know to be quiet?

CAMILLE: I indicated to you to stop talking.

THERAPIST: Did you? How did you indicate that – because I didn't catch that?

CAMILLE: This is universal sign for "stop". [holds up hand towards me]

THERAPIST: Oh! You know what I thought that was? I thought that was you responding and saying that you were hearing me.

CAMILLE: No. That was stop.

THERAPIST: I completely misunderstood that.

CHRIS: I thought the same!

THERAPIST: When I was asking you questions I was sort of trying to see if you could hear me. And, when you put your hand up, I interpreted that as you saying, "Yes, I hear you". So, I completely misunderstood that. I'm so sorry. I wish I had understood that better. So, my continuing to talk then was just more kind of . . . overwhelming stimulus.

CAMILLE: Yeah.

THERAPIST: Could you actually hear what I was saying?

CAMILLE: Yeah.

THERAPIST: You could. Okay. But you assumed I knew what that meant?

CAMILLE: Does that really matter?

THERAPIST: It absolutely does. Because I can imagine, if you thought I knew and I kept talking, you would feel quite hurt and angry.

CAMILLE: I didn't assume. I was just hoping you would get it.

THERAPIST: So, you were hoping I would – and I didn't. I let you down. There was something you needed from me that I didn't understand and, instead, I did something that made things worse for you in that moment. I'm so sorry for that. I know that your experience has been, when you send signals to people about your distress, you often don't feel like they're received in a way that you need them to.

CAMILLE: [crying] I don't want to talk anymore.

[LONG PAUSE TO SIT WITH THE SADNESS]

THERAPIST: I'm sorry about what happened between us, Camille and I'm glad that you were able to tell me about what it was like for you. Your history has been that people haven't taken you seriously. . . . And that began, I think, before the sexual abuse – that your experience was that your emotions weren't really taken seriously and considered.

CHRIS: Well, I wish she would understand that I do take her emotions seriously.

THERAPIST: Can you tell her that?

CHRIS: I take you very seriously, Camille, all the time, when you're emotional and upset. And I always look at ways to try to help you.

CAMILLE: [takes his hand] I know.

THERAPIST: Camille, I know that was really cringey for you, pushing through all of the messages and feelings that there is no point in talking about it, but how would I ever have learned this important thing about you that you need quiet when you are distressed and that that hand signal means – please be quiet?

CAMILLE: I guess; I think you should just have known.

THERAPIST: I wish I could have just known. And I wish your parents could have been more able to help you, that when you told them how much pain you were in after the assault, that they could have given you the care that you needed, and I understand why, after so many failed attempts, talking about your distress feels not only futile but also very painful. That's a hard lifelong lesson to try to relearn, but sharing your distress with Chris, and with me, can only make us more helpful to you when you are in distress.

Camille softened a bit as the session wound up. She never took off her coat, but she did loosen her grip on her mittens and hat, looked up at me, and started to talk more openly about an upcoming event that both partners were looking forward to. Camille and Chris never missed another session after this, and there was a discernible change in how they responded to one another. Camille was more able to use words to signal her distress, and Chris was more confident in his capacity to listen and respond. Camille also became a better carer – one must have some kind of internal model of caring to be a good carer. She became much more able to respond to Chris in his distress with curiosity, openness, tenderness, and patience. This was a massive change.

These processes can take years, when relational expectations and traumatic memories from the past live deep in the unconscious and wrap their slithery tendons around all of a couple's present-tense interactions. Most survivor couples do not have the resources, especially financially, to stay in therapy for years. The best we can do in the short time we have with them is to help them safely rub up against these DTRs in such a way as to say, "hey, you, get out here, I want to talk to you", to try to pry apart the ways in which past and present are tightly intertwined and make a mess of opportunities for new loving engagements. We also hope that the couples will take away their newfound skills, insights, and capacities for engaging and continue to learn and grow together.

Stage Three

Disclosure – telling the stories

The process of DCTCT guides couples slowly, gently, but clearly along the path to building the context for closeness by developing skills in emotion regulation and mentalizing and challenging the underlying internal working models of attachment, shifting habitual attachment strategies and behaviours towards more security-enhancing behaviours. Each step tries to break down the barriers of avoidance created by the ravages of a traumatic childhood where sharing, being close, trusting, and intimacy could be deeply dangerous. While continuing to break through barriers to closeness, safety, and intimacy, it is also essential to break down secrets between the partners, including secrets related to their traumas. The most important purpose in telling these trauma stories is that the survivor's partner comes to understand the scope and magnitude of the trauma and becomes more able to empathize and mentalize about their partner in relation to areas of ongoing pain and struggle. Understanding more about the specifics of the trauma also helps the partner to contextualize trauma triggers and specific aspects of their attachment relationship that might be more or less challenging.

While partners may have heard the title of the story of the traumas their partners have experienced, many do not know the story itself: the flesh and bones of their partner's most terrifying and vulnerable experiences. Often a partner can say what, and who, but not much more. In a previous study I was involved with, all of the partners could say that their partner had been sexually abused in childhood, and some partners could identify the perpetrators. Fewer could say anything about how old their partners were when the abuse occurred, and none of the partners knew the details of the trauma or much about the impact (MacIntosh & Johnson, 2008). Over the course of couple therapy, couples showed more improvement in trauma symptoms and couple satisfaction when a survivor was supported in telling their story of sexual abuse. These couples became closer and partners were often more empathic and better at mentalizing with their partner; this was likely due to understanding more about the context of triggers and emotional responses that had previously just seemed weird or difficult to understand (MacIntosh & Johnson, 2008). Women appear more likely to disclose to their partners because they feel that their partners should know that they are getting "damaged goods", while male survivors often only tell their partners when forced, such as when the police come knocking on the door looking for testimony in a large-scale abuse case (MacIntosh, Fletcher, & Collin-Vézina, 2016). Keeping secrets creates distance, a barrier against ever letting down your guard lest something seep out, as well as shame and challenges with closeness. In the short run, it feels impossible, shameful, frightening, and risky: "what if my partner really does find out how damaged I am and leaves me?" Safely talking through the traumas and sharing the stories with someone close to you increases feelings of competence, decreases trauma symptoms, decreases shame, and increases intimacy in the long run. In spite of the sense of risk and the feelings of fear, therapists need to help the couple share more of their stories and provide them with opportunities to be the safe haven and secure base for one another that these couples so desperately long for, and at the same time, fear.

Begin by exploring what the couple already knows. Have them tell each other the stories that they already know, as they understand them. Check out errors, omissions, and confusions. Close to 100% of the couples where I have worked through trauma disclosures with one or both partners have some incorrect information about the trauma history of their partner; information that they have cobbled together in attempting to make sense of the gaps and holes in the stories that were told. Explore these known stories in the context of how they help the partner understand the impact of these traumas on their lives and relationships. Take as much time over this process as the couple needs, to feel that they have said all that they need to say. This is a new form of exploration that is more direct and specific than previous discussions of trauma and may be more distressing for the survivor. Keep bringing emotion regulation exercises back into the session to help keep the process emotionally safe and encourage active, flexible, and curious mentalizing so that each partner may engage, as fully as they are able, in this process of understanding their partner in a new way.

In a couple where only one partner has experienced childhood trauma, this process is one-directional and will vary depending on the duration, severity, and frequency of abuse. If the abuse was chronic and severe, this may involve sharing model scenes of traumatic experiences. Such a model scene could be defined as one particular episode or experience of abuse in the context of a caregiving relationship that particularly exemplifies the ways in which the abuse or trauma "typically" occurred. The goal of this process is not to share the gritty, graphic, or gory details of each traumatic event but rather to fill out the story with feelings, thoughts, sensations, and relational themes, to help the partner understand the trauma story and to help the survivor lift the veil of silent secrets that has stood between them.

Telling the trauma story begins with a description of the events that occurred, the feelings associated with those memories, and the relational templates that were forged in fear and vulnerability. At this point you may feel the need to have individual sessions with survivor partners. You may need to help them to organize their thoughts, decide which pieces of their history they would like to tell, and perhaps even help them write out the details on paper to share with their partner in a session. If there is a partner in the couple who has not experienced trauma, you may need to help them process their anger, despair, and pain about finding out more about what happened to the person with whom they share their life and with whom they are trying to build new intimacy. This process may also bring up feelings about their own histories – events that they had not identified as being traumatic, which now feel more problematic – and feelings about the ways in which their relationship has been shaped by trauma. It is important for the couple to learn to externalize the trauma as a negative force that has impacted both partners and which they can tackle as a team.

Many survivors will object to the process of disclosure, believing fervently that it is essential to maintain aspects of their lives separate and secret from their partners: an echo of protecting oneself from an abuser who might use knowledge against you. These kinds of secrets can often reflect more about the need to hold the partner away, rather than a need to hold information away from the partner. This will need to be broken down, slowly. The role of therapists includes scaffolding survivors, as they tell these painful stories, as well as partners, so they can hear and respond to their partners in ways that enhance attachment security and safety. These are new opportunities to try out security-enhancing behaviours; the survivor shares the story, the partner is able to listen and respond with concern and comfort, and the survivor is able to complete the circuit by tolerating the support, caring, and soothing concern of their partner.

In a couple where both partners identify as survivors of childhood trauma, the process of telling their stories may need to be slower and more attention paid to ensuring that both partners feel as though their stories have been heard and received. You might ask the couple to decide who should go first, or you can start by identifying similarities and differences between traumatic experiences, attachment impacts, and long-term effects. Of course, the goal of this is not to compare in a "mine was worse than yours" kind of way, but rather to help couples mentalize about the trauma and its impact on themselves, their partners, and their relationships, in a deeper, more profound way that is fully inhabited by details, a way that was not possible at the beginning of treatment.

For many survivors, even the initial disclosure of the presence of a history of childhood trauma can feel shameful and difficult, to be avoided almost at all costs. By the time couples reach my door, at a clinic focused on working with couples dealing with trauma, clearly some disclosure has already been made. In the following segment, Anush and Amira discuss Anush's first disclosure, just over a year ago and 9 years into their marriage. During the first years of their marriage Amira had been in the dark, thinking that Anush's lack of sexual interest in her reflected something wrong with her, or with him. They kept hitting a wall of silence, as Anush's trauma and the impacts ran amok in their relationship, and neither of them could find a way to open the door and talk about the origins of the growing distance between them. The context for the initial disclosure was highly connected to Anush and Amira's cultural and familial background. Anush shared his story with his sister before anyone else, long before turning to a mental healthcare provider: in the culture these partners share, family is a source of support before outsiders. As the firstborn son, Anush devoted his life to being the good son, brother, husband, and father he believed he was expected to be. However, when things were crashing down and Amira was threatening to leave, Anush knew that he no longer had a choice, and he trusted that his sister would be a safe person to help him with the disclosure to Amira.

THERAPIST: Did you have any idea what he was going to tell you?

AMIRA: No, no, I didn't know. When he said we needed to meet at his sister's house, just out of the blue, I knew it was a big deal. He said he wanted to talk to us about something. I remember feeling something is up, but I didn't know what. And then when he started talking, I honestly thought he was going to come out and say he was gay. I was ready for it.

THERAPIST: You knew it was big.

AMIRA: I knew it was big.

THERAPIST: You were ready for something serious, which would have an impact on your marriage, but you weren't expecting this.

ANUSH: I just had a big knot in my stomach. I wouldn't say I was scared, because I felt I was ready to say it. I felt comfortable, and it was the right situation, and nothing was getting better between us. I knew we had support, I was confident that I could say it, but I didn't know how I would be after I said it. More importantly, for me was what was she gonna feel or say. She was not one to come out with her feelings. She holds things back, and of course with the years of issues we've had, it's not something she would bring up. I know that she is not emotionally and physically satisfied. That was another reason why somebody else needed to know also, I needed to know that Amira had someone to turn to. I was very concerned about how I would be after I said it and how she would take it.

THERAPIST: You did everything you could to make it as okay as possible for both of you.

ANUSH: Not just that, if we both needed somebody else to talk to, we both could talk to my sister.

THERAPIST: So it felt to you like disclosing to Amira, with your sister, someone you both feel comfortable and safe with, that would be easier than doing it just the two of you on your own.

ANUSH: I put a lot of thought into it.

THERAPIST: You didn't turn to a therapist, you turned to family. In your culture, family is who you turn to before therapists?

ANUSH: Yes, I needed for her to know that we have somebody for us, close to us where sometimes it's easier to say it than even in an environment like this. In my family you don't talk to strangers and, I, well, I didn't talk to anyone!

THERAPIST: And how was it for you, how did you feel afterwards?

ANUSH: Oh God! I just felt like, I don't even know, I don't even know how. I can't even describe to you the emotion, I just remember that huge knot. I don't even know how it sounded when it came out, I felt like, I was talking but I was like, can they hear me, I was so knotted up. When I was actually able to say it, I just felt like a huge burden, like a ton of bricks coming off of my shoulders.

THERAPIST: So, you got it out, it took a while, but you felt some immediate relief. What was it like for you, Amira?

AMIRA: I felt really bad for him. It made me feel really upset, angry, not at him, but that he had to go through something like that, I felt really sorry for him.

THERAPIST: And to know him for so long and not know something like this. . .

AMIRA: So after he told us in the evening, as that night went on, I started to have all these other questions, and that feeling of sympathy started to change to a little bit of anger. Not outright anger, but like he held this from me, this feeling that I am having of being stuck in something, it's your friggin' fault I've been stuck in this.

THERAPIST: Hmmm.

AMIRA: You pretty much held me in something because of your stupid issues and secret. I started feeling that. . .

THERAPIST: So you started to connect the secret and the withholding to the stuckness you'd been feeling.

AMIRA: And I felt very upset with myself for feeling that way. I remember telling my sister-in-law how horrible I felt. And I think it was the pressure, my telling him that I was going to leave if things didn't change, that maybe led him to finally come out with it. He did say, to all of us, that "there is something that's affected our marriage and now it's gotten to a point that it's really become a problem and I need to talk about it". I still had questions and I wanted to know if every time that we were intimate, did it ever really mean anything? If I think back, we never looked in each other's eyes, we never said "I love you" during making love, not the way – I know movies and stuff are one thing, but it just wasn't the way you hear how it's supposed to be right? So I asked him and he said yes, every time we were intimate it was usually something planned, and the times he agreed, he said he would feel it before, during and after, the whole thing would just play in his mind. Like the trauma he went through and that hurt me more, it's never really been anything more than what he went through. It's never been enjoyable for him either, he's always been this. . .

THERAPIST: This shadow?

AMIRA: Yeah.

With Gary and Geoffrey, it was difficult to begin the disclosure stage. While Gary's levels of dissociation had diminished significantly, it was still challenging for the couple to engage in conversations about their emotional lives in general. Adding disclosures of trauma histories to the emotional load was a difficult next step. The following segment outlines the set-up conversation, outlining how much the couple has already shared about their traumas and how they frame those disclosures within their current relationship struggles.

THERAPIST: As we become more able to talk about things here, it's time to start to talk about your experiences of trauma, the things that have happened to both of you, and to try to do some processing together to decrease triggers, increase your ability to turn to each other, and to support each other. If there are things you're not comfortable talking about yet, we will regroup and look at how we can make these conversations feel safer and think about what stories need to be shared and those that won't, based on what you feel is standing between you. It's really important that you know that at any point you can say, "I think I've reached my tolerance; I don't think we can go any further".

GARY: Okay.

THERAPIST: How does that feel?

GARY: It's good, just. . .

GEOFFREY: Yeah.

THERAPIST: How much do you know about each other's experiences? Do you feel like you have a pretty full picture or there are missing pieces?

GARY: I know he doesn't have a full picture because I'm still having memories myself.

THERAPIST: But the things you do know, you have disclosed?

GARY: I have, but I don't expect him to remember everything.

THERAPIST: Why don't you expect him to remember?

GARY: It's just a lot.

THERAPIST: Okay, and Geoffrey how much do you feel Gary knows about your growing up and the traumatic experiences you have had?

GEOFFREY: A fair amount. I don't think we talk about it a lot, in general.

GARY: I'm also pretty uptight and touchy about it sometimes, when he talks about his childhood – well, even though he had some hard times, I don't really have memories like his and you know, I didn't get to have those experiences and I start to feel really selfish. Part of why he doesn't share is because I'm not that great of a listener.

THERAPIST: What is that like? Geoffrey might be sharing a story that might have been difficult for him, but you can't relate to it because your experiences were so different? What happens inside of you?

GARY: Well, I just feel alienated and I – like I'm on a different planet.

THERAPIST: And how does that make you feel about yourself?

GARY: Me? Well, in the moment I'm patient with myself and I'm not judging myself for being selfish because I know that it's a coping mechanism.

THERAPIST: So when you feel that way, you remind yourself that it's the way that you cope.

GARY: Yeah.

THERAPIST: And then what happens when you try to bring yourself back to Geoffrey or to refocus on what he's saying? What happens inside of you?

GARY: [silence] Well I mean, I don't want to be on another planet, I want to be in an intimate relationship with him, so if I can, I remember that I don't need to feel jealous of other people's experiences and that I love him and want to be with him. . .

THERAPIST: What is it like to be thinking about that now as we talk about it?

GARY: I would like to, maybe experience what it's like to not be a survivor of childhood trauma so that I would know what it's like for other people also.

THERAPIST: To be able to have that experience.

GARY: Yeah, like I don't wish that they would know what it's like for me because I would only wish that on my enemies, but I still would like to know what it's like for them. It's hard to hear about the times that Geoffrey had good experiences growing up. I guess, in a way, it's easier for me to hear the stories of when he had a hard time growing up.

THERAPIST: It's painful not to be able to imagine what it would be like to not have had those horrible experiences. It sounds like, in a way, it makes it possible for you to really be with Geoffrey and understand his traumatic experiences, but it's really hard to be with him when he talks about his positive experiences.

This is an example of how even the preparation for disclosure may bring up feelings in relation to one's own trauma history and also that of one's partner. For Gary, it is a struggle to disclose because he is both still dealing with new memories and also feeling like his traumas are so extreme that he is an alien no one can understand. Gary's shame also overshadows any possibility of Geoffrey sharing his own traumatic experiences which, in essence, renders them invisible. To be able to find some balance in this relationship where Gary's trauma and dissociation already tip the scales towards him needing more support, space will need to be made for Geoffrey's stories, even if they are not as gruesome and life annihilating. We wrangled with this for many weeks, as I supported Gary in trying to be present for Geoffrey, to respond to Geoffrey's distress and his need for his life stories to be heard and understood, and for Gary to find his way to comfort him. The transcript demonstrated that, while Gary was expressing high levels of distress, he did so with clarity and emotional intensity that matched his current emotional state and showed some capacity to understand how this might impact Geoffrey. He was having a tough time, but regulated his distress without dissociating, and he was mentalizing well as he tried to see Geoffrey's perspective and the impact that he was having on his partner. Things may not become easy when survivors' emotion regulation and mentalizing capacities are engaged, but things become possible that were simply not possible without them.

In the following segment, Anush discloses details about his abuse to Amira, with my help. Over the course of the therapy Anush gradually became more willing and open to thinking about and talking about his traumatic experiences. However, this opened a door inside of him that had previously held back additional memories of abuse; here, he recounts new memories that returned to him in flashbacks. This time, it only took a few weeks for Anush to be ready to talk to Amira. Here he is telling Amira more about a particular experience of trauma, and the thoughts and feelings that go along with it, to bring her into his inner torment.

ANUSH: It was hard. It was gut wrenching.

THERAPIST: What can you say about it?

ANUSH: It was just images, feelings in that moment. Running away from the house, because it didn't feel right, and I knew it was wrong. How did it get to that, how did it even get that far?

THERAPIST: Say more.

ANUSH: I ran a block to get away from him, I got home, and I just kinda forgot about it, like it never happened and that's that, until now. It's been a long, long time and it's been in and out of my mind. . .

THERAPIST: For years and years.

ANUSH: For years and years and years and years. I can't turn on the TV anymore without being reminded of it.

THERAPIST: You can't get away from it. You and I talked about these new memories in our individual session last week, so I have a sense of what you have been working through. I'm wondering if you can tell Amira a bit more about what you are remembering?

ANUSH: I started feeling all of these things in my chest and my shoulders. I didn't get around to telling her: I wanted to, but we were incredibly busy and I just kept forgetting. Um, I am just realizing that it wasn't just the one time I told you about. Do you remember that there were friends with a pool who lived right behind our house?

AMIRA: Yes, the house with all the toys?

ANUSH: No, this was a house that was behind, if you remember, there were two French boys who lived there. We used to go to their pool. I would have been between 7 and 9, in that age. One of the brothers, I don't remember which one, he was older, but he also was, it's tough for me, it was wrong, but it's just what it was. He was curious, but he ummm – I don't remember exactly what happened, how it happened, but anyways, there was some inappropriate behaviour on his part. Then there was, I don't remember how old I was, there was a family gathering there, and there was a family friend's son, older and. . .

AMIRA: Him too?

ANUSH: Yeah, him too. I mean, it was again, inappropriate behaviour on his part. But both times, I just kinda got out of the situation,

AMIRA: You didn't think to tell your mom and dad?

ANUSH: No, it didn't occur to me to tell them. I don't know why it didn't come to me before, why I'm only remembering now. It's perfectly clear that it happened, but the images of what specifically happened, that wasn't there clearly before the last couple of weeks. I guess they were in the background and reading that book just blew them to the forefront. Like, I didn't tell.

THERAPIST: It's not unusual for someone whose strategy for coping is to not think or not tell anyone, to push it away, that when you start therapy, when you start reading and stop avoiding thinking about the abuse, that the cover comes off of everything that you've tried to not think about.

AMIRA: How often did it happen?

ANUSH: It happened a few times at the pool and just the one time with the family friend. That was the first time I was able to get that off my chest but it didn't take me long. I was young, naive, and when she [therapist] was explaining how abuse happens and how you remember it or try to not think about it, I've just been having these memories ever since.

THERAPIST: It's better to have it all out. Anush, can you tell Amira a bit more about what happened? You've told her that they were "inappropriate" but that could mean many things. It's important that we don't leave that to the imagination or potential misunderstanding.

ANUSH: I wish it was easier to get off my chest, it's still hard. I guess, well, the older boys, they were going through puberty and, I guess, they were just playing around and stuff, you know.

THERAPIST: I know this is super hard to talk about but it's possible that Amira and I don't know. Could you put it in words for us that would help us understand better and still be tolerable for you?

ANUSH: Well, you know, this happened a bunch of times where they were sitting around and jerking off and showing off and I guess I was confused but also curious so I did watch and it made me feel kind of weird but I kept going back. But then, one time, they, well, they wanted me to touch them when they were doing it. I didn't want to, but the oldest boy got kind of mean, so I did. I touched his penis and he grabbed my hand. . . [long silence in which we all attend quietly to the time Anush needs. Anush begins speaking more loudly and more quickly] Anyway, he grabbed my hand and forced me to jerk him off. I couldn't get my hand away and I couldn't get away. After he, well, you know, after he finished, I ran away. I never went back. That's it. The family gathering thing was just a boy showing me his penis and he wanted me to put my mouth on him, but I ran away. That's it, there's nothing else.

THERAPIST: Anush, I'm so sorry you had to go through that, that's just so yucky and scary for a little guy. How are you feeling now, now that you've told us more about what happened?

ANUSH: Kind of gross but I'm glad I was able to do it, able to tell Amira and not wait 9 years again!

THERAPIST: Amira, what are you thinking, feeling?

AMIRA: I feel horrible. It's not a good feeling. I feel hurt for him. I feel angry at his parents though. I don't know why. I have so much anger for them. I feel like they should have known. I know exactly where my kids are all the time, or what's happening with them.

THERAPIST: Your first question was, "why didn't you tell your parents?" That's what you hope, that parents would protect their kids. And not only did they not protect you, back then kids did roam more freely, but you didn't tell them, or anyone else, which we need to understand more about. It didn't even occur to you to tell them. Not, "I thought about it, but I was afraid", or "I told them, and they didn't believe me". But it didn't even come into your mind, to tell them.

ANUSH: It would have been, "how do I explain this to them?" I didn't know what to say, how to say it – I was 7, 8, or 9 first time.

THERAPIST: That puts a lot of the duty of responding on you. Because it didn't occur to you to go to your dad or mom and show them you were upset.

ANUSH: I can understand how you can be angry at mom and dad, but I don't hold them accountable or responsible.

THERAPIST: You don't seem to hold the people who abused you accountable or responsible either. There is some way in which you have worked hard to make it okay, maybe so you could not be decimated.

ANUSH: I just probably just, as I got older and started understanding that this was wrong, looking back, it was probably because I didn't know how to deal with it or say something. They were young, they were growing, you know, puberty and everything, maybe they were just curious.

THERAPIST: I think that your attempt to understand their abusive behaviour in terms of puberty, and development, and curiosity, is reasonable, and important, but we also have to remember that at no point when you were in puberty, did it occur to you to touch a younger child.

ANUSH: No.

THERAPIST: You are curious when you are going through puberty, and you might look for whatever you can find to help you understand things, especially if you are in a family where there is not a lot of openness about sex or sexuality. But to touch a younger child and take advantage of them because you are curious is a whole other thing.

ANUSH: I know, for sure, that was wrong, I guess I was able to create a justification for them.

THERAPIST: And that protects you from feeling all of the feelings you might feel.

ANUSH: But I don't hold mom or dad responsible, they used to have gatherings galore, there used to be so many people at their house, all the time. I mean, it's not . . . mom and dad could not have been next to me, or know where I was all the time.

THERAPIST: I think all the things you are saying are reasonable, the boys were curious, my parents were busy, all of those things are true, but what Amira seems to be responding to is the emotional part which is: here is this man, this man who is my husband, the father of my children, someone I'm very close to. Someone I wish I could be closer to, who's had these experiences that have changed the course of his life, and there was no one there to help him, with or without all these justifications, there was nobody there to help him.

AMIRA: [silence, hanging head] I mean, this pretty much affected us all these years. I shouldn't be, but I feel that anger.

ANUSH: I think it's okay that she feels the anger.

THERAPIST: She feels what she feels. But for you, there are these secrets, some of those secrets might even be new to you, that have changed the course of your marriage. I guess you imagine or wish that it could have been different had these things not happened, or had you been able to talk about them and get therapy earlier.

ANUSH: I mean, I wish I could have told you, it was just locked up tight. I've always been sorry, when you used to come to me, I wanted so much to be able to get through how stuck I've been and just go to you, to be with you but, it was just there and I couldn't make myself . . . I've always thought of myself, you know, as being able to tackle difficult things. But, this, well . . . it's beat me.

THERAPIST: Well you have tackled many difficult things and, in a particular way, you've tackled this, but the way you tackled it was by shutting it down deep inside of yourself to keep yourself from being overcome and overwhelmed by the memories and all of the feelings that come with them. You must have felt very alone, having all of that inside and not even considering the possibility of talking about it.

ANUSH: It was hard; it has been extremely hard. I mean, I started feeling better about myself after I was able to finally get it out in the open. There was the relief of being able to tell somebody, that made me feel better. That didn't fix all of my difficulties, but it's been better.

THERAPIST: We have a couple of jobs to do here. One is to work through the feelings of guilt and shame that you've been carrying, and feelings of anger and hurt that you've been carrying, together, and the other is to try to work on getting your marriage shifted so you are not just friends who parent children, but romantic partners, lovers. That part of your marriage got broken, but it can get healed again. Those two things have to happen at the same time, they can't happen separately from each other.

You'll note that the level of detail provided by Anush was not high, but it was enough to provide bookends to the nature, severity, and chronicity of the abuse. Amira does not need to wonder about the extent of what happened and how long it went on. It is not necessary to provide a lot of details but enough that the partner has provided a beginning, middle, and an end to the trauma narrative.

Trauma processing in a dyadic context

There are many different approaches to trauma processing, differing based on the theoretical models espoused by the therapist, the nature of the trauma, the age of the survivor at the time of the trauma, and many other factors. All of these processes have one underlying goal, to help the survivor transform traumatic memories held as sensory, somatic, emotional, and cognitive time capsules – locked away in the body as if they were living in the present tense and experienced as still happening when they emerge in response to triggers or reminders of the original event (MacIntosh & Whiffen, 2005). The goal of trauma processing is to shift the experience of the trauma from a present reliving to a past memory, a part of the survivor's life story. Traumas cannot be memories until they no longer affect the survivor as if occurring in the present tense. The goal is not to transform these memories somehow into benign, painless, or formless pieces of history; these traumatic experiences will always be "bad" memories. However, if these memories become a part of the story of the survivor's life narrative – sad and painful to be certain, but no longer deeply embedded and embodied, no longer living as in the present moment – then the goal is achieved. The survivor would no longer live in fear of trauma popping out without advance notice, sucking them into the past masquerading as the present, sweeping them away from the life they are trying to build and into a past that needs to be put back in its place.

Trauma processing unfolds fairly seamlessly from the process of disclosure; these are not separate processes. As the stories are told, the thoughts, feelings, triggers, and rough patches that may previously have been avoided are laid bare. Healing begins through the experience of telling the story. The predominant approaches to trauma processing, which are shown to be most effective, are exposure-based interventions. These interventions focus on helping the survivor recount their traumatic experiences in detail, without avoiding the accompanying emotions and sensations, until the experiences are no longer emotionally overwhelming. However, many survivors struggle to tolerate the intensity of exposure-based treatments without the aid of skills building and psychoeducation; for them, exposure-based interventions can cause severe emotional flooding, functional backsliding, and serious retraumatization (Cloitre et al., 2006). Ensuring that the traumatic memories are disclosed and processed only after the preparatory work to build up emotion regulation and mentalizing self-capacities, and at a point when couples have begun to shift to security-based strategies to meet their attachment needs, tends to protect the survivor from being completely overwhelmed or retraumatized. Newer models of trauma treatment propose that the partner be included in the treatment to help the survivor persevere with the exposure work, work that they might otherwise abandon due to conscious and unconscious drives to continue to avoid such painful memories (Brown-Bowers, Fredman, Wanklyn, & Monson, 2012). Engaging in trauma processing in the dyad also includes the partner in the experience of healing and provides new opportunities for security-enhancing experiences. The goal, here, is to help the couple *both* resolve trauma symptoms *and* improve intimacy, closeness, mutual emotion regulation, and overall relationship satisfaction.

The initial psychoeducation sessions explored triggers with the couples, through to the skills-building processes, and on to working on building attachment security. Each of these steps in the process looked at trauma triggers from a different angle, with an emphasis on identification, communication between partners, and strategies for managing the trigger itself, and were not focused on processing the traumas fuelling the triggers and bringing survivors back into states of reliving and flashbacks. As the therapeutic process moves into trauma processing, the sessions explore these triggers again, this time in the context of the traumatic memories, sensations, and feelings that are at their core, and consider how these traumatic reliving experiences impact the couple relationship. This is also a way to examine, more deeply, the ways in which the trauma is intruding on the current relationship and to begin working through traumatic memories using basic exposure-processing strategies, with the partner's support. Through this process, we also develop strategies to manage those triggers that persist even after the processing work. You will need to move in and out of the exploration and processing as the need to titrate exposure to traumatic material impacts emotion regulation and mentalizing both within and outside of sessions. As with all of this work, take your time.

In looking at triggers, it can be helpful to impose some structure on the conversation. You might begin with questions such as:

What sensory triggers pull you back into the trauma?
What happens to time/feelings/body when you have a flashback?
Are there particular things that your partner may do or say that can trigger you?
Are there particular ways that your partner might speak/touch/respond to you that trigger you?
When you are having a flashback, are you aware of what is happening around you?
If your partner tries to speak/touch/hold you during a flashback, what is that like for you?
When you are triggered, what helps you get grounded?
Are there particular things that your partner does/says that you find very helpful when you are triggered?

For this dyadic process, ensure that there is time set aside to explore the triggers relationally. It can be difficult for a partner to hear that their attempts to soothe and care for their partner in distress are themselves experienced as triggers. Slice it thin as you try to find ways in which the survivor partner does find the response of their partner to be helpful, soothing, reorienting, or comforting. Continue to work on externalizing the trauma by examining the ways in which the trauma is embedded in their interaction cycles, those DTRs, and explore how the traumas – things done *to* the partners – are impacting their relationship. Once a full list of triggers has been developed by each of the traumatized partners, help the couple work together to develop another list of possible ways to work with the triggers. The goal of this is to reduce distress, re-experiencing, and arousal in response to reminders of the traumas, not necessarily to extinguish triggers completely. We need to help couples work together to address triggers related to traumatic memories, and reminders of the trauma, so that they have strategies that turn them towards one another, providing comfort, and working through the long-term impacts rather than avoiding them. Therefore, for some triggers, avoidance responses might be appropriate, such as no longer engaging sexually in ways that are triggering, and not expecting that startle responses related to sensory stimuli outside of the partner's conscious control will disappear with processing. While not advocating avoidance, I want to emphasize the importance of developing strategies that work, with balance and common sense. For most triggers, exposure with support is the most appropriate response. It is essential that trauma survivors understand that only through exposure will these triggers or traumatic responses eventually be extinguished. The goal is to help the couple actively develop strategies to address triggers head-on. For instance, one partner might be particularly triggered when he is standing at the sink, doing dishes, and his partner comes up behind him to bring him the remainder of the dishes from the dining room table. Perhaps the sound of the feet approaching reminds him of his father approaching him from behind in the lead-up to brutal sexual abuse. Or maybe it is simply that when he cannot see someone coming, he becomes startled and afraid but cannot quite put his finger on why this is a trigger. So, how can the couple work together to solve this? One way might be for them to develop a strategy to manage situations where one might startle the other. They could agree to say something to each other when entering a room or when approaching their partner from behind. Usually, once the frozen paralysis of a trauma response has dissipated, couples can come up with simple and effective solutions. The capacity to mentalize will be most acutely called on here as couples find their way into one another's experiences and wend their way back to themselves, considering how to build new, more expansive, and effectively contextualized relational responses and cycles of engagement.

Once these triggers have been explored in depth, the couple can begin to explore aspects of their relationship that are changing in response to their greater understanding of each other's histories and traumas. Some trauma survivors will already have engaged in extensive psychotherapy prior to their arrival for this treatment. For those survivors, it may be enough to recount their traumas and work on triggers with their partner. However, in spite of having engaged in psychotherapy, many survivors will continue to show trauma symptoms that interfere with their daily living. For them, this stage allows for some processing of these traumas in the context of their couple relationship and therapy. This manual deals with traumas that have occurred in the past, primarily during childhood, rather than such shared traumas as when a couple experiences a devastating loss or accident, such as a stillbirth or death of a child. Where traumas are shared, the process shifts from one where one partner is sharing and another is supporting to one where both partners are processing the same trauma but each from their own unique vantage point.

It is important to monitor the emotion regulation capacities of both partners quite closely as you work through painful trauma memories in sessions, pushing but not exceeding boundaries of tolerance. One approach is to use exposure paradigms: the survivor makes a list of memories about which flashbacks, intrusions, and nightmares still occur and then orders those memories based on the level of distress they feel when remembering and retelling them. Based on this hierarchy, the survivor can be supported to recount these memories in detail, starting with the least distressing. Each subsequent memory should begin to yield its traumatic power and shift from the present tense to the past, from intruding to recalling, from overwhelming to manageable. This approach to trauma processes has the advantage of being very clear, easily understood, and easily implemented. However, when looking at traumatic memories that continue to cause distress, it is also important to consider the relational impacts of these memories as well as the impact the retelling will have on the partner. These considerations will affect the order in which memories are approached. Also, using exposure-based paradigms requires that the therapist keep a very close eye on the therapeutic window – the window of emotion tolerance – to ensure that the survivor is feeling the feelings associated with their traumatic experiences but is not flooded, numbed out, or dissociated. It is essential to avoid retraumatization and emotional flooding or dissociation, as any of these could jeopardize the excellent work of building skills and capacities that has been done to this point and risk damaging the fragile safety and trust within the therapeutic relationship.

For many therapists, exposure-based paradigms feel too structured and scripted. These therapists may prefer a more intuitive, emergent approach to the processing of traumatic memories, one that involves ordering the traumatic memories based on what is happening in the lives of the couple, when strategies for dealing with triggers fail or result in the resurrection of other traumatic memories. However, regardless of the approach chosen, it is essential for traumatic memory processing to be thorough, and for the survivor to be able to tell the stories of their experiences clearly and with emotion, within the safety of the session, without becoming reactivated and triggered into re-experiencing. Throughout this process, it is important to keep checking in with the survivor, to keep engaging the survivor in the discussion of the memories and the impact of the traumas, and to maintain the ongoing process of empowering the couple to improve their relationship both through decreasing trauma symptoms in the survivor(s) and also by increasing their capacities for mutual regulation, mentalizing, and secure attachment, as they solve problems and resolve traumas together.

Staying with Anush and Amira and the memory of the older boys at the pool, our session on disclosure was followed by a session on processing this trauma memory which had only recently emerged for Anush. The goals were clear: to reduce avoidance and increase the sense of the traumatic memory as being a story about one's life, an awful story but one with a beginning, a middle, and an end, felt and known to be a part of one's life history. For a traumatic memory to be "translated" away from being a flashback or intrusive memory, it has to make the shift from a primarily sensory memory – sights, sounds, smells, tastes, touches, feelings and flooding – to an autobiographical memory: words, feelings, thoughts, and ideas. No one is ever going to say that these are good memories, but with enough processing they do, indeed, become a part of one's integrated life story (MacIntosh & Whiffen, 2005). Given the extreme efforts Anush has gone through to avoid thinking about his traumas, it is important to help him with emotion regulation as he faces these incredibly painful and shameful memories, to help him to integrate his emotions with the sensory and cognitive aspects of the memories and pull them out of the fuzzy, avoided space they currently inhabit and into his life story.

THERAPIST: In the last session you shared some of the details of these new memories that have resurfaced with Amira, to bring her into the picture of what you are going through. I'm hoping that today we can work our way through the central memory that you have told me about in such a way as to take some of the edge off of it, to bring it more into your memory of yourself and less as a memory that is uninvitedly intruding on you.

ANUSH: Okay, that's not going to be fun. [both laugh]

THERAPIST: Amira, how do you feel about spending some time together working on this memory?

AMIRA: Okay, I just don't know what to do. How can I help him?

THERAPIST: Anush, what do you think would be helpful for Amira to do or be as we are working on this memory?

ANUSH: Just being here. Maybe you could hold my hand?

AMIRA: Of course.

THERAPIST: Okay, so, Anush, let us know if what you need from Amira and me changes as we move along. Let's start at the beginning. Let's flesh out the context first: how old were you, where were you living, what time of year was it, things like that.

ANUSH: First, I was, seven or eight. It was summertime and we were living in the house with my uncle. I had a friend that lived behind our house and they had a pool. We'd go over often to play outside in the pool. Looking back, there were two brothers, they would have been in their early teens.

THERAPIST: So they were like 13–14, and you were like seven or eight. That would be four to five years difference between you. These were the older brothers of your friend?

ANUSH: No. These were just older friends.

THERAPIST: Okay, they were boys who lived in the house with the pool and you went over to play?

ANUSH: Yeah, and sometimes we'd play street hockey, but mostly we were swimming.

THERAPIST: Did your sister or anyone else in your family know these neighbours and go over to the pool or was it just you?

ANUSH: It was just me.

THERAPIST: And you'd play hockey with them?

ANUSH: I don't remember their names. They were close in age, within a year or two of each other. They were in their early teens, they were probably at the age where they were very curious and just becoming aware of – starting to go through puberty, maybe I'm just trying to justify, I don't know. But one of them was.

By setting the context, I was entering into the traumatic memory by referring to aspects of the experience that are remembered more calmly and do not trigger overwhelming emotions. I was also creating anchor points to come back to when emotions become overwhelming. These anchor points – the swimming pool, the hockey, the ages of the other boys – offer places to return if the survivor finds their way into a fuzzy no-thinking zone and enter the traumatic memory more experientially, especially if they lose their capacity to knit together the beginning, middle, and end pieces of the story.

THERAPIST: What do you remember happened and what can you tell us about that?

ANUSH: Well, we were swimming at the pool and, like I said last time, someone started jerking off. I didn't really know what they were doing, I didn't get it.

THERAPIST: Let's just fill out the picture a bit. Where were you, exactly, while this was happening?

ANUSH: I was still in the water with my friend. I think we were both watching.

THERAPIST: Do you remember what you were wearing?

ANUSH: No. I don't remember what I was wearing, I don't remember what the other boys were wearing. I do remember from the flashbacks, the guy who started it wasn't wearing anything.

THERAPIST: So he wasn't wearing anything. Do you remember the progression from having his clothes on to not having his clothes on?

ANUSH: No, I don't seem to. I just picture us as friends, playing by the pool, and it had like a little diving board.

THERAPIST: And can you tell me what happened? What he did?

ANUSH: Ack, all I remember is – well, I don't recall him touching me, but I remember him grabbing my hand and having me touch him. I can see a picture of him grabbing me. I don't recall him touching me, it was him having me touch him.

THERAPIST: And do you remember how you felt?

ANUSH: I don't, I don't remember how I felt. I just know – I mean, at that age what I should or shouldn't feel – I mean, if I compare it to that last event when I was older, I knew for sure at that time, when it happened, that it didn't feel right. Like I just knew it wasn't right, I didn't feel comfortable, but I don't know then how I felt.

THERAPIST: Okay, so when you say it was a flashback, pictures of seeing him and you. . .

ANUSH: Yeah, I mean, pictures of us playing by the pool.

THERAPIST: So you see the pictures, you think there was confusion but you're having a hard time finding any of the feelings that go along with those pictures and thoughts.

ANUSH: No, I really don't.

Remembering that Anush's primary emotion regulation strategy is emotional avoidance, I was trying to slice it more thinly, to ask as many questions as possible that would pull him into the sensory aspects of the memory – the part that will help him access the experience, not just the cognitions. So, I was asking about senses, colours, clothing, what he saw, feelings, and sensations and trying to expand the story to include as many moment-by-moment details as possible.

THERAPIST: Okay. When you were talking about it last week you told us that the grabbed your hand and forced you to touch him. How forceful was this?

ANUSH: It was pretty forceful. Like I can remember feeling my arm jolting and hurting but I don't really know, I was pretty little.

THERAPIST: When these flashbacks happen, how do you feel?

ANUSH: No. I can't say that I know how I felt.

THERAPIST: And in the moment of having the flashback, how were you feeling?

ANUSH: Like how would I picture myself?

THERAPIST: So, in the actual moment when a picture comes up, in that moment, what are you feeling?

ANUSH: I guess, I don't really know, the pictures just come and go, and I feel kind of drowned by them.

THERAPIST: Let's see if we can get a little closer to the memory and the feelings that go with it. I want you to bring your mind back to the moment in the pool. You were in the pool, playing with your friend, and then . . . in as much detail as you can call up, tell us what happens moment by moment, picture by picture, feeling by feeling.

ANUSH: I'll try.

AMIRA: Are you worried about me hearing?

ANUSH: No, no, that's not it, I just get so, I don't know, fuzzy, when I try to think about it. It's all in bits and pieces.

THERAPIST: One of the goals of this is to find a way to take those bits and pieces and make them into a story that has a beginning, middle, and end. So let's just go step by step and see how we do.

ANUSH: Well, the next picture after just playing in the pool is seeing the older boy take his pants down and start kind of dancing around.

THERAPIST: Can you describe that?

ANUSH: Well, I guess like, shaking around and kind of trying to push his penis in everyone's direction. I remember kind of startling and turning around to see what was going on.

THERAPIST: Keep going, what was next?

ANUSH: He was dancing around and then he started touching himself. I didn't really understand it at the time but when I had the flashbacks, I realized that he had an erection.

THERAPIST: Can you remember what you were feeling, thinking, when you saw his erection?

ANUSH: I guess I was curious because I had never seen one before. I remember feeling surprised, I guess, and curious.

THERAPIST: It makes sense that you would feel surprised and curious. Many boys would also feel a bit aroused, even though they didn't understand it. What about you?

ANUSH: I don't know; I don't think so. It all happened so fast. I remember that it was almost right after that that he came up to me by the side of the pool and grabbed my hand and put it around his penis and started rubbing it back and forth. I wasn't steady in the pool so he was doing that with my hand and I kept slipping and I hit my chin on the side of the pool. It really hurt.

THERAPIST: Oh dear, that sounds scary and painful.

AMIRA: [Amira is crying at this point] I can't imagine how I would feel if someone did that to our kids. I would lose my mind. [Amira reached for Anush and put her hand on his knee, firmly]

ANUSH: It was scary, I was afraid I was going to go under the water and I didn't understand what he was doing.

THERAPIST: You were afraid, you were so little and so afraid. Can you stay with those feelings and tell us what happened next?

ANUSH: The memory sort of stops there. I remember what I now know is he ejaculated but I didn't know what it was and I was really scared that something bad had happened, that he was sick or something. As soon as he was done he pushed me into the water, he pushed my head under the water and I couldn't breathe for a second and then, when I came up, he was gone and my friend was just looking at me.

THERAPIST: Do you remember what you were feeling when he pushed you into the water, when you couldn't breathe?

ANUSH: I was really scared.

THERAPIST: What happened next? What do you remember feeling in your body?

ANUSH: I just remember running home in my wet bathing suit and that's it.

THERAPIST: It sounds as though there were many frightening things about this experience, not just the sexual violation but also him grabbing you, hitting your chin on the poolside, pushing your head under the water. It also sounds as though you were too young to really understand the sexual part of what was happening just that it was weird and confusing and felt frightening. All of these things put together made it a very frightening event for you and one that you worked really hard to push away from your mind for a lot of years. How are you feeling now that you've told us about this experience?

ANUSH: A bit wobbly, I guess.

THERAPIST: Amira, what are you thinking and feeling as Anush tells us about this experience?

AMIRA: Well, I just feel like, I wish I had been there, I wish I could have helped him, protected him. I guess it really helps me understand what we've been going through all of these years. How could he have felt okay with sex and being close to me having had all of these experiences?

THERAPIST: It sounds as though understanding more about what Anush has been through is helping you understand the difficulties you have had as a couple. It also sounds as though you are feeling a lot of sadness and anger for what happened to him. Anush, what is it like for you for Amira to know more about your story and to understand what you've been through and feel sad and angry about that?

ANUSH: It feels okay, I think, maybe even good. It feels better that she knows and that it's all out in the open. I didn't think I could feel better by talking about it, but I do feel a weight lifted off of my shoulders.

Throughout this process, Amira was attentive both physically and emotionally to Anush. She was perched in her seat, holding his hand, reaching for him and sending him lots of non-verbal messages of love and support. In hearing more about his experiences of trauma, some of her anger melted away. She was able to see more clearly, by feeling the details through her love as a wife but also as a mother, how paralyzed he was and how impossible sex and closeness might have become for him. As the session came to an end, Anush appeared proud, more relaxed, and visibly more comfortable sitting with Amira close to him.

You will notice that I took a few runs at trying to ask questions that might help Anush identify, feel, and express his emotions in relation to this memory. I asked directly, what feelings came up for him in the memory, and also indirectly, how he felt when he had the flashback. Neither of these proved successful. One of the challenges Anush faced in his trauma processing was that his memories were very fragmented: they skipped in time from one image to the next. His memories were predominantly visual, with little other sensory detail: no sounds, no feelings, just a picture coming and going in his mind. When trying to recount the memory, he kept coming back to thoughts and could not find his way into the feelings. We would then go back and try again to break the memory down into smaller segments, to focus on sensations that might help make a bridge between the traumatic memory of the past living in the present. I was trying to help him get closer to the memory in a way that would allow for the integration of past and present, feeling and thinking. When we tried this, Anush did seem to be more able to find a narrative by putting the fragments in a line, moment by moment in time. Once this had occurred, some of his feelings became more accessible to him: the pain of hitting his chin, his fear and confusion, the wet bathing suit, the surprising erection and ejaculation.

I have chosen to highlight a trauma processing session in a couple where only one partner has experienced sexual abuse and a memory that is not as violent as many we hear. This trauma was also not committed by an attachment figure. I chose this memory to illustrate a partner who was not triggered by the retelling and who could be very present and emotionally regulated for her husband. I am also aware that many of the clinicians who are reading this book are trauma survivors themselves, and did not want to expose them to more graphic violence than was necessary to illustrate the point. However, I will say it again: this is tough work, we hear absolutely gruesome, horrible things, and it will be necessary to hear gruesome horrible things to help these couples work through their traumatic experiences, so be careful and take care of yourself at every possible step. When the memories are more horrible and when the partner is also a trauma survivor, you will need to go more slowly, break memories down into smaller chunks, support partners who get triggered, take turns with trauma processing so both partners have equal time in the driver's seat, and make sure to take care of yourself after sessions in which a lot of blood, guts, and gore are spilled.

Working with sex and sexuality

For many couples, conflicts and challenges around sex are at the forefront of their concerns right from the first session. For others, discussions about sex and sexuality are on the back burner, behind their more primary concerns about closeness and escalating conflict. Amira began her first session with Anush indicating that their primary goal was to address their sexual relationship, whereas Gary and Geoffrey very rarely discussed their sexual relationship, describing it as rich and vibrant and a place where their conflicts disappeared. Childhood trauma couples, especially those that have experienced sexual abuse, have unique struggles in their sexual relationships that require gentle, compassionate, and skilled interventions. The section that follows will outline strategies for dealing with sexual secrets, reducing any bifurcation of sexuality, dealing with triggers, and increasing sexual intimacy. When the couple is ready to begin working together on their sexual relationship, it will be necessary to go slowly and to titrate exposure to triggering, shameful, or conflict-causing sexual material. This work involves finding gentle paths to navigate the way through explorations of the couples' current sexual life, and working to gradually shift avoidance and reduce dissociation. Eventually, the work involves building bridges between the partners as they begin to rebuild their sexual relationship.

The first step in the process of addressing issues in sex and sexuality is to gradually confront sexual secrets and any bifurcation of sexuality. Through a combination of individual and couple sessions, you will work to unpeel the many layers of sexual conditioning and avoidance, along with layers upon layers of secrecy. Some authors argue that individual sessions can be dangerous to the therapeutic alliance and cause unnecessary anxiety about what is being shared. However, uncontrolled, uncontained, and premature disclosures of sexual secrets in the context of couple sessions can lead to greater damage and pain being inflicted upon partners. Moreover, individual sessions may be necessary, as sexual secrets are not easily disclosed when they are surrounded by a garrison of guilt and shame. Therapists may find themselves trying to navigate unplanned discussions about sex and sexuality in couple sessions, in the middle of a minefield of undisclosed compulsive sexual behaviours or extra-dyadic sexual contacts beyond the agreements the couple may have had. For some couples, individual sessions are held at the outset of work on sexual issues and continue throughout treatment, when it seems important to provide an opportunity to bring new disclosures to the therapist or to help explore and plan for challenging disclosures to the partner (MacIntosh, 2017c). Unplanned disclosures of painful sexual secrets, especially those that violate a couple's implicit or explicit relational values, can be very destructive.

Decreasing sexual secrets

The first step in addressing issues in sex and sexuality is to gradually confront sexual secrets and any bifurcation of sexuality. As reviewed in the psychoeducational section on sex and sexuality, the sexual challenges of trauma survivors, especially sexual abuse survivors, can run the range from difficulties with initiation and arousal, to deeply entrenched, painfully shameful, sexual compulsions and reenactments that may be lived out in dangerous and unsafe circumstances. When survivors are steeped in sexual secrets, they can end up leading a double life involving a distant, disconnected, and traumatically deadened sexual relationship with their spouse, along with a shame-filled, chaotic, compulsive, or traumatically reenacted sexual life lived out in dissociative fantasy outside of the relationship.

While partners often have a strong feeling that there are sexual shadows lurking in the corners of their relationship, avoidance is not a one-way street. While struggling with the feeling of distance from their partner, however, there is often a great deal of ambivalence about breaking the silence: maybe knowing more will make things worse, bringing more grief, more anger, or more pain. And, when the secrets come out, partners who have been sheltered from secrets, including secrets about sexual compulsions and reenactments, can feel betrayed in ways that feel like they cannot be healed, so that relationships may fall apart. Many partners can stick it out in the face of careful, compassionate, and contextualized disclosures to work on healing their relationships, but this is a long, hard road.

In the case of Geoffrey and Gary, I held individual sessions with Gary to give him the opportunity to tell me, for the first time, about his feelings of shame and anxiety in relation to sexually compulsive behaviour. These drives had pulled him into a dark cavern of compulsive reenactments with men he did not know and who were often violent. While the couple aspired to a healthy polyamorous relationship, his extra-dyadic sexual activities did not fall within the couple's agreed-upon parameters, and were kept a secret from Geoffrey. He was in torment, filled with shame about his inability to stop reliving his abuse over and over again through these sexual nightmares with strangers. These disclosures were made to me first, to protect both partners. Gary needed to have the opportunity to share these secrets first to someone who would not be devastated and betrayed, to have space for exploration and understanding of his compulsions and the nature of his reenactments, before making decisions about how, when, where, and how much to disclose to Geoffrey. Working on such challenging material without the emotional challenge of an attachment figure in the room allows the survivor space to try to disclose and discuss things that have been hidden in their deepest recesses, without becoming dysregulated or dissociated. Individual sessions are also important for partners, to give them an opportunity to share their anger, hurt, pain, and fear about the sexual issues they are facing with their partner. Sexual secrets have a particular potency: the potential for irreparable rupture is high, and careful planning of disclosures is essential for the well-being of both partners and the relationship.

When it is time for disclosures, they must be well-timed and carefully prepared, with a focus on emotion regulation, ongoing mentalizing, and preserving the fragile attachment. Decisions must also be made about how much to disclose. On the one hand, secrets stand between the couple and will get in the way of rebuilding attachment. On the other hand, some secrets have the potential to devastate the partner. As discussed in the section on disclosure, the question of whether the partner needs to know all of the nitty-gritty details is one that deserves careful scrutiny. It is often enough to share the model scene of the sexual secret: enough that the secret is unveiled but not so much that the partner is torn open. Once sexual secrets have been shared, it is essential to make enough time to explore the injuries to both partners in the relationship and to the relationship itself, time to explore the possibility of healing. Sexual secrets have a unique potential to cause pain; how can the partner tolerate not feeling desired while their survivor partner is engaging in a secret sexual life elsewhere, even if that life is unwanted and disavowed.

Reducing bifurcation

Once the secrets have been told, and the partner is brought into the hidden sexual life of the survivor, healing the divide between the two sides of their sexuality can begin. Early sexual conditioning through sexual abuse is powerful and not easily changed. In fact, it is unlikely that sexual conditioning to traumatic stimuli will change. Helping survivors turn towards their partners to have their sexual needs met, rather than away and into a dissociated double sexual life, involves finding ways to develop a sexual life together that both find arousing and satisfying. However, when secrets are broken down and the partner is brought into discussions about sexual needs and struggles, it becomes possible for the couple to navigate and negotiate how they will deal with conditioned sexual arousal that does not fit into their sexual comfort zone.

Looking at the case of Anush and Amira, individual sessions were held with each of them to pry apart the impact of sexual secrets on their relationship. Sessions with Amira helped her work on her anger, hurt, and betrayal at the long-term impacts of being in a marriage with someone who had been hiding a huge secret the entire time. She was able to discuss her affairs in more detail, to discuss her reasons for staying in the marriage, and to dive into the anguish she experienced over those many years. For Anush, individual sessions were geared towards helping him integrate his divided sexuality, reduce dissociation and compulsive sexual behaviour, and prepare to bring his wife into his process of sexual healing. Anush struggled to connect with Amira in any sexual way in spite of his deep love and strong attraction for her. While he was terrified of losing her, he was also terrified of pushing through his own smokescreen. Try as he might, Anush could not initiate any sexual contact with Amira. Every time he tried to approach her, he became paralyzed with fear and shut down completely. His sexuality was channelled into a state of dissociative compulsive masturbation to Internet pornography. He would find himself sucked into a quagmire of masturbation for hours and hours to pornography that repelled him, seemingly without any understanding of how he got there. While Anush was deeply attracted to his wife and identifies as heterosexual, his pornography choices were predominantly homosexual. Over time, the pornography had shifted from consensual and erotic portrayals to non-consensual, violent, and painful ones.

The first step in this work with Anush was not disclosure, but rather to help Anush become less dissociative in relation to his compulsive sexuality. This started with asking Anush to try to monitor his masturbation: when, where, what, for how long, and so forth. He was to track when he masturbated, to what kind of pornography, how long it went on, and where he was at the time. Eventually he was asked to track back as much as he was able, to identify the moment when he became aware of the urge to masturbate, what was happening at the time, what he was thinking and feeling, at what point he started to dissociate, and what happened when the episode was over. Over time, the simple task of tracking his sexual compulsions expanded his awareness of the complexity of his sexual compulsions; with awareness and decreased avoidance came decreased dissociation and an increasing ability to contain and control his unwanted compulsive sexual activity. It was at this point that we were able to bring Amira into the conversation. Feeling more in control of his compulsions, Anush also felt more able to disclose one factor that was standing between them. Amira was more understanding than Anush imagined she would be. At the point of disclosure, Amira had a strong understanding of the impact of Anush's trauma and even felt a sense of relief that more secrets had been let go. In a transcript from an individual session, Anush describes turning away from his fear of sexual engagement with an Amira who is eager for a sexual connection, towards masturbation and pornography. It is best for practitioners to be as straightforward in these conversations as possible; I find that the less fluff, the better when it comes to talking about sexual issues that are shameful or embarrassing to the survivor.

THERAPIST: And when you masturbate on your own, what are the feelings that go with that?

ANUSH: Just to release, you know.

THERAPIST: So, masturbation is how you take care of your sexual needs when you feel aroused?

ANUSH: Yes.

THERAPIST: And when you masturbate what are you thinking about, feeling?

ANUSH: Nothing really, I guess; it's just mindless.

THERAPIST: And what about pornography or Internet porn, do you use any of that?

ANUSH: Yes, that's there, I mean, I'm interested in sex, that's not gone.

THERAPIST: It's not gone.

ANUSH: It's not gone.

THERAPIST: It's just with other human beings that it's impacted.

ANUSH: Yeah. I am just starting to understand, from these sessions, things are really making so much sense, that – you know, I'm not the only one – it's just more clear. But, I can't seem to make myself . . . to be with her, I – and, she has no idea; if she knew, she would be devastated that I don't touch her but then. . .

THERAPIST: And what kind of porn is it that you watch?

ANUSH: I don't know how to describe it. . .

THERAPIST: Well, men with women, men with men, women with women, adults?

ANUSH: Definitely adults! But, well, I guess it's men with men stuff. I like women, I mean, I am attracted to Amira but, I've always, I guess, it's just what turns me on.

THERAPIST: And, how often are you masturbating to pornography?

ANUSH: Well, I guess, most days, when she goes to bed, I stay downstairs and. . .

THERAPIST: And?

ANUSH: Well, sometimes I just get lost in there, I sort of wake up and it's two or three in the morning and I don't really even know what I've been doing.

THERAPIST: And how do you feel when you "wake up"?

ANUSH: Disgusting.

THERAPIST: Disgusting, you find yourself lost in the pornography but terrified of being close to your wife. There is nothing inhibiting you at the level of your own sexual arousal, your erection, being stimulated, but it's all separated, dissociated from your wife, even, in a way, from you. It's disconnected.

In another session, Anush and I discussed the results of our efforts to decrease dissociation and compulsive masturbation to pornography through tracking, expanding awareness, and rending the veil of secrecy. Anush is a Muslim man from a culture where the divisions and roles between men and women are very clear and prescribed. While he grew up and lives in a western context, it was still difficult for him to talk to a woman about his sexual compulsions. However, in many ways, it was healing for him to be able to open up to me, a female therapist, and break down his avoidance of even thinking about his hidden sexual life. While these particular working sessions were one on one, they were very much a part of the couple process, preparing Anush for the couple sessions and titrating exposure for Amira to this new information.

THERAPIST: How did you do with the tracking last week?

ANUSH: Okay, I guess.

THERAPIST: What did you notice?

ANUSH: Well, it's worse than I thought it was. I don't think I had any idea how often it's happening and how out of it I am.

THERAPIST: Can you tell me about how often, where you were, what you were watching when it happened and how you felt when it was happening?

ANUSH: It definitely happened every night after Amira went to bed and it always happens in the basement. I don't remember what I felt.

THERAPIST: And the porn? Can you tell me about it?

ANUSH: I'd rather not, actually.

THERAPIST: What makes it hard for you to talk about?

ANUSH: Well, it's . . . I guess, it's embarrassing.

THERAPIST: Yes, I get that, but we aren't going to get rid of the shame and dissociation if we don't talk about this stuff. The more we expose the things that happen in the darkness, the more we lift off the cover of the things that are standing between you and Amira.

ANUSH: I know, it's just super uncomfortable.

THERAPIST: Yes, I know but, here we are . . . this is the work we are doing, and we've just got to keep going and push through the uncomfortable to get to a better space. So, let's take another run at that one – what can you tell me about the porn you were watching last week when you were tracking?

ANUSH: Ugh; okay, well, mostly it was just guys fucking guys, like I said.

THERAPIST: Can you tell me more about what it was in the porn that you found arousing?

ANUSH: I'm not sure, there is something about their huge erections and the rawness to it, it's just so out there.

THERAPIST: When you say you don't remember how you felt, do you remember how you didn't feel?

ANUSH: What?

THERAPIST: Okay, I know, weird question, but sometimes, through the fuzz of the dissociation, we can see something about what we are trying not to feel. Does that make sense?

ANUSH: Well, I guess that makes sense. I think I'm trying not to feel so revolted but it's not working.

THERAPIST: Revolted, that sounds really awful. I'm curious, when you said that you were aroused by the big erections it brought to mind what you told Amira and I about what you felt during the abuse at the pool, that you were surprised by the size of your abuser's penis and what an erection looked like. Do you think there could be any connection there?

ANUSH: Um, I never thought about that. Maybe. I don't know.

THERAPIST: Okay, well, this week when you are tracking what I want you to start noticing is the things that happen before you start watching the porn and masturbating, what was happening before you felt the urge, what you were feeling and thinking as you started to sink into that place where you start to get fuzzy and turn to the porn. I also want you to start tracking your awareness of your arousal so that we can start looking at patterns and try to connect it up to some of the struggles you are having with your relationship with your sexuality and with Amira.

ANUSH: I do want to work on this, but it is pretty awful.

THERAPIST: I know, it's really hard, and it's hard to imagine that things can change, but we have to slow but steady this by going a little deeper each week.

Navigating triggers

During the psychoeducational module on sex and sexuality, the couple had the opportunity to begin discussing their sexual triggers, the relationship between these and their trauma history, and the impact of sexual triggers on their relationship. Now is the time to deepen those conversations. As we delve into the ways that the survivor may be triggered by sexual contact with their partner, therapist and partners will work together to develop strategies to manage the triggers and, eventually, to desensitize and diminish them.

As the couple discusses their triggers, ask survivors to place them in the context of their traumatic experiences to ensure that their partners understand the relevant context. When partners understand the origins of a trigger, there can be a shift from hurt or anger – why doesn't she want me? – to empathy and compassion. Most likely, the trauma memories that unfold through this process will have been disclosed and discussed already through the therapy process, but an extra layer of understanding results when the pieces are brought together to link past trauma to current sexual triggers. When triggers have been linked to traumatic memories, it is important for the couple to talk together about how those triggers have infiltrated their relationship and how this has impacted the two of them and their sexual connection. This is an opportunity for them to really flex their new mentalizing capacities: it can be very painful to hear your partner talking about their trauma and how you, a person who loves them so deeply, could remind the survivor of anything related to such horrors. Examining each trigger in detail will most likely produce more than one list. There will be a list of triggers that are related to sexual stimuli that are unavoidable, a list of those that are avoidable, and possibly a list of triggers connected to sexual activities that are particularly arousing for one or both partners and represent a loss to them if the triggers cannot be worked through and desensitized. Many survivors find the experience of sexual arousal itself to be triggering, so this process needs to start with the basic building blocks of sexual connection. For the couple to have a rich and pleasurable sex life, this is an example of a trigger that needs to be worked through.

Once the lists of triggers have been put together, the couple will work together to go through the list and develop strategies for each one, with your help. For unavoidable triggers, you will help them develop skills for gradual exposure and desensitization, as will be discussed below. For avoidable triggers, the couple can decide if they want to remove them from their sexual repertoire or work on desensitization. In the end, the process aims to create safety in their sexual relationship. If survivors feel that their partner fully understands the impact of their sexual trauma, that strategies are in place, and that they can talk about issues as they arise, this goes a long way towards developing a sexual relationship that is flexible, fulfilling, and fun. It also creates the context where mistakes can be made safely and conflict is reduced; if you really feel that your partner understands you and has taken you seriously, when triggers do get aroused it does not feel like an injury but rather an opportunity to use those secure base behaviours and let your partner comfort and soothe you.

In the following segment, Camille is trying to help Chris and me understand how she gets triggered by both sexual and emotional arousal, and how she responds to this in their sexual relationship. Chris is flexing his new mentalizing and attachment capacities by being able to listen and give some words to her experience as they explain it to me.

CAMILLE: It's like I – it's too – intense. As soon as I feel too much. . .

THERAPIST: Like too turned on?

CAMILLE: Not necessarily just turned on but, even if it's too much going on, like too much moving and breathing and bodies all over the place, I get stressed.

THERAPIST: Okay. Can you say more?

CAMILLE: And then I just can't. I get freaked out.

THERAPIST: What does that look like?

CAMILLE: Well, I don't know how to describe it, I just, I just get scared, or I get – I'm not comfortable.

THERAPIST: And would Chris know that that was happening?

CAMILLE: Usually, yeah.

CHRIS: Yeah, she usually starts to cry, and then she looks away from me, or she tenses all up, and I just have to kind of, like, remind her that I'm not hurting her, and that it doesn't need to be scary.

THERAPIST: Does that help?

CAMILLE: Sometimes. Like, it usually helps. But sometimes it's just too much, and I don't want to continue.

THERAPIST: And you're able to say so?

CAMILLE: Yeah.

THERAPIST: Okay. And are there particular triggers, particular positions or activities that trigger you?

CAMILLE: Well, recently it's just weight, on top of me that sometimes is triggering. Umm – it's usually feeling too much. Also, it's triggering, um, when my hair gets pulled, either by accident or on purpose.

THERAPIST: Okay.

CAMILLE: Umm, yeah. It's just mostly that.

THERAPIST: And are you able to orient yourself, like: you know where you are, who you are, that you are with Chris?

CAMILLE: No, I lose. . .

THERAPIST: You lose that.

CAMILLE: Yeah. Sometimes I can't even see.

THERAPIST: And what do you do?

CAMILLE: Well, I get sucked into freaking out.

THERAPIST: So, when you say freaking out, are you like screaming and yelling?

CAMILLE: No, usually it's just sad.

THERAPIST: So you cry?

CAMILLE: Yeah.

THERAPIST: Okay.

CAMILLE: Or I tense up.

THERAPIST: And do you have any sense of what is connected to that response? Do you have a memory, or, some kind of body flashback, coming into you when you start to get overwhelmed and freaked out?

CAMILLE: Sometimes I do. . .

THERAPIST: Yes.

CAMILLE: And sometimes I don't. Usually, when I do have a memory, it's the feeling of being held down by the man, like being smothered and then I just have to get out, I can't think, I just have to get out.

THERAPIST: Okay. So, sometimes it's really clear what the trigger is, and sometimes it's just feelings?

CAMILLE: Yeah.

THERAPIST: Okay. And has that changed over time?

CAMILLE: Hmmm.

CHRIS: I'm able to calm her down more than I used to.

THERAPIST: Yes?

CHRIS: Because when I first started, she – we'd have to stop a lot more; now – now, it's like, I can – I can calm her down and then keep it going.

THERAPIST: So you have learned how to help her? Like you understand it more?

CHRIS: More often, yeah.

THERAPIST: More often.

CHRIS: And sometimes, like she said, it's just too much, and she can't. . .

THERAPIST: So, you just stop.

CHRIS: Yeah.

THERAPIST: And how's that for you?

CHRIS: Well, it sucks, but, it's okay. I don't want her to be so upset.

THERAPIST: It is what it is?

CHRIS: Yeah.

THERAPIST: So, Camille, would you say it's changed over time? Chris is saying it's a little better than it used to be.

CAMILLE: The feeling doesn't change.

THERAPIST: Okay.

CAMILLE: How he deals with it, has changed.

THERAPIST: Oh, I see. Okay. Can you say more about that?

CAMILLE: Well, he does seem to be more understanding, and he notices sooner and he backs off.

THERAPIST: And that feels better for you?

CAMILLE: Yes, he doesn't get angry anymore, he just stays with me. He still wants to hold me, but he seems to be getting better about not holding me when I can't stand to be touched.

THERAPIST: Chris, would you agree?

CHRIS: Yes, that sounds about right.

THERAPIST: So it sounds as though the two of you have made a lot of progress on this on your own through talking and understanding. I'm wondering if we could work on developing a more specific strategy for this trigger with the goal of being able to work through it before it gets too overwhelming and, maybe, to even be able to continue with the sexual experience without having to abort it. Camille, do you think there is a way that you could signal to Chris that those feelings are starting well before you get to the point where you are freaking out?

CAMILLE: I feel like I try but I start to get so overwhelmed that I can't talk or anything.

THERAPIST: Okay, what about a hand signal or gesture? Might you be able to make a sign like "time out"? [shows hands with T like a coach]

CAMILLE: Yeah, I could probably do that, but it would have to be before it gets too far.

THERAPIST: Chris, do you think you would be able to respond to that signal, stop and be with Camille for a bit until it settles?

CHRIS: Totally, that would be fine. I just wish I could hold her when she is feeling like that.

THERAPIST: I know. It's still really hard for you to understand that Camille needs to not be held when she is upset and triggered. I guess even though you get that being held down during the assault gets triggered, that part of you that feels like you would want to be held still doesn't quite compute Camille's need.

CHRIS: Yeah.

THERAPIST: Okay, so, can we try that the next time it happens? Camille, you signal, as soon as you are aware of feeling the feeling of suffocation and being trapped; Chris, you respond by shifting your focus from a sexual one to a supportive one, and we'll see if you can find a way to be together that would help avoid this big trigger response. Eventually, once you feel really confident about that strategy for reducing and avoiding that big response, we can look at ways to shift from managing the trigger to then shifting back into the sexual experience together in a way that feels safe and good. How does that sound?

CHRIS: Good.

CAMILLE: It's worth a try.

Chris and Camille did try this, and it worked well for them. The biggest factor in its success was how responsive Chris was. In terms of security-enhancing behaviours, Camille was able to make a clear signal of her distress and Chris was able to hear it, respond, and provide comfort to Camille in a way that was comforting to her, not to him. Chris really needed to get to a place of feeling that he had a role, a purpose, and the capacity to support and help Camille when she was distressed. It had taken him a long time to mentalize with her well enough to be able to do this in a way that fit with what she needed and not what he might need were he in a similar state of distress. Eventually, they were able to manage this trigger well enough that they could shift back into the sexual experience, most of the time, and develop greater flexibility, openness, curiosity, and playfulness in their sexual relationship.

Gradually restoring sexual relationship

One of the biggest hurdles we face in working with childhood trauma survivor couples, especially those with a history of sexual abuse, is finding ways to push through avoidance – all kinds of avoidance. In this sense, the sexual relationship is no different than any other area of the couple's life together. For many couples, the vibrant, exciting, and pleasurable sexual dynamic that came so easily at the beginning of their relationship becomes virtually non-existent once feelings of home and family get integrated into their attachment. By exploring sexual secrets and triggers, therapy helps the couple learn to communicate directly about their sexual needs and the things that arouse and bring them pleasure. They can move gradually from talking to doing by incorporating scaled exercises to overcome the barriers and avoidance that have built up over time – moving from talk to touch, to help them find safe, slow, and stimulating ways to re-engage sexually starting with a focus on non-sexual and gradually moving to sexual touch (Maltz, 2002; Maltz & Arian, 2001; Maltz & Maltz, 2009). For many couples, a period of conscious abstinence removes pressure and gives the partners breathing room to start again and rebuild their sexual relationship from the ground up. Where there has been a lot of conflict within the relationship around sex, simply taking that issue off of the table to work on other areas of their relationship can provide the couple with a fresh, secure base from which to begin this hard work.

Once triggers and secrets have been worked through, most survivors will have difficulty identifying specific, conscious reasons why they are struggling to get through the invisible sexual barrier that lies between them and their partner. As discussed in the section on attachment, therapists can help the couple by coaching them in shifting their strategies and behaviours as they confront their resistance to engaging sexually once again. We then confront the disconnection between partners that lies outside of their awareness. Sometimes we never know what it is that shifts and why, but for that shift to occur the partners need to be looking directly at the thing they have avoided, disavowed, or suppressed. For Anush and Amira, their sexual relationship was at a standstill at the start of the therapy. For months I tried to help Anush and Amira develop strategies to come together sexually. First, I worked separately with each of them on sexual secrets and their impacts, next we looked together at triggers and Anush's struggles with certain kinds of arousal, and then we worked very concretely on avoidance.

This step started with work to help the couple change some of their daily routines. At that time, Amira was putting their children to bed alone and then going to bed by herself without checking in with Anush. Meanwhile, Anush would slink away to the basement, also alone and return to his compulsive sexual dissociation. There was no communication about spending time together or going to bed at the same time. If a couple is never in the same place – especially the bedroom – it is very difficult to break through the avoidance that is hindering reengagement with sex. The couple agreed to start going to bed at the same time and to check in with one another after the children were in bed. This was a huge shift, and also one that quickly activated unconscious barriers to connection. This provided us with an opportunity to talk about the feelings and thoughts that arose when they tried to change their routine.

THERAPIST: The only way you are going to get back to being ready to be sexually intimate is to be in proximity with each other and to start to get more comfortable with one another. So what does that arouse in you when you think about putting your things away, heading up to the bed and going to bed at the same time? Even if you are not ready to sleep, but to just be together, what does that bring up for you?

ANUSH: Well, I definitely know it's important, it's key. I don't know, I – avoidance, maybe it is subconscious; it's certainly not intentional.

THERAPIST: Well when you think about . . . intention, and you have been clear about this, you want to be close to your wife again, that's your intention. But what is happening at that other level of trauma and anxiety, the feelings deep inside you that keep you away, that avoidance response? That's been a consistent response that you have had for so long and we are trying to tackle it head on. The only way you are going to know how you feel is if you put yourself into the situation and face that avoidance and see how you feel.

I then took another angle and worked with the couple on non-sexual touch and sensate focus exercises, starting with short windows of time where the couple looks into one another's eyes, moving to gentle non-sexual touch that both partners focus on and try to really feel both giving and receiving, gradually growing to reintegrating more sexual contact starting with reciprocal erotic touch and moving to genital contact (Maltz, 2002). From there, the couple was encouraged to build up their level of sexual contact until they "broke the seal" and "did it". This process took over a year. We just kept backing down the hill and starting up again until enough momentum was gained, and the couple was ready, willing, and able.

At a cognitive level, the barrier between Anush and Amira, the thing that shifted and allowed Anush to finally reach for Amira, was never fully explained, but with steady, consistent, and gentle but firm forward movement, the situation eventually shifted. With Anush and Amira, this slow sexual reintegration began early in couple therapy because the couple had little conflict over other aspects of their relationship and both partners already demonstrated capacities for emotion regulation and mentalizing. They started with simple things: a touch here or there, a kiss on returning from work, and more physical contact in general. Eventually, after the work of disclosure and trauma processing, they were able to talk about cuddling and moving towards greater physical intimacy, without going as far as initiating sexual contact. Here the couple is discussing the experience of initiating any physical contact after having a years-long dry spell.

ANUSH: I know; we've been trying to be a little bit more affectionate.

THERAPIST: Hmmhmm.

ANUSH: And a little bit more cuddly. She pretty much didn't cuddle, but it depends. I mean I am just trying to be more affectionate.

AMIRA: He's rubbing my back and giving me little massages . . . that's cute. He's being cute.

ANUSH: She wants more than that of course, but we're trying to start somewhere.

THERAPIST: Somewhere is good place to start. So these massages, what did you say, they were cute?

AMIRA: [laughs] It's just kinda like teasing cuddling little baby things.

ANUSH: It's a type of affection that we had when we first met, that she used to like.

AMIRA: Now I like it because it feels good.

ANUSH: I don't know how she takes it now, but. . .

THERAPIST: Why don't you ask her?

AMIRA: Now, it feels good because it is like a massage, but, also, because he's touching me. He's more affectionate, which is just something that he's never really been. I like to be held, and caressed.

THERAPIST: What about when you are in bed? Do you hold each other, do you cuddle each other; is there any contact in bed?

AMIRA: He started touching my back, or giving me little massages, which is nice. He puts his arm on me, so that feels nice. First it was a bit uncomfortable, but I can get used to it.

THERAPIST: Maybe even like it?

AMIRA: Yeah.

THERAPIST: So the little things you are doing are being noticed. What's it like for you to be trying these new things?

ANUSH: Hmm. I feel good. Like, I feel warm. I feel happy touching her, holding her hand, it's different, just walking on the street, holding her hand, it's more intimate. So, I mean, yeah, it feels nice to and she lets me.

THERAPIST: Sounds like she's actually kinda liking it.

AMIRA: [smiling] Yeah, I like it.

THERAPIST: And the effort is being made.

AMIRA: Yeah. I know he wants to and that is everything. I know I don't respond – it's been so hard for me.

THERAPIST: Hmmhmm, you've built up a wall to protect yourself from the pain of feeling so rejected.

AMIRA: Yes, it's been awful.

THERAPIST: So it's important for us to go slowly and if ever there is discomfort, something doesn't feel right, say something. Don't just walk away or disconnect, say something, talk about it. Something like "it's nice when you do that, but it always reminds me of all the time that we've lost". Whatever the words are, just say them.

AMIRA: I'll try.

Anush continued to try to push through his avoidance of sexual connection with Amira, in spite of being unable to put any words to the feeling of stuckness. Eventually, he started to try to initiate some sexual contact when Amira was sleeping. She did not find this triggering or distressing, and it opened up a small window for us to peek in and take a look at his fears of arousal and rejection.

ANUSH: I know when I come to bed, she may be asleep, but I feel more comfortable being affectionate, like cuddling, when she's asleep. Like I'll hold her, so she knows I'm there, but it feels better when she is asleep.

AMIRA: I know. This week I was asleep, but a couple of times, I noticed that you touched my hand, I knew he was there.

ANUSH: I rub her down a little bit, and it was nice to know that she acknowledged that. She likes that little massage.

THERAPIST: But if we look at it, in terms of levels of intimacy, and levels of anxiety, right now, what works well for you is a sleeping wife. You can initiate some physical contact, you can rub her back, you can touch her hand, you want her to know that you are there. So when she is asleep, you can tolerate whatever anxiety might come up, while initiating contact. It's not necessarily sexual. But it's affectionate and loving. What would that be like, if she was awake?

ANUSH: Well, you know, when we drive home from work we are talking about work, stuff we have to do at home, our kids, things happening with our families. It's busy. But, you know, it's nice being closer to Amira and stuff.

THERAPIST: Hmm, so I asked you a question about what it would be like to be more physically initiating if your wife was awake, and you started to talk about your conversations with Amira in the car, you took me somewhere else. And that's something that you often do, when you are trying to regulate your anxiety, you talk around the issue, but you get back, you get back there eventually, you take me on a little tour. I think that helps you manage your anxiety. But I didn't really hear the answer to that question. Could you take a minute to reflect on how it feels to imagine that after your kids are in bed, you hear Amira go to bed and for you to close the computer, to go upstairs, to get into bed at the same time and to be awake together, whatever that looks like, what does that feel like when you think about that?

ANUSH: I think it feels good.

THERAPIST: So, what makes that hard to do at this point?

ANUSH: Hmmm, it's something like system shut off, she's taking our kids up to bed, I am listening for that, the signs that she's going to sleep . . . that's obviously something I can work on.

THERAPIST: Okay, so something shuts down when you hear her go to bed and you think about going up to be with her and so you end up going to bed after she is asleep, and this feels more comfortable and you are able to initiate some contact with her. You've had a long time in your marriage where you've suppressed your desires, and you haven't been aware of doing that in any conscious, intentional sense. The suppression has happened at such a deep level that you are not even consciously aware of your sexual desire, and of what holds you back. And that's a long time, that avoidance response. You have dealt with the anxiety by not even feeling it. And it strikes me that there's something similar about this, that you know that she's feeling more open, reinitiating some contact, but the automatic response is to turn off. And it's not conscious, it's not intentional, but there needs to be a process of making this whole experience more within your awareness. Something like, if I hear those cues, the cues that tell me she is in bed and still awake, then I need to try to go to her so that the unconscious thing, which is the fear and the anxiety about sexual contact with someone that you really love, that that becomes more conscious. And as much as that's really uncomfortable, the only way through this is to keep pushing through. Does that make sense?

ANUSH: Yeah.

THERAPIST: So what is a ritual that we can build in between the two of you that would make that more conscious?

ANUSH: Umm, well, the easiest thing I guess would be to pay attention to those indicators.

THERAPIST: Do you have a bed time?

ANUSH: Usually by 10:00 I'll be in bed.

THERAPIST: What about setting an alarm on your watch for 10:00 to go up and then you don't have to even be listening, the alarm goes off and up you go. And you are okay with him bringing things with him?

AMIRA: Yeah.

THERAPIST: So you bring whatever that you are working on and then you can rub her back while she goes to sleep so she can actually enjoy it. That gives you a lot of points too.

ANUSH: Yeah, it will be a change in my sleeping pattern but okay, we can try that.

THERAPIST: You don't have to go to sleep until you want to. But you are saying "I want to do this. I want to break through this thing that's stuck, setting an intention and I want to change how my marriage works, I want to be more intimate, want to have a sexual and loving relationship". You set that watch, it wakes you up and prods you out of your avoidance, and it makes you face whatever feelings are there. As you go upstairs, as you brush your teeth, as you get into bed, those feelings are going to come up, and that's what we want.

AMIRA: We need to address them. I think that's true for me. I have avoided any situation that would allow us to be close, like that's just the norm.

Over the next months, Anush and Amira were more able to connect on an emotional and physical level with increased cuddling, hand holding, kissing, and generally feeling closer. However, Anush continued to struggle with invisible forces, which held him back from going to bed with Amira while she was still awake and from making any further moves sexually.

ANUSH: Well . . . not so much success on the homework aspect of it . . . however, there was some more emotional interaction, like touching, feeling, the whole thing. Cuddling was in the homework list.

THERAPIST: Cuddling is a big improvement.

ANUSH: It wasn't just getting in to go to sleep. There was interaction, but even when I went up to bed early, she would be asleep. I still gave her a hug and soothed her, rubbed her arms and stuff like that and she enjoyed that . . . she was responsive to it.

AMIRA: Yeah, it was nice.

THERAPIST: So you've been going up more early to bed?

ANUSH: Yeah.

THERAPIST: That's great. That's part of the homework. You are coming along. So what's it like to be closer, physically, and more engaged?

AMIRA: It's nice.

ANUSH: Yeah, I even spooned her a couple of times.

THERAPIST: Wow!

ANUSH: Yeah, and I didn't feel any resistance. It was comforting.

THERAPIST: Slow and steady. What do you think is shifting inside you?

ANUSH: I think what is helping a tremendous amount is her response to this. It doesn't feel like a forced response. It actually feels natural. It feels like when we first met. And cuddling, hand holding and stuff like that. It had a different feel.

THERAPIST: So your own internal tug of war, if we look back on it, in the time in your relationship, when things really started to move apart, a lot of that tug of war was about fear?

ANUSH: Yeah. I was just in a rut. I was stuck.

THERAPIST: It strikes me that there's been you feeling stuck around your sexual abuse, how to initiate, even fear about your sexuality, being overpowering or being too much or not being enough, not being adequate, all that internal fighting. That was going on, which you tried to push away and not think about, which turned you away from her. And you [to Amira] were approaching and not finding him there, he was not really home and you continued and then got tired . . . and you [back to Anush] knew she was coming to you but you couldn't go back to her.

ANUSH: I couldn't reciprocate.

THERAPIST: You couldn't reciprocate, you were stuck stuck-stuck-stuck, you start to try to push yourself, you tried and tried and tried. You saw that your marriage was getting worse and worse and worse in terms of your intimacy and closeness and at a certain point you were trying and you went over the edge, and you pulled right back, and then you tried and tried and tried some more but, eventually, you got to expect that she would reject you. And then you were frozen, and there was no movement, and you became a solid block of terror. And then you got to this place of, enough already, I've had enough, and you were feeling stuck, and everything shut down. And that's where you were when we started, when you came here. Everything was just shut down.

ANUSH: Yeah.

THERAPIST: And now there's a softening. You *are* trying to be more responsive. You *are* trying to be more initiating, but that dance around the anxiety is still there. It's less big. It's more tentative, but there's a softer, warmer quality to your interactions.

In a later session, we were able to talk more about the growth in their emotional and physical connection and how they could move things up a notch.

THERAPIST: Good, we are moving in a forward direction, but we haven't yet crossed the line where your growing affection and physical contact becomes a sexual contact.

AMIRA: Yeah.

THERAPIST: Kissing, feelings of arousal, being turned on, allowing those feelings back into your relationship since they've been removed, is our next goal.

AMIRA: Yeah, for sure.

THERAPIST: The way you have been moving is really positive, so gradually you are trying to reach for her more and you are responding . . . that's super! How can you push that another inch?

ANUSH: I mean, like we've come to this point, and I know I can do more, but it doesn't feel okay – I can't connect that I think I can do more with the feeling I can't.

THERAPIST: So, there's a bit more confidence growing inside, but there's also some conflict?

ANUSH: There is confidence. I guess what's helping is the responsiveness.

THERAPIST: So where we are now is spooning, cuddling, holding hands: what's the next increment?

ANUSH: Kissing more often? We do sort of kiss when we go to work.

THERAPIST: Okay, how close to the lips of one another. . .

AMIRA: Sorry?

THERAPIST: How close are the lips when you have that off to work peck?

AMIRA: It's a little closer, our lips touch.

ANUSH: Our lips – they've touched. . .

THERAPIST: Well, then, you are in the zone. . .

ANUSH: There's that, feeling. . . . Like, I know I did kiss her. It's not just a peck

THERAPIST: And were you tonguey kissers ever?

AMIRA: No.

THERAPIST: No, not your thing? Okay, so maybe extend the time, maybe a little smooching.

AMIRA: I can be a tonguey kisser, but . . . I don't know. . . [to Anush] are you a tonguey kisser?

THERAPIST: See, these are things we should know about each other. [everyone smiles]

ANUSH: I'm not a tonguey kisser.

THERAPIST: Doesn't turn you on?

ANUSH: No.

AMIRA: There's always room to experiment. [more smiling all around]

THERAPIST: This is true; there is always room to experiment.

AMIRA: Experiment with kissing!

Speaking directly and with plain language about sex and sexuality can be a challenge, especially for those who grew up in families and cultures where sex was not discussed openly. However, I have found that couples very quickly engage with talking about their sexual thoughts, feelings, and experiences when provided with an open forum. Anush and Amira continued to come up against a big wall. They had moved from no contact to much more comfortable and frequent physical contact, including kissing, with satisfying emotional intimacy, but they just could not get past that block and move into sexual engagement. We just kept exploring the wall – the shapes, textures, sounds, and sights of that wall – until it gradually came down. Having patience and trust in the process that if everyone sticks in there, if everyone can tolerate that the unconscious does what it does and takes its own time to unravel its mysteries, only then will that moment of change come, a moment that cannot be predicted, only coaxed.

THERAPIST: But I think it's important to look at the question of the thing that you are afraid of. You are afraid of something that has never happened so, inside of you, you are expecting the something that did happen, your abuse and the aftermath: rejection, embarrassment, shame, shame about your sexuality, all of these are tied into your experiences growing up. And one of the things you've never been able to articulate because your memories are so fuzzy is how you felt during the episodes of being molested. You've not been able to describe how you felt, only some of the flashes or images, those embedded feelings that stay with us even if we can't remember them. Many boys, when they are molested, have erections, and depending on the age, sometimes they ejaculate and that, for many men, translates into huge shame and embarrassment. They ask themselves, "why did I get a hard on, why did I come?" But here's the thing, penises do what penises do, that's their job. And as we have talked about these memories, you've never been able to say whether or not that happened for you. So, all of those feelings, whether you had erections or arousal when you were abused, those memories become embodied and stuck and somehow you learned that your erection, your arousal, your sexuality is something to be ashamed of and to be hidden because it's dangerous.

ANUSH: [nods] Yeah, I guess that's true. I do always feel like, it's definitely not like I don't get erections, I wake up and, well, you know – but I don't know where it came from. I had to have been thinking of something or dreaming of something,

THERAPIST: Maybe, yes, but a lot of guys do wake up with hard-ons because they have to pee.

ANUSH: Then I ask myself, is it just because of that or did I dream of something. Like, I know, I definitely do have to pee, but was it also there for another reason?

THERAPIST: Would it matter?

ANUSH: No, it shouldn't, but it just seems. . .

THERAPIST: Does it seem suspect? If this erection just came out of nowhere, it is somehow suspect?

ANUSH: No, I ask like how long has it been there, did I have it for another reason?

THERAPIST: What does it mean if you've had a really hot dream, and you've got a really big hard on, when you woke up, what would that mean?

ANUSH: That I am normal?

THERAPIST: Ah. . .

ANUSH: That it's there, that I could do something with it.

THERAPIST: It works! Are you afraid that you are not normal?

ANUSH: I don't think I am afraid I am not normal, but I am having trouble with it. It's something that should be happening, I just wish that I could get there with Amira.

THERAPIST: So when it comes into human relationships, it gets difficult. When you're watching a movie or waking up with a hard on, your arousal is fine, it works, it's easy. But actually taking initiative, and letting her know about your arousal, letting her know that you want her, that is where things fall off the wagon.

ANUSH: I don't know, we're watching a movie and I'm totally turned on and I want to show her and tell her and I'm just frozen and she has no idea.

THERAPIST: So the idea of taking Amira's hand when you are watching a movie and putting it on you, showing her your erection?

ANUSH: I haven't tried that. . .

AMIRA: Nope, he's never tried that. [both laugh]

THERAPIST: It'll probably work to show her you are turned on.

AMIRA: Probably . . . that would work! Sure, I'd be shocked if he tried that, but it would be a good shock.

THERAPIST: A playful shock, if you were to take her hand and show her, put it on you, you would also be saying, hey, let's do something with this thing, you don't have to say a word.

ANUSH: Actions speak louder than words.

Something shifted and allowed Anush to talk more openly about his arousal and his fear of his own arousal, and to be playfully engaged with Amira about initiating sexual contact. The very next week, Anush took Amira's hand, put it in his lap and kaboom: off to the races. Many months into our slow but steady process of breaking down avoidance and building up comfort with contact, the couple had sex for the first time in years. They were thrilled and presented this news to me with excitement and pride. I was thrilled for them and received their progress like a proud mama.

ANUSH: I actually did it!

THERAPIST: Yay!

AMIRA: Yeah!

THERAPIST: So, tell me more. As much as you want to tell me.

ANUSH: We had sex!

AMIRA: Yeah, it actually happened. There was a pig flying, we saw it flying . . . I went to bed, he came to bed, and he was cuddling me up a little. I was really tired that day too, but then he started to kiss my back. And I was like oh . . . but I didn't want to push it. I told him it was good.

THERAPIST: That you were enjoying it?

AMIRA: I told him how I was feeling, and then it progressed and then after a little while . . . he took my hand and did what you suggested he do last week!

THERAPIST: Well done, you showed her that you were ready and you wanted her.

ANUSH: Yeah, I was like, is that proof enough that it works? [everyone laughs] She started laughing.

AMIRA: It was nice. It was a start. All the parts work!

ANUSH: Yeah. It felt like her reactions, feelings, when I remember like how she. . .

THERAPIST: How you used to be together?

AMIRA: How we used to be together.

ANUSH: How she would be, physically: her responses, her motions.

THERAPIST: That must have been nice for you.

ANUSH: Yeah, it was nice, it felt nice. I had trouble sleeping after that, my mind was racing. She was knocked out.

THERAPIST: What were you thinking?

ANUSH: I don't even know where my mind was. I just knew what just happened.

THERAPIST: You were there.

ANUSH: I was there; I was happy about it. I didn't have an uncomfortable feeling, like it felt good. It felt natural, it didn't feel. . .

AMIRA: Forced. . . ?

THERAPIST: You didn't feel like you were pushing.

ANUSH: I didn't feel like I was trying to overcome something.

THERAPIST: That's a big shift.

ANUSH: I was comfortable in my actions. When she asked me if I was okay, I responded, "I am okay", and it felt genuine.

THERAPIST: You were there.

ANUSH: I wanted to reassure her too, to show her that I was there.

THERAPIST: You were aware of your own needs, desires and hers as well.

ANUSH: Yes. It took a little bit of getting into it, but I kinda knew that I was going somewhere with it and I didn't feel like I was fighting it. I was just working my way into it. It didn't feel like I really had to overcome a hurdle.

THERAPIST: You were just connecting with your wife, and one thing led to another. Nice. So when you had the communication of the kissing of the back, which was something we talked about last time, and you felt her enjoying it, you just kept going.

ANUSH: Yeah, I do remember that she used to like that. I remember that she would enjoy that feeling, kissing on the back.

THERAPIST: So you now have to build a new reality. This is what she used to do, now you are building a new reality, this is what we do now.

ANUSH: Yeah, I think I'm excited about that.

AMIRA: I really hope so. I really hope this isn't just a one-off.

THERAPIST: You've broken the seal, you've popped the cork off this wine that's been in the bottle for a couple of years. So how do we help the two of you with developing a new rhythm of give and take, approach and avoid – a new way of initiating that will help you with finding ways to be more comfortable, more natural, ways to make sex just a part of your daily life as a couple.

ANUSH: I feel like it was a good starting point because I felt comfortable about starting and comfortable after the fact, so I feel like I'll be able to continue and expand.

Over the remainder of the process of therapy, Anush and Amira continued to build their sexual relationship from the ground up. They learned new ways of initiating, of signalling their arousal, and of communicating about their wants, needs, and desires. It was not a straight path – the couple had dips and dives, times when they could not find their way to one another – but these were short-lived and they came back from these times stronger and more able to navigate the challenging waters of Anush's traumatized sexuality. Every couple will have different needs but the principles will be the same: exploring the impacts of trauma on sexuality in straightforward ways using plain language, a non-judgemental stance and an open mind, and slowly moving towards rebuilding the sexual relationship devoid of destructive secrets and painful triggers.

Note

1 For me, it's all about listening to music, singing and directing choirs, spending time with my partner, cats, and horses, and enjoying the company of good friends . . . well, and chocolate . . . I cannot leave out chocolate. These things bring me back to life after gruelling clinical times. Figure out what your requirements are and make sure to stock up on them.

Chapter 7

Stage Four

Consolidation

The goal of Stage Four is to consolidate everything that has come before. The process of DCTCT is challenging and at times gruelling, but childhood trauma survivors are remarkably resilient: they have to be. If you have made it this far with survivor couples, you are doing very well. You have probably been to the depths and back, heard the unimaginable, and held yourself in the spaces of pain and longing with couples who are willing and able to lay themselves bare in therapy hoping that their relationship will grow strong, close, loving, and safe. When a couple makes it to this point in the process, we expect that when they find themselves in conflict, they are able to draw upon their new mentalizing and emotion regulation skills to navigate conflicts with clarity, tolerable and manageable emotions, and the ability to see one another's perspectives, to find their way to a co-created solution that both can uphold. Having worked hard to push through the stuck spots, which are often forces outside of their awareness blocking the smooth path forward, the couple has become more able to engage in secure attachment-enhancing cycles of interaction. They are now empowered to feel confident and to help one another to regulate their emotional states even when the going gets tough and to continue their movement from insecurity to security in their attachments with one another. Overall, in Stage Four our goal is to help the couple more easily access these self-capacities when faced with interpersonal stress, especially when their attachment systems are activated due to couple conflict. We do not expect that life will become easy because they have completed this therapy; we hope, rather, that the couple will be able to support and soothe one another when the going does get rough, to turn towards each other instead of away, when the challenges of life press heavily down upon them. Over time, we hope that the couple will be able to draw upon their newly developed self-capacities as internalized and automatic, and to trust their newly earned secure attachment with their partner.

If the foundational work of the first three stages has progressed smoothly, this stage will look like couple therapy with couples where developmental traumas are not at the forefront. In fact, it is only in this stage where self-capacities such as mentalizing and emotion regulation are strong and consistent enough to allow for deeper representations of self and other to be explored along with relevant, but non-trauma-related developmental experiences. This allows for current couple-related issues to be processed live, in session, without the need for emotions to be contained out of concerns for dysregulation and overwhelming conflict. However, if at any point the couple reverts to non-mentalizing stances, experiences failures in emotion regulation, or faces the intrusion of latent trauma symptoms, circle back to the appropriate step in the treatment and reinforce relevant skills, explore the trigger that activated the challenge to emerging self-capacities, and reprocess or process traumatic memories and emotions in the dyadic context as needed.

You will know that it is time to begin decreasing the frequency of sessions when couples begin to turn towards one another in their distress, are able to comfort one another, and are able to tolerate their differences and differing needs without losing mentalizing and emotion regulation capacities. With these capacities, couples become able to demonstrate the capacity to compromise and solve problems on their own and to report these successes back to you. For the first time in their relational life, the couple is living in the present, dealing with the usual ups and downs, stresses and strains of life, not being pulled back by traumas that are being reenacted within their relationship. As you work through the stages of treatment, the role shifts from being a teacher in the first stages, to a containing trauma therapist in the intermediate stages, to a couple therapist, coach, and validator in this consolidation stage. Sessions will be shifted from weekly to bi-weekly, to monthly, and then slowly tapered off after six to eight months. It is essential that couples not feel that their success in the couple therapy is directly tied to losing you as their therapist. Go slowly, help them pull out of challenges when they find applying their new skills and abilities to be too difficult, and cheer them on as they move towards autonomy.

The couples

I suppose you might want to know how the stories end for each of the three example couples. For two out of the three couples, the story ends well. Anush and Amira progressed through DCTCT smoothly and steadily; they came in to treatment with reasonable self-capacities, both could regulate their emotions and mentalize well, both had had reasonable developmental experiences with "good enough" families who did their best to care for them. They grew up in a family and cultural context where loyalty and family is everything. Given their ages, the years of unhappiness that preceded treatment, and their painful sexual estrangement, this is a couple who might not have stayed together had they not come from families and a culture that valued marriage, but they did stick it out: they risked and dared and came through the therapy having built a stronger, closer, and more loving marriage. While they did not have the frequency of sexual contact that Amira might have wanted, even at the end of treatment, they did have more frequent and more satisfying sexual interactions that were not bogged down by the ravages of past trauma. The couple left therapy with new skills and capacities; stronger, more secure attachment to one another; and a determination to navigate any struggles ahead of them. They felt very proud of the work they had done together and ready to face the future as a strong, united couple.

Chris and Camille came through DCTCT stronger than they were when they began; they stayed together and completed the entire process. They were both young, and they had very high levels of conflict and distress when they began therapy. Both struggled with emotion regulation and mentalizing difficulties, and both had significant challenges with the ways in which trauma was living in their relationships in the present. The therapeutic process was challenging, with many switchbacks and reviews of previous stages to ensure that they had an opportunity to firmly establish the capacities they needed to work through the barriers that continued to get in their way. Both partners were able to work through some very significant enacted relational expectations that were constantly being kicked up in the relationship and causing distress. At the end of therapy, I did not feel confident that this couple was going to live happily ever after, but I did feel that both partners were far better prepared for the challenges of relational life and for any future relationships that might come along.

You might have noticed that you have not heard much about Gary and Geoffrey since early in Stage Three. That would be because Gary and Geoffrey left therapy prematurely. They got stuck, and they could not become unstuck. Gary and Geoffrey did stay together, but they did not stay in the couple therapy together. Gary was unable to tolerate the process of examining his own history and the ways it continued to come alive in his relationship. He was flooded with shame when he did face his current level of functioning square in the face and how it was affecting Geoffrey and their relationship. However, the main factor that led to the impenetrable "stuckness" was Gary's anger about having to do work that he did not feel he should have to do. In essence, the couple ended up out of sync. Geoffrey continued to work hard in therapy and came to a place of feeling ready to become more connected, and he hoped that Gary could meet his needs and let him get close. Gary got stuck. He described feelings of hopelessness and despair at what was coming up for him in therapy and that it was simply too difficult for him to continue and maintain his fragile self-cohesion.

In the second to last session, Gary reached his limit and expressed his unwillingness to continue with therapy. I struggled with the delicate balance between continuing to challenge and explore in the face of deep shame that quickly turns to anger and backing away to provide a bit of breathing room.

GARY: It was annoying . . . maybe I should have more patience, but I just don't, so I hang out with people who are not stressed about how much attention I'm paying to them.

THERAPIST: What do you think that's about?

GARY: I don't like pressure on me on how to act and how to respond.

THERAPIST: So when someone needs you, when how they feel about themselves and the relationship is affected by how you behave, that feels like a lot of pressure.

GARY: Yeah.

THERAPIST: How does it affect you when that affects Geoffrey so deeply?

GARY: I don't know, it makes me feel like he has these big dreams about what it's like to be in a relationship and they're never going to be met.

THERAPIST: With anyone or with you?

GARY: Probably someone else is into that kind of thing but that's not me.

THERAPIST: What do you mean by that kind of thing?

GARY: You know, how a relationship is more important than other things in your life.

THERAPIST: Can you say more?

GARY: Your relationship is the most important thing in your life, over everything else in your life. It's just not balanced.

THERAPIST: Okay so, help me out here. What I heard Geoffrey saying was that sometimes he needs you to be interested in him, curious about him, listen to his stories. . . . And what I'm hearing you say is "he wants me to think that my relationship is more important than anything else in my life and my self-esteem will be crushed as a result".

GARY: Yeah.

THERAPIST: Do those things feel equal to you?

GARY: I don't know.

THERAPIST: What's your sense of it? 'Cause that's a big jump! To compare from interested in him to make the relationship more important than anything else. Do you have a sense of what made that jump happen?

GARY: What jump?
THERAPIST: The jump from Geoffrey saying he needs you to be interested in him to your belief that he's saying that your relationship has to be more important than anything else in your life.
GARY: I don't know. I don't know if I can really focus on that.
THERAPIST: What can you focus on?
GARY: Just. . .

[long silence, Geoffrey starts to cry]
THERAPIST: Geoffrey, what's happening?
GEOFFREY: It just hurts to hear Gary say that he doesn't want to do . . . he doesn't want to change.
THERAPIST: And how does that affect you?
GEOFFREY: Like he doesn't want to give me anything. I don't know; sometimes we're getting along really great. Like when we were at the cottage we had a really nice time, it was so easy just to chat. It's not like I need him to be paying attention to me 24 hours a day, but I just like being with him, talking to him.
THERAPIST: It sounds like what you're saying is "I don't need much; I do need something".
GEOFFREY: Yeah, I really don't need much, I don't. [Gary gets up and looks out the window]
THERAPIST: Gary, the impression that I get – and again, correct me if I'm wrong because I think sometimes it's really hard for you to identify what you're feeling and thinking when you're upset – but the impression that I get is that when Geoffrey feels hurt by you, you feel very ashamed and very angry. And then the anger comes from shame and there's a part of you that's like "well fuck this noise"; I worked very hard to feel okay about myself and I don't want him to make me not feel okay about myself. And then, on the other hand, there's this part of you that's feeling bad about how he's feeling and that gets eaten by the angry feelings. Is that anywhere near what goes on?
GARY: Not really, I don't feel bad about how he feels anymore, because the way he brings it up to me is not really conducive to sorting it out anyway.
THERAPIST: So when Geoffrey brings up an exercise that I've given you and wants to explore that with you, what makes that difficult for you?
GARY: Well he hasn't really brought up the exercise. I don't know. I don't really feel like doing this anymore, it's too hard. [gets up] Sorry guys.
THERAPIST: When you say you don't want to do this anymore, what are you referring to?
GARY: This . . . therapy.
THERAPIST: It feels too difficult for you?
GARY: Yeah.
THERAPIST: Can you tell me what makes it so difficult?
GARY: I don't like feeling like I wanna kill myself. It's not really enjoyable.

I never saw Gary again. For Gary, the shame he experienced at the challenges he faced in managing the stressors of therapy and being in a relationship with someone who was coming into the belief that they were worthy of receiving care was unbearable. Gary referred to himself as a "rescue dog" who should not have to change, who should not have to take care of anyone else because his life had been full of trauma and who had what he referred to as mental illness. For Gary, a lifetime of being at the mercy of the needs of others, his mother's mental illness, and the ongoing sexual abuse he experienced were all enough. At a conscious level, Gary talked about being fed up with providing care for others and feeling like he had done the caretaking work of a lifetime during his childhood. Outside of his awareness, I can only imagine that the demands of therapy, which caused him to unleash feelings of shame, pain, and deeply embedded memories of how caring for others was the most dangerous thing in the world, began to cause him to lose self-cohesion, to feel horrible about himself, and to be overcome with a desperate need to flee. For Gary, a part of his identity and self-cohesion was tied to being a survivor of trauma but was also tied to being mentally ill and a victim of trauma. As Geoffrey began to make progress in therapy and ask for Gary to be a full participant and partner with him, rather than someone he provided unconditional care for with little expectation of reciprocation, this challenged Gary's self-cohesion, his identity, and his ability to maintain the tentative hold he held on his emotional stability. Gary needed things to move more slowly, perhaps too slowly, and Geoffrey was at a place where he simply could no longer tolerate not having any of his needs met. Neither wanted to end the relationship. The solution was simply to take the heat off of Gary and to go back to the way things had been; Geoffrey needed to accept his role as Gary's caretaker, and Gary needed to settle back into the one comfortable identity he had. This is not an unfixable dilemma. It simply means that for Gary and Geoffrey, change would have to be infinitesimally slow. Had Gary been able to continue to tolerate slow but steady, gentle nudging in the direction of becoming a reciprocal partner in his relationship, therapy could have continued. It would have taken a long time, but that would have been okay. I was not about to give up, and Geoffrey was okay with how long it would take, but Gary quit. When Geoffrey came to the following session alone, I was informed that the couple had decided that it was too hard for Gary to continue in therapy. Geoffrey was referred to a close colleague and continued in individual therapy for another eight months.

THERAPIST: Okay, do you have any sense about what it is about the process that triggers those feelings?

GEOFFREY: I think it makes him feel stupid 'cause he can't do it. Like he tries to do it, he wants to do it . . . he's tried to do it for me, but he just can't . . . like every time we talk about it he just goes straight to bed for a couple hours. It makes me stop trying to get him to come. I could convince him to come . . . I guess.

THERAPIST: How do you think you could get him to come?

GEOFFREY: Just really insist, I guess. I can see he wants to do the right thing, he wants to do it for me but when I see his reaction . . . like I see that I have the power to convince him to come or to insist and he would do it if he saw that I really, really wanted him to do it . . . but like it's pretty clear from his reaction that it's not that he just doesn't want to, it's physically hard to be here.

THERAPIST: And what does that do to you?

GEOFFREY: To me? It makes me back down, it makes me try to remember, to feel or understand what he's going through because I'm not like "oh we have to do it, we need it we need it". I need it. But I have to remember what's it's like to do something that's really hard and I understand it's really hard for him.

THERAPIST: Yes, it sounds like it is incredibly hard for him. And so you back down, you stop . . . and then?

GEOFFREY: I comfort him or just lie down with him or leave him alone. I back down.

THERAPIST: And where does that leave you?

GEOFFREY: I don't know what's gonna happen. Sometimes it feels impossible, and then we have some nice days, and then it's like: okay, maybe we can make it. It's clear that we've hit a wall here, and I think maybe if we just draw it out longer – this process of trying to make things more functional – maybe we can figure it out. We have figured some things out too from the therapy here but also on our own. When it's bad it feels like it's always gonna be bad, but sometimes when it's good I think, maybe we can make this work.

THERAPIST: And where are you now?

GEOFFREY: Where are we now? Nervous but . . . I'm still hopeful. I think he's really into trying again in a different context like maybe in a year or something after a break if we make it through that.

THERAPIST: Does he have any idea of what he thinks might be helpful? Something different than this kind of therapy?

GEOFFREY: He talked about maybe going back on antidepressants or maybe me going on antidepressants. That's just trying to be better and stronger on our own.

THERAPIST: What does all of this do to you? I know it's easy for you to talk about him and it is reasonable for us to talk about how it's affecting him but what does all this do to you?

GEOFFREY: Like the stopping therapy?

THERAPIST: Well stopping therapy is one part of your experience of finding it very difficult to navigate with Gary around your needs, and one of your needs has been to try therapy, to be able to try to get a voice for yourself and the relationship, to talk about your desire to feel like he cares, like he's interested, like he's able to sustain some attention on you, sustain some kindness to you. And therapy has been a place where you've been able to talk about those things with some help, successfully or otherwise, but with some help. And without that platform, those conversations might change. I guess I'm just curious about how you feel about therapy and how you imagine you'll be able to continue to talk about your needs in this relationship.

GEOFFREY: This whole process has definitely been rewarding for me. I did need that space to talk about what was going for me. I'm going to miss having that space.

THERAPIST: How are you feeling?

GEOFFREY: [crying] Nervous. Still hopeful about what will happen. Although that changes very quickly when things get bad. I don't know – I guess I don't know the feelings. Nervous, sometimes hopeful and sometimes hopeless. Scared about what's gonna happen but scared about giving up too and what would happen if that happens.

THERAPIST: What might that look like?

GEOFFREY: Devastating. At the beginning it was so wonderful, so passionate, so amazing. I couldn't believe how lucky I was. I feel like all of our stuff is coming out and. . . [deep crying]

THERAPIST: That's what happens. The idea of finding someone who's different, who's not the same as the people who hurt you is really exciting and brings out the best in us and our hopefulness for being different in a relationship and having different experiences, and then we find ourselves reliving things because that's what's inside us and that's what we need to tackle. It can be very challenging for couples.

GEOFFREY: Yup, that's it for sure.

THERAPIST: I'm so sorry it has been so difficult for both of you, and I'm sorry you're losing the therapy that has been a space for you to talk about your hopes and pains in this relationship.

GEOFFREY: Yeah, I'm going to miss this.

As Geoffrey moved steadily forward, Gary started to pull back and, in the end, quit therapy. With survivors whose trauma continues to haunt them, trauma-related distress can pull them inwards and make it hard for them to tolerate focusing on anything other than managing their distress (Whiffen & Oliver, 2004). For Gary, even within a model of treatment focused on specific developmental needs and impacts of trauma, the pain of looking at the impacts of his trauma on his life and his relationships was just too much for him to bear. DCTCT is a model that requires the survivor be able to tolerate looking their trauma squarely in the face, even if the titration of that process takes a very long time. Therapists can always go slowly or move backwards and around, but we can never close the door to forward movement.

Who decides what makes a good outcome?

It is not up to practitioners to decide what a positive outcome is for any particular couple. It would be wonderful if all of the couples could leave therapy feeling safe, happy, and close to their partners, ready to face the challenges of daily life with intimacy and joy. This is not realistic for any couple therapist to expect, but it is especially unrealistic for therapists who work with trauma survivor couples. When couples enter therapy, they have often been experiencing significant conflict for years, or they have found themselves in a state of suppression where one or both partners has hived themselves off into dormancy to survive their unhappiness in the relationship. Working with consistency and persistence to reduce high levels of conflict and increase attachment security, or waking partners up to work actively on their relationship may lead to them coming together to build a stronger, more loving relationship, or it may lead to a healthy decision to move into separate lives as whole and conscious humans. Nothing is lost; survivors will have developed new skills and capacities, had the opportunity to explore and process traumatic experiences, and taken risks to break open scabs and scars that have covered over internalized expectations based on old traumas. All of these places of growth accompany survivors into their new lives and relationships, should the couple decide to part ways. All of this to say, you can create a safe space to work with couples, but you cannot keep them together.

Over and over, I have talked about the importance of going back, reorienting, and continuing to flesh out any area that has been covered in therapy but continues to collapse under attachment stress. Ultimately, however, even with these adaptations, the model may simply demand too much from some survivors as the therapy, even when paced carefully, challenges their self-cohesion in potentially harmful ways. As much as we may put slow, steady pressure on the gas pedal, we also need to respect the limits placed by survivors for the maintenance of their basic daily functioning. Therapy would not be of much use if it were to break through traumatic barriers but leave survivors unable to function in their own lives.

Final thoughts

If you are still reading, you are clearly committed to providing the best possible care to your highly vulnerable, deeply distressed couples. This manual, like any set of clinical recommendations, is only as good as the clinical judgement and humanity of the person doing the actual work with the couple. This is not a bible, it is not a rigid set of instructions, and it certainly will not be the definitive last word on working with traumatized couples. It is simply a guide to help you in your work. Use it as a buffet: leave sections out, take it in a different order, trust your strong clinical skills and knowledge to know what will help you and how to use these ideas in your own work with your couples.

Childhood trauma survivors have experienced the worst that life has to offer at a time of life when they should have been carefree and never had to doubt their safety and security in their families and the world. Trust that they know their limits, are stronger than you can imagine, and will show you the value of putting in the time and care to build a relationship of healing. Your authenticity is the most powerful intervention you have at your disposal. Maintain your humanity, take care of yourself, find a good peer supervision group or consultant, and make sure to heal your own traumas as you move along in your clinical work with survivors. Give me a call if you want to chat.

I wish it were possible to create a manual that would answer all the questions, would be helpful with every couple, and would help you feel confident and skilled in all situations. I have shared with you what I have gleaned from my research and practice in the hope that it will provide you with support for your work, new ideas to explore with your couples, and strategies to add to your arsenal of clinical skills. I would like to be able to tie it all up for you in a neat bow and tell you that if you care enough, are persistent enough, and engage with this material diligently and with determination, the couples you work with will come out the other end happy, harmonious, and healed. However, the ravaging impacts of childhood trauma may take a lifetime to heal. If you think of the process like a relay race, it can take a bit of the pressure off. You may be the couple's first therapist or the one who takes them over the finish line with arms waving. For those couples who come to one session, and for those who continue to the beautiful end, you have an opportunity to be a new experience: to be the responsive, empathic, understanding attachment figure who sticks it out even when the going gets rough. You can be a model for what it means to be the safe haven and secure base, as the couple learns to provide these experiences for one another.

Bibliography

Alexander, P. (2009). Childhood trauma, attachment, and abuse by multiple partners. *Psychological Trauma: Theory, Research, Practice, and Policy, 1*(1), 78–88. doi:http://dx.doi.org/10.1037/a0015254

Alexander, P. C. (1992). Application of attachment theory to the study of sexual abuse. *Journal of Consulting and Clinical Psychology, 60*(2), 185–195. http://dx.doi.org/10.1037/0022-006X.60.2.185

Alexandrov, E. O., Cowan, P. A., & Cowan, C. P. (2005). Couple attachment and the quality of marital relationships: Methods and concept in the validation of the new couple attachment interview and coding system. *Attachment and Human Development*, 7, 123–152.

American Psychiatric Association. (2013). *Diagnostic and statistical manual of mental disorders: DSM-5*. Washington, DC: American Psychiatric Association.

Anderson, S. R., & Miller, R. B. (2006). The effectiveness of therapy with couples reporting a history of childhood sexual abuse: An exploratory study. *Contemporary Family Therapy: An International Journal, 28*(3), 353–366. https://doi.org/10.1007/s10591-006-9015-x

Archer, J. (2000). Sex differences in aggression between heterosexual partners: A meta-analytic review. *Psychological Bulletin, 126*, 651–680.

Augusta-Scott, T., & Dankwort, J. (2002). Partner abuse group intervention: Lessons from education and narrative therapy approaches. *Journal of Interpersonal Violence, 17*(7), 783–805.

Babcock, J. C., Green, C. E., & Robie, C. (2004). Does batterers' treatment work? A meta-analytic review of domestic violence treatment. *Clinical Psychology Review, 23*, 1023–1053.

Bacon, B., & Lein, L. (1996). Living with a female sexual abuse survivor: Male partners' perspectives. *Journal of Child Sexual Abuse: Research, Treatment, & Program Innovations for Victims, Survivors, & Offenders, 5*(2), 1–16. https://doi.org/10.1300/J070v05n02_01

Bales, D., van Beek, N., Smit, M., Willemsen, S., Busschbach, J., Verheul, R., & Andrea, H. (2012). Treatment outcome of 18-month day hospital Mentalization-Based Treatment (MBT) in patients with severe borderline personality disorder in the Netherlands. *Journal of Personality Disorders, 26*, 568–582.

Banyard, V. L., Williams, L. M., & Siegel, J. A. (2004). Childhood sexual abuse: A gender perspective on context and consequences. *Child Maltreatment, 9*(3), 223–238.

Bartholomew, K., & Horowitz, L. M. (1991). Attachment styles among young adults: A test of a four-category model. *Journal of Personality and Social Psychology, 61*(2), 226.

Bateman, A., & Fonagy, P. (2008). 8-year follow-up of patients treated for borderline personality disorder: Mentalization-based treatment versus treatment as usual. *The American Journal of Psychiatry, 165*(5), 631–638. https://doi.org/10.1176/appi.ajp.2007.07040636

Bateman, A., Fonagy, P., & Allen, J. G. (2009). Theory and practice of mentalization-based therapy. In *Textbook of psychotherapeutic treatments* (pp. 757–780). Arlington, VA: American Psychiatric Publishing, Inc.

Baucom, B., Epstein, J., Kirby, J., & LaTaillade, J. (2015). Cognitive-behavioural couple therapy. In A. Gurman, J. Lebow, & D. Snyder (Eds.), *2015 clinical handbook of couple therapy fifth edition* (pp. 23–61). New York: Guilford Press.

Beitchman, J.H., Zucker, K.J., Hood, J.E., DaCosta, G.A., Akman, D., & Cassavia, E. (1992). A review of the long-term effects of child sexual abuse. *Child Abuse & Neglect*, *16*(1), 101–118.

Berthelot, N., Godbout, N., Hebert, M., Goulet, M., & Bergeron, S. (2014). Prevalence and correlates of childhood sexual abuse in adults consulting for sexual problems. *Journal of Sex & Marital Therapy*, *40*(5), 434–443.

Bograd, M., & Mederos, F. (1999). Battering and couples therapy: Universal screening and selection of treatment modality. *Journal of Marital and Family Therapy*, *25*, 291–312.

Brennan, K.A., Clark, C.L., & Shaver, P.R. (1998). Self-report measurement of adult attachment: An integrative overview. In J.A. Simpson & W.S. Rholes (Eds.), *Attachment theory and close relationships* (pp. 46–76). New York: Guilford Press.

Briere, J. (2006). Dissociative symptoms and trauma exposure: Specificity, affect dysregulation, and posttraumatic stress. *Journal of Nervous and Mental Disease*, *194*(2), 78–82. https://doi.org/10.1097/01.nmd.0000198139.47371.54

Briere, J., & Scott, C. (2006). *Principles of trauma therapy: Guide to symptoms, evaluation, and treatment*. Thousand Oaks, CA: Sage Publications.

Brown-Bowers, A., Fredman, S.J., Wanklyn, S.G., & Monson, C.M. (2012). Cognitive-behavioral conjoint therapy for posttraumatic stress disorder: Application to a couple's shared traumatic experience. *Journal of Clinical Psychology*, *68*(5), 536–547. https://doi.org/10.1002/jclp.21850

Chauncey, S. (1994). Emotional concerns and treatment of male partners of female sexual abuse survivors. *Social Work*, *39*(6), 669–676.

Chris Fraley, R. (2002). Attachment stability from infancy to adulthood: Meta-analysis and dynamic modeling of developmental mechanisms. *Personality and Social Psychology Review*, *6*(2), 123–151. https://doi.org/10.1207/S15327957PSPR0602_03

Cloitre, M., Cohen, L.R., & Koenen, K.C. (2006). *Treating survivors of childhood abuse: Psychotherapy for the interrupted life*. New York: Guilford Press.

Cloitre, M., Koenen, K.C., Cohen, L.R., & Han, H. (2002). Skills training in affective and interpersonal regulation followed by exposure: A phase-based treatment for PTSD related to childhood abuse. *Journal of Consulting and Clinical Psychology*, *70*(5), 1067–1074. https://doi.org/10.1037/0022-006x.70.5.1067

Cloitre, M., Stovall-McClough, C., Zorbas, P., & Charuvastra, A. (2008). Attachment organization, emotion regulation, and expectations of support in a clinical sample of women with childhood abuse histories. *Journal of Traumatic Stress*, *21*(3), 282–289. doi:http://dx.doi.org/10.1002/jts.20339

Collins, N.L., & Feeney, B.C. (2000). A safe haven: An attachment theory perspective on support-seeking and caregiving in intimate relationships. *Journal of Personality and Social Psychology*, *78*, 1053–1073.

Colman, R.A., & Widom, C.S. (2004). Childhood abuse and neglect and adult intimate relationships: A prospective study. *Child Abuse & Neglect*, *28*(11), 1133–1151. https://doi.org/10.1016/j.chiabu.2004.02.005

Crawford, E., & O'Dougherty Wright, M. (2007). The impact of childhood psychological maltreatment on interpersonal schemas and subsequent experiences of relationship aggression. *Journal of Emotional Abuse*, *7*(2), 93–116.

Crowell, J.A., Pan, H., Gao, Y., Treboux, D., O'Connor, E., & Waters, E. (1998). *The secure base scoring system for adults*. Unpublished manuscript. Stony Brook: State University of New York.

Crowell, J.A., & Treboux, D. (1995). A review of adult attachment measures: Implications for theory and research. *Social Development*, *4*, 294–327. https://doi.org/10.1111/j.1467-9507.1995.tb00067.x

Dattilio, F.M. (2009). *Cognitive-behavioral therapy with couples and families: A comprehensive guide for clinicians*. New York: Guilford Press.

Davila, J., & Kashy, D.A. (2009). Secure base processes in couples: Daily associations between support experiences and attachment security. *Journal of Family Psychology*, *23*(1), 76–88.

DiLillo, D. (2001). Interpersonal functioning among women reporting a history of childhood sexual abuse: Empirical findings and methodological issues. *Clinical Psychology Review*, *21*(4), 553–576. https://doi.org/10.1016/S0272-7358%2899%2900072-0

DiLillo, D., Peugh, J., Walsh, K., Panuzio, J., Trask, E., & Evans, S. (2009). Child maltreatment history among newlywed couples: A longitudinal study of marital outcomes and mediating pathways. *Journal of Consulting and Clinical Psychology*, *77*(4), 680–692.

Dimitrova, N., Pierrehumbert, B., Glatz, N., Torrisi, R., Heinrichs, M., Halfon, O., & Chouchena, O. (2010). Closeness in relationships as a mediator between sexual abuse in childhood or adolescence and psychopathological outcome in adulthood. *Clinical Psychology & Psychotherapy*, *17*(3), 183–195. https://doi.org/10.1002/cpp.650

Feeney, J. A. (2008). Adult romantic attachments: Developments in the study of couple relationships. In J. Cassidy & P. R. Shaver (Eds.), *Handbook of attachment: Theory, research, and clinical applications* (pp. 456–481). New York: Guilford Press.

Feeney, B. C., & Collins, N. L. (2004). Interpersonal safe haven and secure base caregiving processes in adulthood. In W. S. Rholes & J. A. Simpson (Eds.), *Adult attachment: Theory, research, and clinical implications* (pp. 300–338). New York: Guilford Press.

Feinauer, L. L., Callahan, E. H., & Hilton, H. (1996). Positive intimate relationships decrease depression in sexually abused women. *American Journal of Family Therapy*, *24*(2), 99–106. https://doi.org/10.1080/01926189608251023

Firth, M. T. (1997). Male partners of female victims of child sexual abuse: Treatment issues and approaches. *Sexual & Marital Therapy*, *12*(2), 159–171.

Fonagy, P. (1991). Thinking about thinking: Some clinical and theoretical considerations in the treatment of a borderline patient. *The International Journal of Psychoanalysis, 72*(4), 639–656.

Fonagy, P. (2010). Attachment, trauma, and psychoanalysis: Where psychoanalysis meets neuroscience. In M. Leuzinger-Bohleber, J. Canestri, & M. Target (Eds.), *Early development and its disturbances: Clinical, conceptual, and empirical research on ADHD and other psychopathologies and its epistemological reflections* (pp. 53–75). London: Karnac Books.

Fonagy, P., Leigh, T., Steele, M., Steele, H., Kennedy, R., Mattoon, G., . . . Gerber, A. (1996). The relation of attachment status, psychiatric classification, and response to psychotherapy. *Journal of Consulting and Clinical Psychology*, *64*(1), 22–31. https://doi.org/10.1037/0022-006X.64.1.22

Fonagy, P., & Target, M. (1998). Mentalization and the changing aims of child psychoanalysis. *Psychoanalytic Dialogues*, *8*(1), 87–114. https://doi.org/10.1080/10481889809539235

Fonagy, P., & Target, M. (2006). The mentalization-focused approach to self pathology. *Journal of Personality Disorders*, *20*(6), 544–576. https://doi.org/10.1521/pedi.2006.20.6.544

Fraley, R. C., & Shaver, P. R. (1998). Airport separations: A naturalistic study of adult attachment dynamics in separating couples. *Journal of Personality and Social Psychology*, *75*, 1198–1212.

Frieze, I. H. (2005). *Hurting the one you love: Violence in relationships*. Belmont, CA: Wadsworth.

Gartner, R. B. (Ed.). (2017). *Healing sexually betrayed men and boys: Treatment for sexual abuse, assault, and trauma*. Routledge.

Godbout, N., Runtz, M. G., MacIntosh, H. B., & Briere, J. (2013). Childhood trauma and couple relationships. *Integrating Science and Practice*, *3*(2), 14–17.

Harway, M., & Faulk, E. (2005). Treating couples with sexual abuse issues. In M. Haraway (Ed.), *Handbook of couples therapy* (pp. 272–288). Hoboken, NJ: John Wiley & Sons Inc.

Hayes, S. C., Wilson, K. G., Gifford, E. V., Follette, V. M., & Strosahl, K. (1996). Experiential avoidance and behavioral disorders: A functional dimensional approach to diagnosis and treatment. *Journal of Consulting and Clinical Psychology*, *64*(6), 1152–1168. https://doi.org/10.1037/0022-006X.64.6.1152

Hazan, C., & Shaver, P. R. (1994). Attachment as an organizational framework for research on close relationships. *Psychological Inquiry*, *5*(1), 1–22. https://doi.org/10.1207/s15327965pli0501_1

Herman, J. L. (1992). *Trauma and recovery: The aftermath of violence from domestic abuse to political terror*. New York: Basic Books.

Holtzworth-Munroe, A., Meehan, J.C., Rehman, U., & Marshall, A.D. (2002). Intimate partner violence. In A.S. Gurman & N.S. Jacobson (Eds.), *Clinical handbook of couple therapy* (3rd ed., pp. 441–465). New York: Guilford Press.

Jacobson, N.S., Gottman, J.M., Waltz, J., Rushe, R., Babcock, J., & Holtzworth-Munroe, A. (1994). Affect, verbal content, and psychophysiology in the arguments of couples with a violent husband. *Journal of Consulting and Clinical Psychology*, *62*, 982–988.

Jarry, J.L., & Paivio, S.C. (2006). Emotion-focused therapy for anger. In E.L. Feindler (Ed.), *Anger-related disorders: A practitioner's guide to comparative treatments* (pp. 203–230). New York: Springer.

Johnson, M.P. (2008). *A typology of domestic violence: Intimate terrorism, violent resistance, and situational couple violence*. Lebanon, NH: Northeastern University Press.

Johnson, S.M. (2004). *The practice of emotionally focused couple therapy* (2nd ed.). New York: Brunner-Routledge.

Johnson, S.M., & Greenberg, L.S. (1992). Emotionally focused therapy: Restructuring attachment. In J. H. Obegi & E. Berant (Eds.), *The first session in brief therapy* (pp. 204–224). New York: Guilford Press.

Kelly, J.B., & Johnson, M.P. (2008). Differentiation among types of intimate partner violence: Research update and implications for interventions. *Family Court Review*, *46*, 476–499. https://doi.org/10.1111/j.1744-1617.2008.00215.x

Kendall-Tackett, K. (2002). The health effects of childhood abuse: Four pathways by which abuse can influence health. *Child Abuse & Neglect*, *26*(6), 715–729.

Kinzl, J.F., Traweger, C., & Biebl, W. (1995). Sexual dysfunctions: Relationship to childhood sexual abuse and early family experiences in a nonclinical sample. *Child Abuse & Neglect*, *19*(7), 785–792.

Kluft, R.P. (1993). *Clinical perspectives on multiple personality disorder*. Arlington, VA: American Psychiatric Publishing, Inc.

Knapp, D.J., Sandberg, J.G., Novak, J., & Larson, J.H. (2015). The mediating role of attachment behaviors on the relationship between family-of-origin and couple communication: Implications for couples therapy. *Journal of Couple & Relationship Therapy: Innovations in Clinical and Educational Interventions*, *14*(1), 17–38.

Kunce, L.J., & Shaver, P.R. (1994). An attachment-theoretical approach to caregiving in romantic relationships. In K. Bartholomew & D. Perlman (Eds.), *Advances in personal relationships* (Vol. 5, pp. 205–237). London: Jessica Kingsley.

LaTaillade, J.J., Epstein, N.B., & Werlinich, C.A. (2006). Conjoint treatment of intimate partner violence: A cognitive behavioral approach. *Journal of Cognitive Psychotherapy*, *20*(4), 393–410. https://doi.org/10.1891/jcpiq-v20i4a005

Levin, S.B. (2007). Hearing the unheard: Advice to professionals from women who have been battered. In H. Anderson & D. Gehart (Eds.), *Collaborative therapy: Relationships and conversations that make a difference* (pp. 109–128). New York: Routledge, Taylor & Francis Group.

Linehan, M.M. (1993). *Cognitive behavioral therapy for borderline personality disorder* (Vol. 51). New York: Guilford Press.

Loeb, T.B., Williams, J.K., Carmona, J.V., Rivkin, I., Wyatt, G.E., Chin, D., & Asuan-O'Brien, A. (2002). Child sexual abuse: Associations with the sexual functioning of adolescents and adults. *Annual Review of Sex Research*, *13*, 307–345.

Luyten, P., Fonagy, P., Lowyck, B., & Vermote, R. (2012). Assessment of mentalization. In A. Bateman & P. Fonagy (Eds.), *Handbook of mentalizing in mental health practice*. Arlington, VA: American Psychiatric Publishing, Inc.

Lyons-Ruth, K., Dutra, L., Schuder, M.R., & Bianchi, I. (2006). From infant attachment disorganization to adult dissociation: Relational adaptations or traumatic experiences? *Psychiatric Clinics of North America*, *29*(1), 63–86.

Johnson, S. M. (2002). *Emotionally focused couple therapy with trauma survivors: Strengthening attachment bonds*. New York: Guilford Press.

Johnson, S. M. (2008). Emotionally focused couple therapy. In A. S. Gurman (Ed.), *Clinical handbook of couple therapy*, *4*, 107–137.

MacIntosh, H. B. (2013). Mentalising: An exploration of its potential contribution to understanding the challenges faced by childhood sexual abuse survivors in couple therapy. *Journal of Couple and Family Psychoanalysis*, *3*(2), 188–207.

MacIntosh, H. B. (2017a). Dyadic traumatic reenactment: An integration of psychoanalytic approaches to working with negative interaction cycles in couple therapy with childhood sexual abuse survivors. *Clinical Social Work Journal*, 344–353. https://doi.org/10.1007/s10615-016-0607-0

MacIntosh, H. B. (2017b). Couple therapy with male survivors of childhood sexual abuse. In R. Gartner (Ed.), *Healing sexually betrayed men and boys: Treatment for sexual abuse, assault, and trauma* (pp. 233–260). New York: Routledge.

MacIntosh, H. B. (2017c). Working with male survivor couples. In R. B. Gartner (Ed.), *Healing sexually betrayed men and boys: Treatment for sexual abuse, assault, and trauma*. New York: Routledge.

MacIntosh, H. B., Fletcher, K., & Collin-Vézina, D. (2016). "I was like damaged, used goods": Thematic analysis of disclosures of childhood sexual abuse to romantic partners. *Marriage & Family Review*, *52*(6), 598–611.

MacIntosh, H. B., & Johnson, S. M. (2008). Emotionally focused therapy for couples and childhood sexual abuse survivors. *Journal of Marital and Family Therapy*, *34*(3), 298–315. https://doi.org/10.1111/j.1752-0606.2008.00074.x

MacIntosh, H. B., & Whiffen, V. E. (2005). Twenty years of progress in the study of trauma. *Journal of Interpersonal Violence*, *20*(4), 488–492. https://doi.org/10.1177/0886260504267836

Maltz, W. (2002). Treating the sexual intimacy concerns of sexual abuse survivors. *Sexual and Relationship Therapy*, *17*(4), 321–327.

Maltz, W., & Arian, C. (2001). *The sexual healing journey: A guide for survivors of sexual abuse*. New York: HarperCollins.

Maltz, W., & Maltz, L. (2009). *The porn trap: The essential guide to overcoming problems caused by pornography*. New York: HarperCollins.

Mikulincer, M., & Shaver, P. R. (2007). *Attachment in adulthood: Structure, dynamics and change* (pp. 251–323). New York: Guilford Press.

Millwood, M. (2011). Empathic understanding in couples with a female survivor of childhood sexual abuse. *Journal of Couple & Relationship Therapy*, *10*(4), 327–344. https://doi.org/10.1080/15332691.2011.613310

Nordsletten, A. E., Larsson, H., Crowley, J. J., Almqvist, C., Lichtenstein, P., & Mataix-Cols, D. (2011). Patterns of nonrandom mating within and across 11 major psychiatric disorders. *JAMA Psychiatry*, *73*(4), 354–361. https://doi.org/10.1001/jamapsychiatry.2015.3192

Novak, J. R., Sandberg, J. G., & Busby, D. M. (2018). Using difference scores to inform therapy practice: Differences in perceptions of attachment behaviors between partners in a clinical sample. *Journal of Marital and Family Therapy*, *42*(1), 106–122. https://doi.org/10.1111/jmft.12303

Oka, M., & Whiting, J. B. (2011). Contemporary MFT theories and intimate partner violence: A review of systemic treatments. *Journal of Couple & Relationship Therapy*, *10*(1), 34–52. https://doi.org/10.1080/15332691.2011.539173

Panos, P. T., Panos, A., & Alred, H. (1990). The need for marriage therapy in the treatment of multiple personality disorder. *Dissociation*, *III*(I), 10–14.

Pelcovitz, D., van der Kolk, B., Roth, S., Mandel, F., Kaplan, S., & Resick, P. (1997). Development of a criteria set and a Structured Interview for Disorders of Extreme Stress (SIDES). *Journal of Traumatic Stress*, *10*(1), 3–16. https://doi.org/10.1023/A:1024800212070

Pietromonaco, P. R., & Feldman Barrett, L. (2000). The internal working models concepts: What do we really know about the self in relation to others? *Review of General Psychology*, *4*, 155–175. https://doi.org/10.1037/1089-2680.4.2.155

Pistorius, K., Feinauer, L., Harper, J., Stahmann, R., & Miller, R. (2008). Working with sexually abused children. *American Journal of Family Therapy*, *36*(3), 181–195. https://doi.org/10.1080/01926180701291204

Putnam, F.W. (1989). *Diagnosis and treatment of multiple personality disorder*. New York: Guilford Press.

Regehr, C., Leslie, B., Howe, P., & Chau, S. (2005). Stress, trauma, and support in child welfare practice. *APSAC Advisor*, *17*, 12–18.

Reid, K.S., Taylor, D.K., & Wampler, R.S. (1995). Perceptions of partner involvement in the therapeutic process by patients who experienced sexual abuse as children. *Journal of Sex Education & Therapy*, *21*(1), 36–45.

Reid, K.S., Wampler, R.S., & Taylor, D.K. (1996). The "alienated" partner: Responses to traditional therapies for adult sex abuse survivors. *Journal of Marital and Family Therapy*, *22*(4), 443–453. https://doi.org/10.1111/j.1752-0606.1996.tb00219.x

Rorty, M., & Yager, J. (1996). Histories of childhood trauma and complex post-traumatic sequelae in women with eating disorders. *Psychiatric Clinics of North America*, *19*(4), 773–791.

Rumstein-McKean, O., & Hunsley, J. (2001). Interpersonal and family functioning of female survivors of childhood sexual abuse. *Clinical Psychology Review*, *21*(3), 471–490. https://doi.org/10.1016/S0272-7358%2899%2900069-0

Runtz, M.G., & Schallow, J.R. (1997). Social support and coping strategies as mediators of adult adjustment following childhood maltreatment. *Child Abuse & Neglect*, *21*(2), 211–226. https://doi.org/10.1016/S0145-2134(96)00147-0

Sandberg, J.G., Bradford, A.B., & Brown, A.P. (2017). Differentiating between attachment styles and behaviors and their association with marital quality. *Fam Process*, *56*(2), 518–531. https://doi.org/10.1111/famp.12186

Soderstrom, K., & Skarderud, F. (2009). Mentalization-based treatment in families with parental substance use disorder: Theoretical framework. *Nordic Psychology*, *61*(3), 47–65. https://doi.org/10.1027/1901-2276.61.3.47

Sroufe, L.A. (1996). *Emotional development: The organization of emotional life in the early years*. New York: Cambridge University Press.

Stark, M. (2002). *Working with resistance*. Lanham, MD: Jason Aronson.

Stein, H., & Allen, J.G. (2007). Mentalizing as a framework for integrating therapeutic exposure and relationship repair in the treatment of a patient with complex posttraumatic psychopathology. *Bulletin of the Menninger Clinic*, *71*(4), 273–290. https://doi.org/10.1521/bumc.2007.71.4.273

Stein, H., Fonagy, P., Wheat, K., Kipp, M., & Gerber, A. (2004). Does mentalizing capacity mediate the relationship between developmental adversity and adult social functioning? *Journal of the American Psychoanalytic Association*, *52*, 1217–1221.

Stith, S.M., McCollum, E.E., Rosen, K.H., Locke, L.D., & Goldberg, P.D. (2005). Domestic violence-focused couples treatment. In J.L. Ludbow (Ed.), *Handbook of clinical family therapy* (pp. 406–430). Hoboken, NJ: John Wiley & Sons Inc.

Testa, M., VanZile-Tamsen, C., & Livingston, J.A. (2005). Childhood sexual abuse, relationship satisfaction, and sexual risk taking in a community sample of women. *Journal of Consulting and Clinical Psychology*, *73*(6), 1116.

Vaillancourt-Morel, M-P., Godbout, N., Labadie, C., Runtz, M., Lussier, Y., & Sabourin, S. (2015). Avoidant and compulsive sexual behaviors in male and female survivors of childhood sexual abuse. *Child Abuse & Neglect*, *40*, 48–59.

Vaillancourt-Morel, M-P., Godbout, N., Sabourin, S., Briere, J., Lussier, Y., & Runtz, M. (2016). Adult sexual outcomes of child sexual abuse vary according to relationship status. *Journal of Marital and Family Therapy*, *42*(2), 341–356. https://doi.org/10.1111/jmft.12154

Vall, B., Seikkula, J., Laitila, A., & Holma, J. (2018). Embodiment and reflective practices: Conjoint therapy for psychological intimate partner violence. *Journal of Family Therapy*, *40*, S45–S62. https://doi.org/10.1111/1467-6427.12142

van der Kolk, B. A. (1994). The body keeps the score: Memory and the evolving psychobiology of post traumatic stress. *Harvard Review of Psychiatry, 1*(5), 253–265.

van der Kolk, B. A. (1996). The body keeps score: Approaches to the psychobiology of posttraumatic stress disorder. In B. van der Kolk (Ed.), *Traumatic stress: The effects of overwhelming experience on mind, body, and society* (pp. 214–241). New York: Guilford Press.

Wampler, K. S., Riggs, B., & Kimball, T. G. (2004). Observing attachment behavior in couples: The adult attachment behavior Q-Set (AABQ). *Family Process, 43*(3), 315–335. doi:http://dx.doi.org/10.1111/j.1545-5300.2004.00025.x

Whiffen, V. E., Judd, M. E., & Aube, J. A. (1999). Intimate relationships moderate the association between childhood sexual abuse and depression. *Journal of Interpersonal Violence, 14*(9), 940–954. https://doi.org/10.1177/088626099014009002

Whiffen, V. E., & Oliver, L. (2004). The relationship between traumatic stress and marital intimacy. In D. Catherall (Ed.), *Handbook of stress, trauma and the family* (pp. 137–157). New York: CRC Press.

Wilson, K., & James, A. L. (1992). Child sexual abuse and couple therapy. *Sexual & Marital Therapy, 7*(2), 197–212. https://doi.org/10.1080/02674659208404479

Woolley, S. R., & Johnson, S. M. (2005). Creating secure connections: Emotionally focused couples therapy. In J. L. Lebow (Ed.), *Handbook of clinical therapy* (pp. 384–405). Hoboken, NJ: John Wiley & Sons Inc.

Zala, S. (2012). Complex couples: Multi-theoretical couples counselling with traumatised adults who have a history of child sexual abuse. *Australian and New Zealand Journal of Family Therapy, 33*(3), 219–231. https://doi.org/10.1017/aft.2012.27

Zlotnick, C., Johnson, D. M., Yen, S., Battle, C. L., Sanislow, C. A., Skodol, A. E., . . . Shea, M. (2003). Clinical features and impairment in women with Borderline Personality Disorder (BPD) with Posttraumatic Stress Disorder. (PTSD), BPD without PTSD, and other- personality disorders with PTSD. *Journal of Nervous and Mental Disease, 191*(11), 706–713.

Zlotnick, C., Warshaw, M., Shea, M. T., Allsworth, J., Pearlstein, T., & Keller, M. B. (1999). Chronicity in Posttraumatic Stress Disorder (PTSD) and predictors of course of PTSD in patients with anxiety disorders. *Journal of Traumatic Stress, 12*(1), 89–100.

Index

For Product Safety Concerns and Information please contact our EU
representative GPSR@taylorandfrancis.com
Taylor & Francis Verlag GmbH, Kaufingerstraße 24, 80331 München, Germany

www.ingramcontent.com/pod-product-compliance
Ingram Content Group UK Ltd.
Pitfield, Milton Keynes, MK11 3LW, UK
UKHW052052230926
475702UK00025B/1133
* 9 7 8 0 4 1 5 7 9 3 6 1 2 *